MESSY
CHURCH
THEOLOGY

Exploring the significance of Messy Church
for the wider church

Edited by

George Lings

Messy Church® is a registered word mark and the logo is a registered device mark of The Bible Reading Fellowship.

Text copyright © BRF 2013
The authors assert the moral right
to be identified as the authors of this work

Published by
The Bible Reading Fellowship
15 The Chambers, Vineyard
Abingdon OX14 3FE
United Kingdom
Tel: +44 (0)1865 319700
Email: enquiries@brf.org.uk
Website: www.brf.org.uk
BRF is a Registered Charity

ISBN 978 0 85746 171 1
First published 2013
Reprinted 2014
10 9 8 7 6 5 4 3 2 1
All rights reserved

Acknowledgments
Scripture quotations taken from The New Revised Standard Version of the Bible, Anglicised Edition, copyright © 1989, 1995 by the Division of Christian Education of the National Council of the Churches of Christ in the United States of America, are used by permission. All rights reserved.

Scripture quotations taken from the Holy Bible, New International Version (Anglicised Edition), copyright © 1979, 1984, 2011 by Biblica (International Bible Society), are used by permission of Hodder & Stoughton Publishers, an Hachette UK company. All rights reserved. 'NIV' is a registered trademark of Biblica (International Bible Society). UK trademark number 1448790.

Scripture quotations marked ESV are from The Holy Bible, English Standard Version, published by HarperCollins Publishers, © 2001 Crossway Bibles, a division of Good News Publishers. Used by permission. All rights reserved.

Cover photos copyright © Helen Jaeger

Every effort has been made to trace and contact copyright owners for material used in this resource. We apologise for any inadvertent omissions or errors, and would ask those concerned to contact us so that full acknowledgment can be made in the future.

A catalogue record for this book is available from the British Library

Printed and bound by CPI Group (UK) Ltd, Croydon CR0 4YY

Contents

Section 3: Messy practicalities

Introduction

The Rt Revd Paul Butler,
Bishop of Southwell and Nottingham

I first heard about Messy Church early on in its life. It sounded great, because it was creative, all-age and committed to reaching out to the de-churched and non-churched. Back then, though, it appeared as one more idea among several that were floating around. The way it then took off, and has continued to grow across the world, has been phenomenal. Rightly, this has attracted masses of interest and research. This book offers some great insights into what has made Messy Church the phenomenon that it is.

It has been my privilege throughout the 'Messy Church years' to have visited quite a number of different Messy Churches in action. I have been on different days of the week, at varying times of the day and in a range of buildings. I have joined it in villages, inner cities and the suburbs. I have observed a variety of quality. I have seen some that appear to be not much more than a varied style of worship for the already faithful, but most have really been reaching out to people for whom this is church for the first time—and it is their church. I can honestly say that every one I have visited has been good to join in.

I have also been privileged to talk with lots of people involved in leading these churches and have been very impressed by the thoughtfulness and commitment given to developing things as they go. It has also been a privilege to talk with the Messy Church national team fairly regularly; they are an impressive bunch!

So by way of getting you, the reader, thinking at the start of this helpful set of essays and reflections, here are my seven 'F' factors that contribute to Messy Church being what it is.

Family: We all know that families come in all shapes and sizes, but it is obvious the moment you walk into a Messy Church that there are families present. Parents and children are either busy doing an activity together or can be seen to have split up to do different kinds of things—only later to be busy showing each other what they have made or achieved. Sometimes there are grandparents there too, even great-grandparents. Dads are in evidence (although not always, it has to be noted). Families love Messy Church because they can do it together. It genuinely caters for all ages. This applies to every element when done well. Songs cross age barriers; a reflection on the Bible story has insights for all ages to consider and take away to put into practice.

Family matters to Messy Church.

Friendship: On one visit I was talking with a 90-year-old lady who has been following Jesus all her life, and has been part of a church throughout. 'This is the best church of my life,' she said quietly. 'Why?' I asked. 'Because it is the friendliest I have ever known, and the most fun.'

She was experiencing friendship in Messy Church that apparently was often either missing or weak in all other expressions of church she had known.

A danger of 'family-focused church' is that those who are not in families can feel excluded; not so in a well-run Messy Church. All ages are welcome, and single people feel integrated and involved. Friendships develop and grow here, including friendship with the one who 'sticks closer than any brother' (Proverbs 18:24).

Food: Eating together has always been a part of how families and communities function well. It was core to Jesus' ministry, and he gave us a meal by which to remember him. And eating together is a vital part of how and why Messy Church works. Where the meal is left out, something is missing. This may be inevitable as some move to meeting fortnightly, or occasionally weekly. But it must not be lost from the ongoing life of a Messy Church. Perhaps those who do start meeting more often need to ensure at least a monthly full-blown meal together. There is something special about community, friendship and family that only happens around eating together.

Fun: Immediately one thinks of all the fun had in the creative crafts and activities. Messy Church has brought out the creative in many a person. It has managed to keep coming up with fun ideas. But there is a holy fun about the whole of Messy Church; when everyone gathers for worship it does not suddenly become sombre. There is fun in the songs while praising God. Christian truth from the Bible is shared in ways that engage and are fun. We all learn best when we are enjoying what we are doing. Remember the 90-year-old lady.

Faith: The whole of Messy Church is about communicating and sharing faith in Jesus Christ. But I want here to highlight that Messy Church was born, has continued, and must go forward, in faith. When Lucy and Paul Moore first tried it out as an experiment in Portsmouth, they were taking a step of faith. They had no idea how it would go, or how people would respond. They certainly had no idea that it would become a worldwide movement crossing denominations as well as continents. At each step of the way, as others asked if they could 'copy' the idea, as BRF agreed to invest time and money in it and as invitations from around the world were taken up, faith has been involved. Steps of faith have been required, involving trusting in God, who calls us to go 'with the wind of the Spirit' and walk into his future. Such faith commitment has been rewarded. The biggest reward is that people of all ages have come to faith in Jesus Christ. They have expressed this faith in baptism and confirmation. Others whose faith had waned have had it brought back to life.

There has been a real willingness, by Lucy and others, to grapple with some of the hard questions that have arisen in this journey. Where does a Messy baptism take place? What does a Messy confirmation look like? And how might Communion be celebrated in a Messy Church? What does growing as a disciple, or community of disciples, look like for Messy Church?

Answers are still being worked on, but this is being done in faith that the God who calls is faithful and he will lead on.

Flexibility: Exploring these questions of faith has demonstrated another requirement of Messy Church, and that is flexibility. From the start, as more churches experimented, there was flexibility about day, time, venue and format. In growing and developing, further flexibility has been demonstrated to allow for different cultural and geographical settings; flexibility in developing ways of exploring discipleship. Yet I am glad that there has been the courage to be inflexible with some aspects of Messy Church: its all-age nature; the importance of the three aspects of creativity, hospitality including food, and celebration in worship. This inflexibility is intended to be for the un- and de-churched, not just transforming the way an existing church operates. There has also been the flexibility to recognise some derived alternatives, like Sweaty Church, although this raises some hard questions too. There is now the flexibility of providing ideas and materials through a magazine as well as books and the web. Flexibility will remain important as Messy Churches become more 'mature' in experience and length of existence—and to avoid becoming too fixed in their ways.

Fruitfulness: My final 'F' factor is the wonderful fruitfulness that has come—the fruit of lives changed by the good news of Jesus Christ; the fruit of families being enriched by joining in worship and fun together; the fruit of friendship that crosses the ages; the fruit of people discovering gifts and using them to serve other people and God; the fruit of spiritual life.

Jesus made it clear to his disciples that the true worth and value of people and their lives is seen in their fruitfulness. Messy Church is being seen to be born of the Spirit and filled with God's life. It has many years of fruitfulness ahead of it.

A note on Lucy Moore

Lucy herself sees Messy Church as a Holy Spirit-inspired idea. She understands herself as somehow being caught up, and blown along by, the wind of the Spirit. I believe she is correct. The glory does and should go to God.

Nevertheless, in human terms we recognise that Messy Church and its growth owe an enormous amount to Lucy herself (and indeed to her family for the way they have supported, encouraged and released her to do this). It has been Lucy's vision, passion, drive, creativity and sheer doggedness at times that have been vital to the growth and development of Messy Church. She has been very skilful in also bringing on board some very creative team mates in the journey.

Why might God have used Lucy in this way? Well, the 'F' factors apply to her too. Her family, and family life, are key to her whole being. She is a wonderfully friendly person who is a friend to many. Food is important to Lucy. She is enormous fun—see her act, and hear her laugh! She is full of faith in her Lord. She has been amazingly flexible as Messy Church has developed—and she keeps thinking flexibly as it grows. Her life is fruitful, with the fruit of the Holy Spirit.

Messy Church is God's work, but thank God who made, saved, called and equipped Lucy to do this particular piece of kingdom work.

Messy questions

1

When is Messy Church 'church'?

Claire Dalpra

Claire Dalpra has worked for Church Army since 1999 as a fresh expressions researcher, writer and editor. Her areas of research include fresh expressions for under-fives and their families, fresh expressions for adults with learning disabilities and the sustainability of spare-time-led fresh expressions of Church. Her role now includes training and review work as well as collecting national data on Messy Churches as part of a fresh expressions of Church research project undertaken by Church Army's Research Unit in partnership with the Church Commissioners. Claire lives in Sheffield with her husband and eight-year-old daughter.

Confused? You're not the only one...

Deciding when something is a fresh expression of Church is a subtle art. As I wrote this chapter, taking care to include all the necessary variables, caveats and provisos, I couldn't help feeling some degree of sympathy for those people befuddled by the definitional confusion that accompanied the term 'fresh expression of Church' when it was coined by the *Mission-Shaped Church* report in 2004.

For the last year, my work at Church Army's Research Unit has involved collecting quantitative data on fresh expressions of Church in the Church of England. There is a significant relational dimension to this piece of research as almost all the criteria assessment and data collection occur in the context of a telephone conversation. A good number of the practitioners that I have spoken with are Messy Church leaders and I continue to be impressed by their commitment, creativity and passion to reach those beyond the fringes of our existing churches. However, from my phone calls I discern that, despite all the efforts of people like ourselves, the national Fresh Expressions team and the wealth of resources that have been made available since 2004, what can be legitimately labelled a fresh expression of Church is still a topic of ongoing debate.

Is it fresh? Is it Church?

The first subtlety in deciding when something is a fresh expression of Church is the need to attend to two different questions simultaneously. One question is 'Is it fresh?' Some people assume that to be 'fresh', it must be something never seen or done before, as if 'freshness' means something new, trendy or novel. In our research project, we are clear that 'fresh' is about being missional, seeking to connect with people outside the church, as well as contextual: that is, we only include fresh expressions of Church that have allowed context to shape the kind of church that grows as a result. As such, 'fresh' does not mean something never done or seen before in church life; rather, it means something more akin to 'refreshing'. Therefore, you may be surprised at a few cases we have included in our research. We have included congregations in residential homes for frail elderly people and two ventures that grew from mother-and-toddler groups.

The other question to address (the question that this chapter will explore) is 'Is it church?' Since 2004, as the understanding of the term 'fresh expressions of Church' has evolved and broadened, both proponents and critics of the movement have noted that the phrase 'of Church' is now often omitted. Indeed, Messy Church is to be commended for using the word 'Church' in its title in a way that means it cannot easily be left out. As this chapter will make clear, fresh expressions of Church were always intended to be ecclesial, growing initiatives to become churches in themselves. Because fresh expressions of Church are intended to be church, they must take seriously their formational[1] responsibility. They must be communities that aim to form disciples of their members as well as bringing them to faith.

Beyond a first glance

The next challenge in the subtle art of deciding when something is Church is to make a deep enough examination of any group or project to be sure that first appearances do not mask deeper realities. Name, location, frequency of public gathering or target demographic alone is not enough to allow an assessment of whether such a group is church. A description of activities alone does not tell you the deeper intentions and values that will hold the clues to identity. This is why our research project involves a fairly cumbersome initial stage of talking with leaders to discern whether their project meets the definition criteria we have set for a fresh expression of Church.

Anyone describing the appearance of a household pet might say it has four legs, two ears, two eyes, a nose and a tail, but on that description alone we are no closer to finding out whether they have a cat, a dog or a rabbit. We all know that, while there are many obvious similarities, a cat is a fundamentally different creature from a dog or a rabbit. In the same way, if someone says, 'I'm part of a group of Christian volunteers who organise a gathering for kids to a format of crafts, story, prayer and food,' that does not tell us whether their gathering is church or not. We have to ask more questions.

Working with aspiration

Linked to the above issue of deep enquiry, another subtlety in decision-making is taking a long enough view. It is arguable that the most effective fresh expressions of church are those that deliberately begin by engaging in listening and loving service.[2] While holding the planting of a fresh expression of Church as a long-term intention, those working with people groups who are at a cultural distance from inherited church show wisdom in resisting the temptation to strive for instant results to meet the full necessary criteria of 'being church' in the early years of their existence. Indeed, if those who are developing a fresh expression of Church claim to know at the beginning exactly how the later stages of discipleship and worship will look, this suggests a flawed process.

We have handled this subtlety in our research project by honouring aspirations. One way to track the diversity that arises when working with aspiration is to use category headings such as 'fresh expressions of worship', 'fresh expressions of community' and 'fresh expressions of evangelism'. These are legitimate forms of fresh expression but are only partial because they address only one aspect of what it means to be fully church. If these partial forms are understood and intended as building blocks in a mission-shaped process of creating indigenous church, this is not simply an unhelpful rebranding exercise.[3] Where there is no intention to develop further stages, we celebrate the work that is done but do not include it in our records. It can be frustrating that this introduces a further set of variables but, on balance, it seems only fair. Drawing on an interpersonal analogy, children are no less human just because they haven't reached an age when they can manage their own finances.

More than one point of comparison

One last subtlety is worth a mention here. In discerning whether something is a fresh expression of Church, there are a number of different alternatives that we would use as contrasts to help our definitional work but would not deem fresh expressions of Church. Firstly, a new venture could be an outreach project of an existing church, effective in mission but not intended to be church or congregation in its own right. Secondly, a new venture may be simply a worship service or an infrequent worship event. We are clear that just because a project is fresh and a worship service, that does not make it church. To be church, it must be something more than a service or an event: we must ask whether those who gather see themselves as a discernible group who congregate.

Where Christians are seeking to connect with different cultural or sociological groups through styles that are contextual, fresh expressions of Church instincts are at work there. Where there are different congregations meeting within the same building but with distinct identities, we would include them. We define 'distinct identity' as a congregation having its own dedicated leadership, its own system of providing pastoral care and discipleship and its own focus of mission. Such aspects reflect instincts to develop congregations as interdependent churches within one wider church set-up.

Not a value judgment

I suspect that mission and ministry among children and young families is one of the areas where confusion about outreach projects, worship services and fresh expressions of Church arises most often. The first two dioceses we worked with presented us with a total of 53 examples of Messy Churches, and we then had to sift them to see if they met our research criteria as fresh expressions of Church. However, one aspect of this definitional work is not subtle but refreshingly straightforward: we are not seeking to promote the idea that those we include in our database are better than those we do not include. No value judgment is being made. Some contexts will need outreach projects and worship services to connect with the people in their communities; some will need fresh expressions of Church.

Messy Church is 'church' when a new ecclesial entity has been created

Tackling the 'Is it church?' question seems to be less confusing for practitioners when they are reminded that *Mission-Shaped Church* in 2004 was a follow-up report to *Breaking New Ground: Church planting in the Church of England* in 1994. In *Mission-Shaped Church*, the term 'church plant' was avoided for its unhelpful connotations of cloning existing forms of church, but the report made clear that the term 'fresh expression of Church' (a noun) should describe the consequence or end result of a church-planting process (a verb).[4] Whether the process was undertaken by a small team or by an entire congregation, the conclusion was the same: what was intended to grow was a church.[5]

Thus, fresh expressions of Church is a mission strategy working to plant churches rather than develop existing ones. One of the most helpful ways I have discovered to make clear that a fresh expression of Church is about birthing a new church is to ask whether the motivation for beginning a Messy Church is to boost the numbers of those attending the 'main' Sunday morning congregation. This instinct we would call 'addition', because it seeks to add numbers to a church that already exists. For example, an outreach ministry of a local church, while acknowledging the need for evangelistic endeavour to enhance the life of the existing church either spiritually or numerically, presupposes that any fruit of that endeavour will be gathered up in the existing church congregation.

With fresh expressions of Church, we are looking for a different instinct. We are looking for the recognition that those who come to a Messy Church are very unlikely to come to the 'main' Sunday morning service of an existing church. This we would call a 'multiplication' instinct, because the number of churches in a parish, deanery or diocese is being increased rather than the number of members at any one church. The instinct for multiplication has 'gone out' to take people on to 'who knows where'.

This dynamic is easier to observe when fresh expressions of Church are developed across a wider geographic area, such as a deanery (as some Messy Churches are) or a diocese, where fresh expressions of Church work outside parish boundaries to complement existing churches, some being granted a Bishop's Mission Order as a legal framework in which to operate. It is harder to see in a single parish context; creating new ecclesial entities is hugely challenging to inherited parish churches. Legal status, financial resources, allocation of leadership, the ownership of buildings and ways of measuring attendance are all determined by the provision of public worship by existing parish churches. As such, the unconscious pull, at a local level, to think in terms of addition rather than multiplication is a powerful one, but there are very different instincts at work in these two approaches that should not be underestimated.

In an Anglican context, a new ecclesial entity within a parish was given organisational room in a number of ways by the *Mission-Shaped Church* report.[6] For example, multiple and midweek congregations were recognised as a fresh expression of Church category with a long history of building on additional Sunday services and midweek services. The report noted the growth of midweek attendance and the increased conviction of those attending that this was their ecclesial community. This change of thinking was becoming more commonplace; more clergy were accepting it and encouraging services to develop into congregations.[7]

It is important to add that this is not about creating fiercely independent churches that break off and cut all ties with their sending churches as soon as possible, needing no other church to survive. Too often, the life-cycle model used in church planting theory has been unhelpfully skewed toward assumptions of Western, male, individual independence that has been interpreted as legal, governmental and financial autonomy with Congregationalist overtones. Carter and McGoldrick point out that maturity in the life-cycle model should be interpreted as interdependence, where relationships with others are vital.[8] Proving an ability to trust, collaborate with and respect others who are different from us is important. Mutual respect and benefit between the existing parish church and the fresh expression(s) of Church that it brings to birth within the parish is the overall goal.

How can we tell if our project is 'church'?

It is not a bridge back into existing church

The first thing to consider when asking if your Messy Church is 'church' is whether you intend it to be a bridge or 'feeder' back into existing church or whether you are growing it as a church in itself. As Messy Church participants grow in faith and commitment to Christ, do you hope that those people will start to come to the 'main' Sunday morning congregation of the parish church? Or are the constraints on people crossing the bridge back from Messy Church to the 'main' congregation so significant that it is unlikely they will ever make it across? It is not unusual to find that there is a mix, and so the proportion of those who cannot make a transition becomes important. If it is recognised and accepted that the majority of Messy Church members cannot cross the bridge back, then, almost by default, you are working with fresh expressions of Church instincts.

Those involved see it as their primary place of church

The next question to ask is whether the majority of those attending Messy Church understand it to be 'their church'. This acknowledgment by members that it is 'their church' is a diagnostic piece of evidence pointing towards it being a church in its own right rather than an outreach project. Do members feel that Messy Church is the place where their belonging to a Christian community is primarily expressed? The answer to this question can be difficult to tease out if 'blending' occurs. Blending is a term to describe the way in which increasing numbers of Christians belong to more than one worshipping community, deriving benefit from and serving the cause of multiple churches that together make up necessary elements of their ongoing spiritual life. We can understand how blending might occur for families where belonging to a church that meets the needs of children and teenagers is important but where parents also derive benefit from belonging to a more adult-focused gathering. However, where the majority of families at a Messy Church see it as their primary place of church, this suggests that you have a potential fresh expression of Church on your hands.

Another useful indicator is the way the people who help to lead the Messy Church think. There is a question about how the volunteers, as well as those who attend a Messy Church, understand their membership of it. Do the team members who plan and prepare for Messy Church see it as their primary place of church? While we can sympathise with the practicalities of resourcing Messy Church, 'borrowing' volunteers on a rota system speaks more of duty or hobby than of membership and sends a powerful signal that the group is not an expression of church in itself. If it is to be a fresh expression of Church, we would expect the Messy Church to be wrestling with questions of how to respond to the longer-term aim of nurturing leadership that is not just 'lending a hand' to something they perceive to be an outreach ministry while belonging to a 'proper' church elsewhere.

Questions of discipleship are handled within the Messy Church

If a Messy Church is not a bridge back into an existing congregation and if the majority of attendees and volunteers see it as their primary place of church, then comes another key indicator. Picking up on the formational responsibilities of any fresh expression of Church, do leaders take responsibility for the long-term discipleship of the members or do people or groups from the sending church take responsibility for this?

Laurence Singlehurst reminds us that any church—existing or fresh—that is engaging evangelistically will need to work in stages, consistent in style, to facilitate an effective discipleship journey.[9] With an outreach ministry, this becomes the responsibility of the existing church as those new to the faith grow towards being involved with the wider life of the existing church. For example, members of a mother-and-toddler group who express a desire to explore discipleship issues further may be invited to join an Alpha course facilitated by the leadership of the parish church.

However, for a fresh expression of Church, the responsibility for the journey of discipleship for its members rests primarily on its shoulders. It may be that a Messy Church is only at the stage of life where it is conscious of the importance of the question. If we detect that leaders have identified this need and are committed to wrestling with the questions of how to do it (even if they have not yet been able to respond to the need), then we are likely to include it as a fresh expression of Church.

This issue of discipleship is especially acute in fresh expressions of Church that aim to connect with children and adults simult-aneously. Can both children and adults develop in their disciple-ship within just one gathering per month? What other dimension to the overall life of the Messy Church will be needed to facilitate the spiritual growth of the adults involved? One church I know began to address this question with an additional gathering to their regular pattern. Every half-term, the adult members met during an evening to reflect on two questions as a way into the discipleship journey: 'How are you experiencing our fresh expression of Church?' and 'How are you experiencing God in your life?'[10]

Messy Church is 'church' when there is evidence of the four marks

If a new ecclesial entity is emerging, a crucial question to ask is how it would demonstrate the characteristic four marks that ecclesiologists agree to be diagnostic of Anglican churches.[11] These are: one, holy, catholic and apostolic. All four marks have undergone different interpretations throughout church history,[12] but *Mission-Shaped Church* uses them as a basis for essential dynamics in determining the health and validation of a fresh expression of Church. Thus, in asking 'When is Messy Church "church"?' we have some helpful interconnected relationships—for short called IN, UP, OF and OUT—to work with.[13]

Because it takes time for a new church to grow, it should be noted that no fresh expression of Church is expected to grow in all four relationships equally and simultaneously. Criticism levelled at fresh expressions of Church often fails to hold in balance the need for them to grow and mature different aspects of their lives at different paces. Furthermore, some inherited churches may measure themselves against these criteria and find that there is much development needed in particular aspects within their church life.

The four marks

The 'one' or IN relationship looks for evidence that authentic community is being nurtured. Are members committing to one another in a way that reflects the loving and diverse oneness of the Trinity? Most activities need the presence of a community dynamic to be effective; any venture that operates too strongly on a client–provider dynamic is in danger of establishing patterns that will be difficult to break out of. However, if a fresh expression of Church is the primary place of ecclesial belonging for its members, a deeper quality of communal life will need to grow.

The mark of church known as 'holy' concerns the facilitation of the UP relationship that helps members to seek God, encouraging their transformation into his holiness. An outreach project of a local church may have an aspect of the UP relationship if it is surrounded in prayer; indeed, many argue that prayer is a vital component of any effective outreach ministry. However, for a fresh expression of Church, it must be the kind of UP that sustains the team and its members for the whole of life.

The mark of 'catholicity' has been interpreted in a number of different ways over the years, but, in a fresh expressions of Church context, the essence of catholicity is interpreted as the instinct for inclusivity, which acknowledges that no local church exists alone but is called to relate to the wider church. This is also known as the OF relationship. As I heard a senior member of the clergy express it, if members of your Messy Church moved away to another part of the country, would they want to connect with an Anglican church in their new locality that might be very different from the Messy Church they belonged to where they lived before?

There is some debate about how crucial the sacraments are in defining what is church in Anglican ecclesiology,[14] but, while scholars deliberate, the intention regarding dominical sacraments (baptism and the Eucharist) remains an important test of whether a new group is staying faithful to what is 'church' in the Church of England. Sacraments are an indicator of not only the UP relationship but also the OF relationship. As authorisation by the wider church is needed for sacraments to occur, this is a healthy sign that those to whom the fresh expression of Church is accountable in the wider structures recognise it to be church.

The last mark concerns the OUT dynamic or the 'apostolic' mark, which asks how a fresh expression of Church maintains its ongoing missional life. The apostolic relationship invites a fresh expression of Church to journey on and out, to continue God's mission.[15] This then begs the following question: in what way is the fresh expression of Church responding to this ecclesiological challenge of developing its own outreach ministry or ministries?

Even if a significant proportion of members are not yet Christians and therefore would not understand their role to be evangelistic, there is still a call on the embryonic church to look for opportunities to reach beyond itself to serve, invite and involve those beyond the existing membership.

How can we tell if there is evidence of the four marks?

A sense of Christian community has been fostered beyond attendance

There might be a number of ways in which this is evident. One way is that participants (those at whom Messy Church is aimed) become involved with the running of Messy Church. No one imagines that this can happen right at the start, but the earlier the foundations for such a dynamic can be laid, the better. This involvement does not mean just helping to put the tables away at the end, although help is not to be refused! Rather, it is in the planning, preparation and set-up that participants should be invited to shoulder some responsibility, because they believe in the importance of what is happening. If, after three to five years, no participants have joined the team of helpers, there is serious cause for concern. While values of hospitality and serving may be important for the Christian team members in the initial stages, never to invite participants to share in the ownership of a Messy Church is indicative of a weak IN dynamic. Such an expression will not only risk developing in a way that is unsustainable but will feel more like a 'service' (in both senses of the word), undermining the sense that it is intended to be church.

Other indications we would look for include the following: all participants understand that they can give something as well as receive, even if they are not committed Christians as yet; new friendships have been formed through Messy Church; participants meet up outside Messy Church gatherings; Messy Church members socialise in each other's homes. These would all suggest that authentic community is being fostered beyond mere attendance.

The worship helps its members to become more Christlike

If a fresh expression of Church is developing, the group will need to look for forms of worship to sustain them through the whole of life. As George Lings puts it, 'What must be characteristic of the worship is that it feeds the life, gifting, calling and aspirations of the growing community.'[16] I have heard it said that, excepting the funeral of a child, all-age worship is the hardest kind of worship service to lead well. If a Messy Church is a fresh expression of Church, it will be wrestling with the difficult challenge of how to consistently and effectively take adults and children on a spiritual journey for the whole of life.

Some have commented that, for adults, Messy Church is like swimming in the shallow end of a swimming pool in terms of spiritual engagement. I hear the warning contained in that comment, but would want to add that most congregations struggle to offer depth of spiritual engagement for the diversity of age groups and stages of faith that they serve. How refreshing that Messy Church offers a counter-emphasis to much existing liturgical worship, which is aimed primarily at intellectually minded adults and those long steeped in the Christian faith! We need congregations that are aimed at children and at those new to the faith; otherwise we in the wider church will be guilty of marginalising them.

At the same time, we must take care in our assumptions about how we encourage people down to the deeper end of the swimming pool. As well as introducing additional meeting points for adults within the monthly pattern of Messy Church gatherings, we might look at three different types of discipleship—formal, informal and socialisation (discussed in Chapter 11 of this book). Messy Church may be stronger in the last two types. My own daughter is seven and I notice that the times of my most enriching spiritual encounters with God are when I am preparing to lead a Godly Play session. I suspect that we underestimate the impact we have on the spiritual nurture of Messy Church leaders and participants when we ask them to take a turn in preparing and leading.

Lastly, if a Messy Church is church, it will be acutely aware of the need for provision for its teenagers when they outgrow the age group of the children at whom Messy Church is primarily aimed. Some Messy Churches have found that their teenagers join the leadership team and continue to be a part of its life in that way, but others may find themselves called to 'birth' something for teenagers that has enough in common with Messy Church values to create a smooth transition while allowing for its own identity and style to emerge.

The sacramental life of the church has been considered

Very few Messy Churches I have spoken to have Communion or baptisms regularly. As most Messy Churches are fairly new and are run by teams of lay volunteers, I am not too surprised. However, it is worth noting that Lucy Moore devotes a couple of chapters in her book *Messy Church 2* (BRF, 2008) to baptism and the Eucharist, welcoming that possibility. While rate of development and frequency of celebration should be allowed to vary in every fresh expression of Church, evolving discussions concerning sacraments and who presides are indicative of how far a Messy Church has moved on the journey of maturing as church. At one child-focused fresh expression of Church, although there is a priestly member of paid staff from the parish team who acts as chaplain to the group and administers Communion, the service is led by extended communion when she is unable to be there. There are two designated mothers who have permission from the Bishop to perform this role.

One of the questions we often ask in our phone conversations is whether a baptism could take place at a Messy Church if requested. If there is no option for a baptism to take place at a Messy Church, this sends out a powerful message that it is not 'proper' church. If a Messy Church meets on a weekday, sometimes there is the constraint of being unable to invite family and friends to a baptism there, so we can understand a family requesting it on a Sunday instead. In this situation, the Messy Church congregation leaders could be invited to run the service on that particular Sunday morning, thereby communicating that the choice to hold it in this context is an expression of their catholicity rather than subservience to the 'main' church congregation.

The church is represented on decision-making church councils

One of the strengths of the Messy Church network is the regional support through Coordinators and Fiestas as well as the books and website resources. Every Messy Church will know that it is part of a wider network of Messy Churches. However, Messy Churches that are church should consider securing representation on the wider decision-making councils of the church. Although few Messy Churches will ever pursue formal governance or legal status such a Bishop's Mission Order or Charitable Trust, there are still informal ways in which this can occur. If a Messy Church is understood to be a church or a congregation in its own right, does it have representatives on the PCC or deanery synod? Where can it express its voice? Where can it learn from others? If the wisdom of Henry Venn and Roland Allen is to be adhered to, a Messy Church that is church must be on a journey to self-governance (even if it is informal) in order to mature.[17] Finance too will be an issue, with a Messy Church needing, over time, to manage its own finances rather than being reliant on handouts from the PCC.

The church community offers outreach, social and evangelistic, to those beyond itself

This diagnostic indicator is potentially confusing. Some may see the fact that they have begun a Messy Church as the sign of a healthy-enough OUT dynamic. However, the creation of the Messy Church is actually the result of a healthy OUT dynamic in the sending church. To mature as a church in its own right, there needs to be evidence of instincts to reach out even beyond the Messy Church. This outreach could be a further fresh expression of Church—maybe a Messy Church in a nearby village or a youth congregation for teenagers who have outgrown Messy Church—or some sort of outreach ministry that doesn't qualify as a fresh expression of Church, such as a soup run or holiday club.

Why does it matter?

If deciding when a venture is a fresh expression of Church is so subtle an art, some might ask if it really matters. Why do we need to include some Messy Churches in our research and leave others out? Using the above criteria in the first diocese where we collected data, we concluded that only eight of 14 Messy Churches were church. In the second diocese, we decided that 17 of the 37 Messy Churches listed were church.[18] But why are we choosing to be so exact? At the end of the day, why is it important whether a Messy Church is church or not?

I believe it is important for any Messy Church to have a clear understanding of its identity and future trajectory because its on-going health and the expectations of its members and supporters will flow from this understanding. For example, the identity and purpose of a Messy Church will affect decisions about who you call on for outside expertise. Someone in the role of consultant or 'mission accompanier' may require missiological insight into effective evangelism or ecclesiological wisdom in how young churches grow most healthily. There is massive potential for misunderstanding over identity. For these young churches, the support that can be offered by clergy, PCC members, funders of the venture and members of the sending church will be hugely significant in helping the Messy Church develop as church, if all are agreed.

I encountered in my research one very scary scenario in which the lay leaders of a Messy Church clearly understood the need to develop Messy Church as a congregation in its own right, but their incumbent did not. Where this combination of views occurs, I worry for the Messy Church's vulnerability in the longer term. It will feel extremely frustrating and painful to know that while your Messy Church is becoming church, your closest supporters still assume it is not. Like a newborn baby, the young church is unlikely, in this context, to be given the affirmation and support necessary to grow into a healthy child.

I noticed something else. Many of the Messy Churches I spoke to were included in our research because they qualified under the most crucial aspects of our research criteria. For example, their members did not attend any other church, and it did not seem as if they would in the future. Participants were reported to have said that Messy Church was 'their' church. Thus the Messy Church leaders had been forced to explore discipleship questions in the Messy Church context. However, I detected that the issues concerning the healthy development of their Messy Churches—such as the four marks, Henry Venn's three-self thinking and the introduction of the sacraments—remained largely unconsidered and unexplored. So there is a sense in which these Messy Churches are stuck on their ecclesial journey: they cannot return to the assumption that Messy Church might act as a bridge to existing church, yet moving forward to see their Messy Church mature as a church in itself seems a very daunting task for these groups of lay leaders.

I suspect that local clergy will need to play the very important role of midwife, supporting and encouraging Messy Church leaders, to ensure that these young churches do not remain stuck halfway down the birth canal or die in the earliest days of their young lives. Such a role for clergy is akin to that of playgroup leaders, who help young children to mature in social skills, discover and harness play and develop patterns of learning for life.

✤

2

When is Messy Church 'not church'?

Steve Hollinghurst

Steve Hollinghurst is a researcher, consultant and trainer in mission and evangelism to post-Christendom culture in the UK and abroad. He has been working for Church Army since 2003. He is author of Mission-Shaped Evangelism *(Canterbury Press, 2010),* New Age, Paganism and Christian Mission *(Grove, 2002),* Coded Messages: Evangelism and The Da Vinci Code *(Grove, 2006) and, with others,* Equipping Your Church in a Spiritual Age *(CBTI, 2005).*

The previous chapter laid out criteria that we use in Church Army's Research Unit when trying to assess if something should be properly considered a fresh expression of Church rather than a modification of an existing church, or an outreach project. This chapter seeks to explore some further issues raised by the combination of components of Messy Church, with regard to answering this question.

Might the name 'church' lead to false assumptions?

There is a cluster of questions here. If we emphasise the idea that fresh expressions are 'church', does that create pressure to call a new gathering 'church' before it has really become a Christian community? Are people assumed to be part of a church because they attend Messy Church, while some of them might see it primarily as a family craft activity? What does this mean for discipleship, both for the adults and for their children?

These questions first arose out of a conversation between several people running Messy Church, in relation to the difficulties they were facing in the discipleship of adults, and were further illuminated during a review of a different fresh expression of Church facing similar issues. All of this suggests that Messy Church, with its combination of various activities, may be church for some people but not for others. If this fact is recognised, it may be a positive outcome. There is, however, a danger that by seeing all these activities as 'church', we make assumptions that hide what is really happening.

The problem of adult discipleship

As early as 2010, a number of Messy Church groups had successfully gathered regular members and were looking at how they taught and discipled the adults who were attending. The teaching offered during the monthly meetings was felt to be accessible for the children present, but this meant that adults might be in need of something more at their level. Not surprisingly, a number of groups explored with their adults the possibility of setting up a further discipleship meeting for them. A common story emerged, however, that established members who indicated that they would be keen to come to these discipleship sessions did not in fact come.

Further exploration suggested that the expressions of willingness to go to a discipleship group might have been expressions of affirmation for the leaders inviting them rather than any real desire to go. There was concern that pressure for them to attend might be putting some people off coming to Messy Church altogether and, as a result, adult discipleship groups that had been started were being stopped. This experience led to questions about discipleship in Messy Church that have become an ongoing thread on the Messy blog, www.messychurch.org.uk/messy-blog/. It also raised questions about how attendance at Messy Church should be viewed. A number of leaders said they had assumed that people attending Messy Church over many months were expressing some sort of Christian faith or, at the very least, a desire to explore that faith and were therefore ready for a discipleship group run in an appropriate way. These leaders were now wondering whether their assumptions had been false or whether they had just gone the wrong way about setting up such groups.

A case study

Ideally, a study of a number of Messy Church groups should be done to explore these dynamics. However, the case study outlined below is offered in the hope that its suggestions can be tested further. It should be acknowledged that this example does not fit the standard criteria of a Messy Church. For example, it doesn't offer a meal to share between the children and adults, only a drink with biscuits or cakes. There are small groups of adults talking in a café environment while children pick up a drink or a biscuit but largely play games. Apart from that, the format of a time of gathered prayer, praise and teaching in a family-friendly style, followed by shared craft activity based on an aspect of the teaching theme, is similar to the Messy model. This, no doubt, affects the dynamics of the event and the way relationships are fostered. Another difference is that the group meets every week during term time rather than on the more normal monthly pattern of Messy Church. So, although one aspect of the contact with adults might be affected by not having a shared meal, relationships are being built up in a far more regular context.

The church and its location are anonymous, but the details described are accurate and the observations were made during a review of its ministry. The church from which this fresh expression of Church arose exists on an estate of social housing in a town that, otherwise, offers high-priced private housing. The parent church is itself a plant from an older Victorian church, and has a relatively modern building which was erected along with the housing that formed part of the town expansion in the 1960s. The church's regular congregations are from a broad age range, with a number of young families, most of whom do not live on the estate but come from the more affluent surrounding areas.

In 2008, the idea emerged of a new event, meeting after school on Wednesdays, that would offer a mix of worship, fellowship and craft activity in a fun atmosphere involving both parents and children. The event took shape in early 2009 and quickly attracted 50 attendees, growing to around 100 in the same year. There were also 20 regular volunteers, drawn mainly from the parent church but also from other churches in the area. At the end of the first year, the parent church, pleased with the success of the new venture, agreed to fund the lead worker but also had questions about the high level of resources being used, in terms of people and now finance, and wanted to understand how this fresh expression of Church related to the existing congregation and their own families and children's and youth programmes. On this basis, a review was set up involving people from the new congregation, the wider church and a member of Church Army's Research Unit. This review took place in the autumn of 2010, reporting the following spring.

Fresh expression of Church or fresh expression of mission?

The questions put to the review team were common ones asked of fresh expressions of Church. Was the new event an outreach project of the church, designed to bring more people into existing expressions of Church, or a fresh expression of Church in its own right? Was it attracting new people or supporting existing members? Was the use of resources wise and was it taking resources away from existing programmes? Were the attendees being enabled to encounter Christ and grow in Christian faith?

These were very pertinent questions because the initial vision did not make plain whether the group was intended to be a fresh expression of Church or an outreach project. However, it was becoming apparent to all that the new people being attracted were not becoming part of Sunday church life, and, for many involved, the idea that this was a fresh expression of Church in its own right was also becoming clear.

As part of the review, questions were applied to determine whether or not the new group was a church. A key issue for those involved was that it had attracted a very different group of people from the existing congregation in that, except for the families who attended because their adults were part of the volunteer team running the event, its members came from the estate in which the sending church was situated. A postcode search engine showed the economic and social differences between those coming to the fresh expression of Church and those attending the existing con-gregations. For the people involved, and the church's leadership, this was felt to be a good reason to say that the fresh expression needed to be seen as a church in its own right and not an outreach designed to enable people to join the existing congregations.

With regard to other criteria, the fresh expression of Church had its own name, met regularly, was building community and offered worship. However, there were issues that needed exploring further. Those attending, apart from the volunteers, were almost entirely de-churched or non-churched. Many, when asked, said that they viewed the group as an after-school club rather than a church. In addition, because it had initially been seen as an outreach project, it was funded entirely by the existing church. Given the suggestion that it was a church in its own right, questions were asked about sacraments (although there was provision for these because a minister from the sending church was part of the volunteer team).

The volunteers expressed how much their involvement had helped them grow in Christian ministry and in their relationships with God and with each other, but it was not clear that the group was 'church' to them, either. For some of the key leaders in the volunteer team, this was their church, but for most it was not. Most of the volunteers saw their primary church as being elsewhere. Some had simply not thought to ask the question; others recognised that the fresh expression of Church did not offer what they felt they needed in terms of fellowship and teaching. This brought back the question of adult discipleship, because the teaching was aimed far more at the children present than the adults. So who really thought it was church?

Were all the adults really part of the 'church'?

It was illuminating to observe one of this fresh expression of Church's weekly gatherings. Firstly, a lot of really good things were happening. There was a great atmosphere; people were having fun; children were mixing well and so were their mums and, in some cases, dads and other carers. Sometimes the adults were talking with each other, sometimes engaged in activities with the children present—and not only their own children. Many, though not all, of the parents (not just the volunteers) were involved with the children in the craft activity that happened towards the end of the meeting. While some volunteers were making and serving refreshments, others were ensuring that the activities went well and that people were included, or were having significant conversations with parents present. Indeed, a number of stories were told about how the fresh expression of Church had impacted the lives of the adults coming, a number of whom had very difficult family situations. This impact also extended to steps of faith from those with no Christian background.

However, what happened during the time of worship, prayer and teaching was highly revealing. The building was a very flexible modern church building, with space at one end for liturgy and at the other for social activity. Most of the meeting happened in the social space, but the worship happened in the 'sacred' space. The liturgical space had an area of floor in front of what, on Sunday, would be the Communion table, with several rows of chairs in an arc behind that floor space. When this part of the meeting was announced, people moved from the social to the liturgical area. However, while all the children went to the front and sat on the floor, the parents did not all follow. Some sat right behind the children and participated fully with them in the singing, prayers and teaching. Others sat some way back and did not participate, but watched the children doing so. Others sat on the very back row and pulled out their mobile phones, which they 'played with' until the worship slot had finished.

Bearing in mind that this group neither claims to be Messy Church not follows completely the Messy Church model, we cannot assume that a generic problem for Messy Church is that adult participation in worship is assumed but sometimes unwillingly given—but the question is worth asking.

At one level, it could be viewed as an issue of layout. Had the worship happened in the same space as the crafts and social activities, the dynamics would have been different. However, if that had been the case, the body language might not have so obviously revealed the way the parents perceived their relationship with the religious content of the meeting. While some were participating with the children, who all participated fully, others were observers on the edge or were trying to be, in effect, not present. We were told that this happened every week and the volunteers who led the worship and teaching found it distracting. They were concerned about how to get the non-participating parents involved. Fortunately, those participating in the worship couldn't see the parents behind them and weren't being distracted.

Part of the DNA of the Messy model (and also part of the case study explored in this chapter, even though the group involved isn't actually Messy Church) is the holding together of elements that most churches keep apart. This is seen in the way the whole event is aimed at both parents and children, and other adults too, but also in the way the social interaction, crafts and worship all form part of the same event. The evidence so far suggests that this enables the children to be full members of the church, but also that adults are attending who otherwise would not. In other churches, a club might be run after school, with crafts and worship, to which parents would send their children. The Messy Church model is that the parents are fully involved, building up family life. Yet the example in this case study raises questions: what exactly are those adults coming to, and what are they saying about their own Christian faith or lack of it in doing so?

For a moment, let us imagine another church running all the components of Messy Church but splitting them into separate events on separate days. (Of course, this would mean that it wasn't properly Messy Church, but thinking in this way may help us to understand the issues arising when all the components are present in one event.) So, imagine that Messy worship happens on Sunday, a Messy meal on Wednesday and Messy crafts on Friday. All of these activities are expressly intended for adults and children together.

This scenario would show which parts of the split-up Messy Church the adults attended. Would some come only to the meal and the crafts? Would many send their children to Messy worship but not attend themselves? Or would they come and sit at the back, watching rather than participating? The question then raised would be, are those who are not part of the worship life of the church really part of the church at all?

Here we have to be careful; there is a tendency, due to our Christendom heritage, to talk about churchgoers rather than church members. Technically, in Christendom thinking, everyone was a member of the state church unless they opted not to be, so attendance on Sunday was seen to mark out faith. The problem with this scenario was that church ceased to be viewed as something people were part of and became something they would go to. The building or the service, rather than the people, ended up being seen as 'church'. The Christendom model would say of those who didn't attend on Sunday that they were 'not going to church'. In a way,

Messy Church, by combining other activities with worship, exposes that attitude by rightly saying that all those activities are part of what we do as the church in this place. A proper understanding would be that the meal and the craft activities are as much part of the church as the worship is, whether these components take place at the same event or at different ones. We need, therefore, to dismiss an inherited reaction that those who do not worship are not going to church and are therefore not part of the church.

Many church activities are designed to be accessible to people of faith and to people with little or no faith. Of the people present at such events, we might reasonably distinguish between those who have faith and those who do not, suggesting that the former are members of the church and the latter are not. This would be a far more theologically robust distinction, viewing church membership as an incorporation into the body of Christ through faith and by the work of the Holy Spirit. We cannot see into people's hearts and minds and fully judge what God is doing in their lives. However, it seems quite likely that those who do not want to participate in worship are expressing a lack of faith in Christ and are probably not to be viewed as church members. As Messy Church combines the different elements, we might suggest that a person can come regularly to Messy Church but actually not be a member of the church at all. It may not be a bad thing—indeed, it may be a key to a Messy model of mission—but this reality may be hidden if we declare that Messy Church is church because it clearly carries the appropriate marks of being a church.

If we think back to other models of church, it becomes clear that this situation is not unique to Messy Church. Many churches, as part of their mission, run events that are accessible to non-Christians and enable them to build relationships with Christians and explore Christian faith. The hope is that such events become part of a journey to faith and that the new Christian then becomes part of the worshipping community of the church. Applying the criteria used to assess fresh expressions of Church, such events on their own would be viewed as fresh expressions of outreach rather than Church. Only if there is also a new or radically transformed worshipping community, for those reached by the church's mission, would the whole project be called a fresh expression of Church—and rightly so. It has a worship life, community life and outreach events showing at least some of the marks of Church.

Messy Church contains all these elements and is thus, if the model is followed, a fresh expression of Church. However, unlike many other fresh expressions of Church, it runs its outreach and its worship within the same event and not separately. What may well be happening is that some (and, in our case study, most) of the adults attending Messy Church are not Christians and are, in effect, coming to the Messy outreach but opting out of the Messy worship. When we recognise this, it becomes clear why such people don't wish to join a discipleship group: they are not disciples.

This situation is similar to the long-known issues of nominalism in traditional expressions. Here, a parallel with traditional church may be helpful. In many churches, there are times when people without a Christian faith attend worship services and either don't participate at all or do so partially. Events such as baptisms and weddings often see many adults present for the occasion who are not truly part of the worship. Some churches have visitors who sit at the back and observe, like the adults in the fresh expression of Church described in our case study. Other churches, of course, run guest services or events like Back to Church Sunday, to which people who don't normally attend are invited. Firstly, this parallel should stop us from criticising Messy Church by saying that many of those attending it are not really members of the church; this scenario is part of much church experience. Secondly, we might ask ourselves whether we think the attendance of non-Christians at traditional church services renders those services 'improper', or whether we see the non-Christians' presence as a mission opportunity. If it is the latter, then the same may be said of Messy Church when the attitudes of adults are unknown or equivocal.

Fresh expression of Church or worship event?

The previous chapter drew a helpful distinction between a fresh expression of outreach, designed to enable people to become members of existing churches, and a fresh expression of Church in which a new Christian community is formed. It is also helpful to distinguish between a fresh expression of worship and a fresh expression of Church. Our research suggests that a number of projects that claim to be fresh expressions of Church are, in fact, innovative and often praiseworthy outreach projects, while others are creative changes to existing worship, rather than an attempt to plant a new Christian community among those who are de- or non-churched. Where does Messy Church come on that scale?

If a Messy Church is designed mainly for existing church members and then attracts others who were already Christians, it might rightly be viewed only as a fresh worship event, not a fresh expression of Church. While Messy Church is certainly designed to attract people who are de- or non-churched, some examples may not do so in practice; thus, individual cases may not be fresh expressions of Church, even if Messy Church is viewed as such overall. However, if it is right to view a Messy Church event as a combination of outreach and worship, and if that combination is attracting non-Christians, it clearly is more than a creative worship service with crafts and a meal for the Christians who attend. The very fact that, for some, Messy Church is a form of outreach means that it is not to be dismissed as simply a fresh worship event.

This, however, raises a further question: would a new worship service that regularly attracted a large percentage of non-Christians be properly viewed as missional and thus be a fresh expression of Church? There are clearly some examples that seem to work in this way: Goth churches, for instance, seem to do it by creating an unusual expression of worship that attracts those who are not Christian but are part of the Goth subculture. But is this an effective form of mission?

Most models of planting a fresh expression of Church suggest that a process of living among the non-churched, listening and discerning what God might be doing and what the 'good news' might be in that culture, is the starting point. Creating worship within the culture comes later, when people from that culture have come to faith and can be part of creating appropriate worship for themselves. When fresh expressions of Church start with worship, it is likely that the worship will be what the Christians *think* is an appropriate expression for that culture, when, as yet, they know far too little to be sure that is true. The Goth model and some local Messy Churches start with worship, despite its being only one of the five stated values (hospitality, creativity, all-age, celebration and Christ-centred). As we have already noted, this is not all that Messy Church does, but, if worship dominates, such an approach invites genuine concern that the worship adopted may turn out to be the existing churchgoers' idea of what will be appropriate for families in their area, rather than what really is appropriate. This issue can be compounded by the provision of online resources for worship.

However, some approaches to mission suggest that attending worship as a non-Christian, even if the worship is not properly at home in that person's culture, may have a missional impact. Over several centuries, a number of Christian apologists have attacked the prevailing idea that coming to faith is a rational decision that people make, and that then they become members of the church. Blaise Pascal, writing in the 17th century, suggested that faith is enabled by experience of the Christian life, not by rational proof. For Pascal, rather than a person's belief leading them to join the church and live a Christian life, those invited to join the church try out what it means to be a Christian, in the hope that this experience will lead them to believe. At the end of the 19th century, French philosopher Maurice Blondel argued similarly that faith could be discovered only through experience, and that the end of faith was not right belief but right living. An experiential approach was also offered by Søren Kierkegaard.

In many ways, these voices anticipated the postmodern turn from truth as facts demonstrated by reason, to truth as experience. Echoes are also present in the debate about whether the pattern of conversion follows a model of 'believing, belonging and behaving' or whether 'belonging' might come first. These writers, however, not only make this suggestion with regard to belonging to a Christian community but also suggest that being present at worship may in itself be a converting experience. Might this be true in a Messy Church context and in the case study described earlier in this chapter?

There may already be examples of people coming to faith because of the worship element of Messy Church gatherings. This doesn't seem to have happened yet in the case study cited, but that doesn't mean it will not; it is still early days when we think of the time it can take for the non-churched to make that faith journey. We might ask how much of an experience of worship is being had by someone sitting at a distance, ostensibly playing with their mobile phone—but the person is at least there, and the activity might be their way of coping with being there, while keeping half an ear open to what is going on. Others are clearly watching and paying more attention, and it is almost certainly the case that they wouldn't be there at all if the Messy model of combining craft, social interaction and worship had not been adopted.

A Messy model of mission?

All of this suggests that Messy Church has taken the normal model of planting a fresh expression of Church and put its own unique twist on it. This twist may or may not be fully worked out explicitly, but it is implicit and worth highlighting. Many would seek to build relationships within a community, then organise separate appropriate outreach events, and later, when people have come to faith, build a worshipping community within the culture. Messy Church has instead created a single event that enables the building of relationships with non-Christians, includes outreach activities and invites non-Christians to join with Christians in all-age worship. Implicit in this is not only an invitation to belong before believing but an assumption that the experience of worship, which may in itself be missional, is open to non-Christians. The genius of Messy Church's approach is that, because these three elements are combined into one event, people who would not otherwise attend worship are doing so, even if they are doing their best to distance themselves from it. If it is right that the experience of worship can lead to faith, then this is a powerful achievement. Once this is understood, the clear advice for those who are concerned about adults not participating in worship is to welcome their presence just as it is and to understand that they are expressing where they are on their faith journey rather than disrupting the worship. Encouraging them to be more involved at the wrong time may cause them to leave and not come back.

Messy Church not only combines the three components of relationship-building, outreach and worship but also brings to-gether children and adults. Some of the adults may be attending because they enjoy the outreach element but are only tolerating the worship aspect and not participating in it. However, their children are there, and, in the case study explored above, the children were participating in the worship. This does not mean that these children are Christians, but it does show that if an event is created that offers teaching and worship appropriate for children, their parents will also come. These children are being raised in church with their parents' approval, which is likely to increase the chances that they will become Christians in the future, either as children or as adults. It also suggests another way in which their parents may come to faith. The Messy Church blog includes an insightful post, quoting a mother who wants to learn about the Christian faith so that she can answer all the questions her children are asking as a result of their Messy Church experience. That woman could, of course, be a Christian who has had little teaching, but she might also be a non-

Christian who is deciding to learn about Christianity because of the impact Messy Church is having on her children. If so, it would not be the first instance of a church in which adults came to faith as a result of the discipling of their children.

Would other fresh expressions of Church, working with other groups, gain by following the Messy model that is working well with families? There may be cases where it might work, but the success of Messy Church in attracting non-Christians, as well as being a product of the model, may be to do with the demographic it reaches. Its appeal is firstly that it offers a fun activity for the whole family; this factor makes it much easier to attract non-Christian children to outreach events rather than attracting adults only. Secondly, it provides time for parents and children to have fun together, which, for many families, is rare. In some sections of society, a fresh expression of Church needs to work at building relationships for a long time before any events can be started, whereas Messy Churches may find that all they need to do is advertise and people will come. Not only that, but non-Christians, who would not otherwise go anywhere near worship, will come because they value the other parts of the package.

If there are positive missional outcomes of the Messy Church model, there are also challenges. The issues raised by trying to disciple adults who are attending Messy Church are, in part, a consequence of confusing their attendance at something called 'church' with actual membership of a church. As we have seen, for some of these adults it is just a craft club (from our point of view, an outreach project rather than church), but this perspective is hidden by the inclusion of worship and the adoption of the name Messy Church.

If this is a possible consequence of the Messy model, it may also be a consequence of the desire to distinguish between fresh expressions of Church and creative outreach projects. It is not that this distinction is invalid; indeed, if not made carefully it may not take account of the fact that many fresh expressions of Church begin life as outreach projects. Some of these projects are clearly intended to plant a new church and thus would be classified as fresh expressions of Church in infancy, aiming for a more mature expression of Church in the future. Others, though not initially intended as a new church, later find that this is clearly what they have become. These too may be seen, with hindsight, as fresh expressions in infancy. In both cases, for many fresh expressions of Church, it is very important to allow enough time for the outreach project stage to develop, without rushing to the worship stage before there are new Christians with whom to form it. There may be a danger that the desire to be classified as a fresh expression of Church rather than an outreach project puts pressure on Christian volunteers to prove they are a church by providing or initiating worship far too early in the story.

Some tentative conclusions

It may be that the inclusion of worship in the Messy package turns out to be a major contribution to its missional impact. However, it may turn out to be damaging to the proper development of worship as an expression of the faith of those who, for now, are engaging with an outreach project. Raising this possibility also highlights a further issue that the Messy Church model may be hiding—the difference between the needs of the Christian volunteers and the needs of non-Christians who are part of the wider Messy Church community. Even if many who are part of that wider community are not ready for discipleship groups, the volunteers will need such groups if the community is to be 'their church'. If Christian volunteers remain primarily as members of other churches because of this lack, it may threaten the long-term stability of young churches. This issue may also be true of the worship: is it for the volunteer team and their families more than it is for the non-Christian families? Again, it may be that by recognising that many families are coming to Messy Church outreach even though worship is included, attention can then be focused on the discipleship needs of the Christian members of the church alongside the very different needs of those who are not yet Christian.

The notion that there are different needs for different groups in Messy Church, which may require extra events such as discipleship groups, also challenges the strong value in Messy Church of doing everything together. Yet does the intention to build an all-age Christian family in Messy Church, in which all are equal members together, have to mean that everything must be done in one event? Real families do not operate that way, even at their best. Much can and will be done together in a good family, but not everything will be or should be. This realisation has implications for a developing Messy Church programme that can offer people what they need at different stages of faith but also at different stages of life. It does not mean an inevitable return to separate adults' and children's churches, but it may mean that if the teaching remains accessible for children at Messy Church, older groups need additional events, appropriate to their age. To make these events additional rather than alternative will be challenging but not necessarily impossible.

The combination of elements in Messy Church, along with its ability to welcome non-Christians into its community, means that in most cases it is likely to be classified as a fresh expression of Church. However, this may hide the fact that many of those who come along to Messy Church are actually taking part in an outreach project, not church at all. If we recognise this, it raises some challenging questions about the inclusion of worship, and there is the added danger of failing to enable Messy Church to be church for its Christian volunteers. Then again, by combining elements that, for many fresh expressions of Church, are different stages of planting a church, the Messy model of mission may make the journey of faith easier and quicker for those non-Christians who are part of the Messy Church community.

✥

Case study: Messy Church Special Educational Needs

Trish Hahn

Trish Hahn runs a Messy Church in Hemel Hempstead, for families that have a child with a disability.

In Luke 14:12–14, Jesus implores us to embrace the gospel message of inclusivity. He tells us not to invite our friends when we put on a dinner party but to invite the marginalised members of society—those living in poverty or with personal experience of disability, who often suffer from a sense of isolation.

In verses 15–24 the conversation turns to heavenly matters as Jesus describes the heart of his Father, through the parable of a house owner who throws a banquet. The master orders his servants to go out and compel 'the poor, the crippled, the blind and the lame... to come in, so that my house will be full' (NIV). God's kingdom will not be complete without the people who are often overlooked, forgotten and excluded.

The ethos and message of Luke 14 are at the heart of Messy Church for families living with disability at Adeyfield Free Church. We are a group of ordinary Christians who have caught the vision for an 'all-inclusive' community and are trying to live by faith to see those on the fringes of society enabled to take their place at the Lord's table.

Statistics show that, within the UK, 72 per cent of families with disabled children are left isolated; half become so unwell that they seek medical help from their GP.[19] One in five has suffered a break-up of family or marriage due to a lack of support, and, according to the Joseph Rowntree Foundation (2009), disabled people are twice as likely to live in poverty.

Our model of Messy Church Special Educational Needs (SEN) originated in September 2011, following a vision given to one of the church members for a new type of church group specifically for children with SEN. She has personal experience of living with a child who has a severe physical disability and needs support 24/7.

Many of our Messy Church families whose children have a disability have a real sense of feeling isolated, and their child's disability and resultant behaviour may make them feel uncomfortable within a community or family setting. Indeed, some of the parents have been emotionally wounded by unloving words and attitudes from other people, even within the church, who have little or no understanding of disability and the many forms it can take. Our aim is to make these families feel welcomed, accepted and loved, no matter what their family situation or their child's condition. Siblings often attend and it has been beneficial for them to mix and play freely with other able-bodied children. We want to provide a safe, secure environment for these families, so that they can experience church in a vibrant, non-threatening way, with emphasis on accessing appropriate sensory and tactile craft activities, interactive songs and stories using puppets, drama and other resources. Many of the resources we use, we adapt ourselves.

At our Messy Church we have children with a range of disabilities including cerebral palsy, Down's syndrome, learning disabilities, epilepsy, and some on the autistic spectrum. We are introducing Makaton (using fingers to speak) into our songs and story time as some of the children cannot vocalise words and some use Makaton at school. Widgit is another communication aid that we have introduced, which uses pictures with written words underneath, further enabling children to understand what activities are on offer. The most recent addition to our programme is a picture timeline to help children feel comfortable and to give some structure to their playtime.

This particular model of Messy Church continues to develop through listening to parents' comments and thoughts, and adapting and evolving our ideas and themes to tailor the programme to meet the specific needs of those attending. Volunteers also attend training courses to learn more about issues such as autism, and skills such as using Makaton in Christian worship songs. Resources used include the *Messy Church* books, information from the charity Through the Roof and sensory toys from our local toy library. A particular challenge is how to engage our families intentionally with the gospel message and lively worship songs while keeping everything straightforward, visually engaging and clear, as visual prompts particularly aid some children in their understanding.

We want the parents to know that they can relax and let their child just be who they are without being afraid that others will judge them, their child's behaviour or their parenting skills. Parents are able to chat freely with others who understand and can empathise with their situation, and we provide current information about support available from within the community and local health service.

Comments from parents include:

Messy Church SEN is opening doors to both Christian and non-Christian families of children with disabilities, showing them love in action, offering fellowship, understanding and care, consideration and kindness. It gives them the opportunity of meeting others in the same boat.

For us it's a very enjoyable time, a chance for both our children to play with others without us having to stress about their behaviour being judged.

We love the atmosphere—friendly, lively and fun. Great to be able to take the children with special needs somewhere where their differences are celebrated and accepted. Also lovely to meet other parents and carers and chat over a cup of tea.

At Adeyfield Free Church we believe that all people, including those with disabilities, are made in the image of God (Genesis 1:27), and we welcome, accept and value every disabled child, sibling, parent and carer, encouraging them through love in action to have a personal relationship with Jesus. We believe that this model of Messy Church is the ideal vehicle to enable us to reach out to those families that society often keeps at arm's length. Volunteers ranging in age from six through to teenage, as well as over-60s, are getting alongside these families, helping to create a fun and vibrant atmosphere in which we meet together with God in a unique and special way.

3

How does Messy Church travel?

Lucy Moore

Lucy Moore works for BRF as Messy Church Team Leader. She is responsible for developing the work of Messy Church nationally and internationally—writing, speaking, reflecting and developing Messy projects. She continues to help lead the local Messy Church in her own church, where her husband is the minister. Before working full-time with Messy Church, Lucy was a member of BRF's Barnabas Children's Ministry team, offering training for those wanting to bring the Bible to life for children in churches and schools across the UK, and using drama and storytelling to explore the Bible with children herself. Besides the Messy Church series, her books include Bethlehem Carols Unplugged, The Gospels Unplugged, The Lord's Prayer Unplugged *and* Colourful Creation *(all Barnabas for Children) and* All-Age Worship *(BRF, 2010), and she presents* Messy Church: The DVD.

Jesus told them another story: 'The kingdom of heaven is like what happens when a farmer plants a mustard seed in a field. Although it is the smallest of all seeds, it grows larger than any garden plant and becomes a tree. Birds even come and nest on its branches.'

MATTHEW 13:31–32 (CEV)

This appropriately tiny parable about a tiny object that becomes unexpectedly huge keeps cropping up (no pun intended) in re-

flections about Messy Church, not least because the black mustard plant was a weed that was impossible to get rid of once it had
established itself, and no farmer in his or her right mind would
deliberately plant a weed. Messy Church is arguably a disreputable,
less presentable member of the church family, an unpredictable and
sometimes unwanted weed that has appeared in the garden and is
spreading with the wild abandon of a dandelion on intravenous
fertiliser.

I often tell this story about the genesis of Messy Church. There
was a gardener—we'll call him Fred—and Fred had a vegetable
garden in which he grew vegetables of one sort or another. Some
years the plot did very well and he got a large crop, and other years
the weather was bad or there was a pest of some sort, and in those
years the crop was less good.

One day Fred went out to his garden with his hoe in his hand
and there, to his surprise, in the middle of the vegetable plot was
a Wild Weed. He'd never seen anything like it before. 'I must root
it out!' he thought. 'It could be something like bindweed, which
will send its root system under my entire garden and I'll never get
rid of it. It could be something poisonous, which will infect my
entire crop. Or it could...' (and here his imagination was going
a little overboard), 'it could have escaped from a GM laboratory
and will grow into some sort of man-eating monstrosity that will
wrap tentacles around old ladies or small children and devour them
mercilessly!' Fred stepped forward with his hoe in his hand to dig
out the Wild Weed before it was too late. But then he stopped.

'What if...' he thought, 'what if this isn't a weed at all? What if
it's actually a gift from someone? What if it grows into something
beautiful and rare, like a black rose or a blue tulip? What if its
seeds provide a solution to world hunger or its leaves are a cure for
some hideous disease?' And Fred stood there with his hoe in his
hand and wondered what on earth he, as a responsible gardener,
should do.

Asked to advise Fred, people happily suggested solutions,

from the curt 'Blast it with weedkiller' to 'Send an email to Radio 4's *Gardeners' Question Time*', to Googling it or isolating it in a greenhouse.

It felt very much like Fred's predicament when Messy Church began to spread, back in 2005–2006. Was this a malignant waste of time that would suck all the creativity and resources of a local church into a process leading to no growth except that of an ungodly or harmful variety? Or was it a gift of God to be cherished and nurtured, that might bring new life, beauty, healing and nourishment?

Several years after the start of Messy Church in 2004, our weed—or, to return to Jesus' original parable, our mustard seed—is still very much in the growing stage. There are plenty of garden plants that are much bigger and better rooted than Messy Church, while the suspicious postmodern birds are only just bouncing on its branches to see if they're strong enough to nest in. It will be some time before we know whether the weedkiller brigade had the right view of it. In the meantime, we rely on good and godly friends, some of whom are contributing to this book, to reflect critically and objectively on what is happening in and through the Mess; and at the heart of it all, in BRF, we do our best to nurture this strange gift wisely and well. Later in this chapter, I'll be considering what it is about Messy Church that makes it readily usable across the denominations and in different countries and contexts, and what BRF is doing to encourage and nurture Messy Church.

Messy Church is indeed growing! New Messy Churches are currently registering at a rate of about one a day on the directory on the website. By July 2010 there were 402 registrations; by July 2011 the number had risen to 785 and by July 2012 there were over 1300. By June 2013 there were 1873. Word of mouth suggests that there are probably about three times as many who haven't yet registered. A review of the directory in early 2012 threw up just seven Messy Churches who asked to be deleted as they no longer run—a fairly negligible 'failure rate'. From its tiny start in a medium-sized Anglican church in the UK, it has spread to every major Christian denomination and into at least 14 countries, predominantly and predictably English-speaking ones or English-speaking communities in countries such as Switzerland, Spain or South Africa, but also into Denmark, Germany and Wales on a larger scale and other countries such as Poland or Norway on a one-off basis.

Are these figures reliable, though? There is currently no 'statement of faith' or 'entry requirement' for Messy Churches to sign up to. BRF hasn't built a wall around the garden and set a bouncer at the gate. We know for a fact that some of the churches on the directory, while they are doubtless doing worthy work, are not doing what we would call Messy Church. They might be leading a toddler group or a craft club and calling it Messy Church. They might be leading an after-school children's club or even a lively family activity session with no food, no all-age aspect and no mention of Jesus from one month to the next, and still calling it Messy Church. We know of one church that has simply rebranded its Sunday school as Messy Church. This interesting situation reveals something about the way in which Messy Church has developed and about the way that BRF has, rightly or wrongly, chosen to nurture it.

Let's consider first how it's growing. How do people hear about it? What makes them start their own Messy Church? What is it about Messy Church that engenders enthusiasm in a High Anglican church in inner-city London as much as in a New Frontiers church in Worthing, a tiny Methodist church in rural North Wales or a Salvation Army Corps in Adelaide?

Personal enthusiasm

News travels on several levels—the all-important personal level of gossiping the good news, then the strategy of BRF and finally the different means that God has put in place to make it spread easily.

We might describe them as the neighbour talking over the garden fence, the landscape gardener and the city planner.

Gossip is a hugely important factor in the spread of Messy Church. Society has never valued this apparently idle chit-chat, particularly by women, but if we take any malevolence out of the word and use it purely in the sense of community storytelling, using a social network to spread an idea or 'viral networking', we can claim that the idea of Messy Church has been spread through gossip as one person simply enthuses about their latest news and ideas to their social circle. One member of our congregation was gossiping to a new acquaintance at the dinner table on a cruise and waxed lyrical about our Messy Church. When she came home, she asked for a copy of the book to send to this person in Australia, who had expressed curiosity, fuelled no doubt by Lori's palpable enthusiasm. People will share what they are passionate about, and Christians in many churches are desperate to share the goodness of God with their local communities, not out of a sense of empire-building or self-protection but because they have experienced what God can do to transform an individual or family life. They've got something good and they want others to share it.

Why then did early Christianity spread? Because early Christians believed that what they had found to be true was true for the whole world. The impetus to mission sprang from the very heart of early Christian conviction.[20]

Organisational resources

The support network that BRF has put in place works alongside this informal, gossipy approach. There is no space in this chapter to describe the work the team is doing to 'listen, reflect and chronicle' what is happening in Messy Churches to enrich our understanding and practice. I will merely describe how we currently resource the spread of the idea. The books and other resources that are available, the face-to-face training on offer across the UK from team members, the commitment to provide articles for publications from other organisations and to lead seminars or actual Messy Church sessions at festivals and big Christian gatherings like Greenbelt and Spring Harvest, and the dense (if messy) website all contribute towards the spread of the idea and the ongoing nurture of the ministry. The enquiry buttons on the website, which are a direct line to the team, are in use every day, with people across the world asking all sorts of questions, from where they can find ideas on the great commission to the stickier points of theological underpinning.

Events such as Messy Meet-ups, gathering leaders to share ideas and problems, or the more ambitious Messy Weekends also help resource the network. Jane Leadbetter's responsibility in the BRF Messy Church team is to grow a team of volunteer Regional Coordinators across the UK and overseas to cascade support and information to individual Messy Churches and to send stories back to BRF so that we can learn from all that is going on across the network. Through regular emails and an annual gathering, Jane 'gossips' the latest news to the Regional Coordinators, who filter it out to their own networks as appropriate. As one of them said when she accepted the challenge, 'It is my utter devotion to the concepts of Messy Church which actually makes it impossible to say no!'[21]

Structural provision

Messy Church has been proved to work most effectively where a diocese has been far-sighted enough to support the 'movement' structurally. The Bishop of Shrewsbury, Mark Rylands, has done just this and appointed a Messy Church Adviser for his episcopal area. We are grateful that, by mid-2013, two of the main denominations had offered a contribution towards core costs at BRF from central funding and continue to work towards wider recognition. A few Diocesan Children's Advisers have been allowed to include the role of Regional Coordinator as a small part of their work. To help their Messy Churches survive over the coming years, churches would do well to learn from the Bishop of Shrewsbury's visionary example and appoint more paid workers regionally to prioritise the nurture and development of Messy Churches.

Of course, the network of support also operates independently of BRF, through the generosity and goodwill of people who simply want to share a good thing around—a very Christian virtue. I say 'independently' but, arguably, the generosity of spirit at BRF that offers Messy Church as a free gift to the church and asks for nothing in return finds an echo in the graciousness of those who have been touched by this open-handedness. Revd Kathy Biles, who ministers in Port Stanley in the Falklands, describes the network of support that helped her to get Messy Church off the ground, from the leaders who answered her questions in the Midlands to the people in the Falklands who had experienced Messy Church already in previous places and were keen to share their expertise.

During a sabbatical last year, I was able to research Messy Church and to visit Messy Churches in Nottingham and Derbyshire. In February I gave an introductory presentation—using the Messy Church DVD— which was attended by members of all churches. Everyone present was interested, enthusiastic and willing to offer help. Since then, with one or two minor setbacks, the project has gathered pace...

It looks as though it will be a steep learning curve, but we are blessed by having Edmonde Openshaw and her husband, Steve Gill, who ran Messy Church at their church in Chinley, Derbyshire, before coming here last August to manage the Lighthouse Seamen's Mission in Stanley. The Entwistle family, now based at Mount Pleasant, have also been involved in Messy Church in southern England—so we have someone to turn to for practical advice.

The DNA of BRF

Why has BRF chosen to nurture Messy Church in this supportive and non-prescriptive way, rather than by setting out regulations and franchise agreements? It is interesting to look through the archives of BRF to discern something of the DNA that runs in our veins as an organisation. At St Matthew's Church, Brixton, Revd Leslie Mannering and his staff were wrestling with the issue of how to nurture the people in their spiritual care. Their concern is summed up in a piece that Revd Mannering wrote in the Parish Magazine of December 1921:

We are so apt to be immersed in organisations, committees and plans, that we become entangled in our own machinery. Even if the machinery is running smoothly and well, there is a danger of it being—just machinery. It is the dynamic of personal faith that really moves men and things. We need to get back to the fundamentals of our faith.

So first we see a rejection of mechanical structures and a call to the personal, relational nature of faith. This cutting to the heart of Christianity and a refusal to become rigid and fossilised finds surprising resonance in the development of Messy Church. The idea of producing Bible reading notes was born and grew very quickly in popularity in St Matthew's and in neighbouring churches who started to ask for the notes for their own use. In 1947, Revd Mannering wrote in an article called 'The story of the BRF', celebrating 25 years of BRF:

Thus the Fellowship entered upon a new phase. There were indications that it might grow rapidly—all the more need, therefore, for prayer and guidance. What might be the purpose of God for this Fellowship? What line ought we to take? In May 1927, again under the leadership of Canon Pym, a group of us met for prayer and conference at the Diocesan Retreat House in Carshalton. It was unanimously agreed that the movement should be left to grow naturally and without publicity. As Canon Pym said, 'the Spirit must have free play'.

During a time of bewildering growth, remarkably like the time of growth of Messy Church, those responsible for BRF felt strongly that God's Holy Spirit should have 'free play', a statement that is startling enough now to modern ears. Revd Mannering made three further statements which have a bearing on the way Messy Church is developing. First, he said, 'What happened? Looking back we can only marvel at the way in which the good hand of God has been upon the Fellowship.' We too spend a lot of time marvelling at what God is doing in Messy Church. Then, 'We belong to a Fellowship; let us see to it that we are a Fellowship. The more this can be realised and implemented, the stronger will be the spiritual life of the BRF.' We too do our best to maintain strong relationships within the core team and with the wider network of Messy Church leaders, Regional Coordinators and leaders in the wider church in order to preserve unity within the church.

Finally, Revd Mannering said:

We hope the anniversary commemoration will lead to the Bible becoming more of a living force in the hearts and lives of men (and women). The last thing we want to do is to blow the BRF trumpet for its own sake. Yet we dare to hope that it may be used to sound a call that may be heard far and wide, rallying men (and women) back to the Bible.

We too see that there may be a danger in getting so tied up with Messy Church that we lose sight of the living God who is behind and over it all. We too want people not just to enjoy Messy Church but to meet the God for whom it all exists.

A small idea in a local church developed into an organisation that celebrated its 90th anniversary in 2012 and has nurtured and resourced the discipleship of countless men, women and children all over the world through Bible reading notes, books, dynamic websites and face-to-face ministry. It is an organisation that places relationships before programme or structure, and that keeps God at the centre. This DNA continues in a wonderfully fresh way some 90 years later in the same organisation.

Not putting up walls

Was it a mistake to refuse to erect walls around Messy Church to make it clear which groups were 'in' and which were 'out'? In the early days of Messy Church's expansion, we had no idea that it would grow so large and so fast. The image we used was of surfing on a wave of the Spirit—being taken somewhere unknown, by a force over which we had no control but which was enormously exhilarating. Put simply, it was (and still is) huge fun—free play, I suppose. Collecting accurate statistics, being 'protectionist' about the concept or making money out of it: none of these elements was a priority for the team, which started off as just one person with office back-up. Helping people to do it effectively, acting as advocates for the many churches starting it and listening to what God is doing through Messy Church certainly were and still are priorities. Messy Church was seen by the team and trustees as a great gift of God to the church, with BRF as the privileged figure that got to distribute the gift. This means, however, that Messy Church is now in the situation of growing in a wide open field with hybrids, lookalikes and mislabelled plants growing up alongside it.

Is this a problem? In some senses, it is not. Just as Jesus was resigned to the way in which life on earth must be a mess, with wheat and weeds growing alongside each other until harvest time, when everything will be sorted out (Matthew 13:24–30), we feel there is absolutely no point in sending some clipboard-wielding 'OfMess' Inspector round to check the purity of the mess that is happening. Apart from the practicalities, we have a growing sense that we need to model what we believe: the medium must reflect the message. The way we 'govern' Messy Church should be an example of how church can be to others. There is a creativity of approach, a generosity of spirit that needs to find expression, and an encouragement of an attitude of service to the local community which needs to be fanned into flame, not extinguished by rules and regulations. 'Are you in or are you out?' is an attitude that Messy Church tries to combat when referring to church-belonging, so it would be ironic to use it in the sense of a policy about the actual organisation of Messy Church. If church teams are finding that the name and network give them confidence and enable and encourage mission and outreach, even if the form that mission takes is not what *we* would call Messy Church, at least mission and outreach are happening where they might not have happened before.

Also, one of the founding principles of starting a fresh expression of Church is that a church should listen to its local community and contextualise its fresh expression of Church, using what it has learned from that listening process. Churches should be encouraged to have confidence in what they discover from listening in their local area. God may have the next brilliant idea for his kingdom waiting to sprout up in another church and they could miss it if they're content simply to deliver a Messy Church package.

If BRF or any denomination starts erecting walls and claiming that such-and-such isn't a Messy Church, that you sign up to a statement of faith or a contract of use of the name or similar binding agreement, not only would there be a huge amount of anxiety and bureaucracy generated, but it would raise the question, 'How do we remain able to change and adapt?' or, in other words, 'How do we stay alive?' No living thing remains static and unchanging; to be alive means to be in a cycle of transformation. Being a living organism is messy. We can say with a fair amount of confidence that our values are those of being all-age, being Christ-centred, creativity, celebration and hospitality, but these are values that we have learned on the way. We didn't start off with them firmly in place: we recognised them as we went along and used them as trellises to help good practice grow strong. Our organic weed is bound to change in appearance as it matures across such a broad range of soils and climates. Do we really want individual churches to do Messy Church in exactly the same way for ever, or do we want them to be free to give the Spirit free play too, perhaps to lead the way in exciting new developments?

An example would be the wonderful Trashy Church, an offshoot of Messy Church in Canterbury Diocese, which claims that its craft is its mission and recycles broken objects for use in the community, or the much-loved Sweaty Church in York,[22] which, while independent of Messy Church, remains a close friend and is breaking new ground in its emphasis on worship through sport and coaching as a metaphor for discipleship.

Anything goes? Quality but not control

There could be a problem, though, when a closer examination of the facts behind the figures reveals that Messy Churches on the Directory turn out to be nothing of the sort, but rather children's clubs or toddler groups that have thoughtlessly appropriated the name. This means, for one thing, that statistics are unreliable. Does this matter? Numbers are fun, but the God of the mustard seed, minute grains of yeast and one pearl has an ambivalent attitude towards figures. However, it does lead to frustration for anyone trying to make accurate claims about what God is doing through Messy Church. It is also frustrating when research done into Messy Church is based on visits to supposed Messy Churches that, in fact, do not share the same core values. One researcher visited two such events in which the adults were actively discouraged from joining in the celebration, and understandably drew the conclusion that, while Messy Church may be good for getting children through the door of a church, it has no effect whatsoever on the discipleship of adults—a finding that could have far-reaching effects if his research is acted upon by his diocese.

It is also a problem when emails such as the following are received, which make us realise that there is an expectation for Messy Church to offer a reliable and consistent 'brand'.

I'm planning to spend the summer in Cornwall with family and am interested in continuing to take my two children to Messy Church throughout this time. Please can you either forward any information or direct me towards where I might find any local event.

It is no longer simply about whether we at BRF think something is Messy Church or not; it's about whether the families for whom it is meant can trust the 'brand'. Is an aspidistra an aspidistra whether it's growing in Scotland or in Cornwall? But then, would we expect a Methodist church service to be identical in two different places? Would we demand our collection money back if a Baptist church we visited in Cardiff sang different hymns from the one we were used to in Carlisle?

Why are Christians so nervous about the word 'brand'? Perhaps because it sounds so crassly commercial; we fear the McDonaldisation of the church against which John Drane warns us.[23] Messy Church is a brand in that it has a clear and recognised identity. BRF protects it insofar as the logo is trademarked and precautions are taken when it travels to environments renowned for pirating good ideas, but the overall ethos is to hold the concept lightly. We are very clear about what Messy Church is and will bust a gut to share that clarity of vision with those who will listen. That's not because we want to control it but because we feel that this is the best way of doing Messy Church, building on years of experience gathered from a wide variety of examples, and we want each Messy Church to stand the best chance of working.

Fingerprints of God

How has God been active in spreading this idea so widely? Jesus was born at a time when ideas could be transmitted speedily across vast distances more easily than ever before in history, thanks in part to the Roman Empire. God put Paul, the passionate intellectual, in place at the right time to spread the news of Jesus to the world of the Gentiles. He brought countless other visionaries, practitioners and technologies along at the right times in history to keep the flame of the gospel alive, to transform society or to give the church a new lease of life.

So, I believe, has God put in place various elements that have made it easy for Messy Church to travel. How likely was it, for instance, that the group starting the first Messy Church would include someone who worked for a Christian organisation that was already set up to deliver high-quality published resources and face-to-face ministry, with the capacity to set up a website, a board of trustees willing to risk finances on extending the ministry by setting that person aside to pursue the work full-time, and a gap in the publishing schedule to allow for the publication of the first *Messy Church* book? What did God need to put in place to make the first Messy Church coincide with the inception of Fresh Expressions, who filmed it and took it around the world as part of the vision day for churches before it was a year old? What cosmic shifts needed to happen in the denominations for permission to be given for it to be seen as genuine church, not as a little club on the side? How valuable has the internet been in sharing information and stories? What about the media of social networking in gossiping the idea across continents? How easy has international travel become, so that inspirational speakers can enthuse about Messy Church face-to-face overseas as well as in the UK? God's plans and timing for giving different churches this new idea are impeccable. What, I wonder, might a modern-day Gamaliel say in the face of such improbabilities?

All can play

Why does Messy Church work in so many different contexts? If nothing else, Messy Church proves gleefully that different denominations have far more similarities than differences. Hooray! The High Anglican church can believe in mission and be passionate about wanting families to grow in Christ just as much as the New Frontiers church. The participation of all the major denominations is a great joy to us. Because the emphasis is on values rather than on programme, there is freedom to give a local flavour to a Messy Church. The qualities of Messy Church are universal Christian ones—love of Jesus, love of the Bible, love of worship, love of creativity, love of family life—rather than specifically denominational ones, and its 'flavour' is one of cooperation and generosity. (What we will do if a group from a less central movement, such as the Jehovah's Witnesses or the Mormons, asks to use the logo, we're not yet sure.)

It also 'works' because people feel confident to start it. It is tried and tested. There is a host of stories about it from churches of all shapes and sizes. There are people of all sorts running Messy Churches, not just clever trained theology students: the large bank of material to draw on gives people confidence to 'just go for it', as Revd Elizabeth Youngson says on Messy Church: The DVD. It's very simple. It uses elements that churches have used for years (meals, hands-on learning, family work), so it feels familiar. It doesn't require an ordained person to take control, but liberates the gifts of lay people who may have been passengers in church and turns them into leaders. It taps into the Zeitgeist in which churches need to reconnect with lost generations, from a new position of creeping ever more towards the edge of society rather than from its traditional place at the centre. In an age of rules and regulations that has led to a fear of being responsible for other people's children, it is liberating for leaders to be assured that they are not responsible for enforcing discipline, but can simply share their faith and skills with families.

For families it makes sense, as it taps into universal needs. Many parents want what is best for their children, and that includes bringing them up with a stake in the church, learning Bible stories and learning to pray. They don't necessarily trust the church implicitly, as may have been the case in times past, so some adults appreciate being there alongside their children to hear what is being said and taught, to be reassured that this is not religious fanaticism or some weird cult but just their local church with people they know from the school gates and the park. Some enjoy learning how to be better parents from being part of this church community. They appreciate somewhere cheap to go as a family. They enjoy having other parents to talk to, and find the 'guided play' helpful when they have no model to look to for entertaining their children. These elements are universal to parents all over the world, from every socio-economic group, all of whom have at some level of their consciousness a sense that childhood is a precious time, that life is fast-changing and transient, and that they want to be the best parents they can be.

In the words of Canon Mannering, again from 1947, 'What of the future? Putting our trust in God and not in ourselves, we should face it with the highest expectation.' Where we have made mistakes, they have sometimes come from setting our expectations of God too low, not expecting him to include us in taking such a massive step to draw families back to him, but relying instead on what we, with our limitations, could achieve. Canon Mannering goes on:

What, then, does the Lord require of us? Out of the distant past a voice speaks to us, bidding us 'walk humbly with our God'. And we know that the prophet Micah is right. All the more is it required of us because God has so signally blessed our Fellowship. We must be ready to learn, and unlearn, and relearn; pressing forward to the fulfilment of Christ's promise: 'the Spirit of truth shall guide you into all truth'.

How appropriate that the roots of the word 'humbly' are so closely linked to the earth in which this Wild Weed is growing.

4

Does Messy Church make disciples?

Judy Paulsen

Judy Paulsen's early childhood was spent in north-west India, where her parents served as Anglican missionaries. She later studied and worked as a speech-language pathologist in Ontario, Canada. Her life took quite a change of path when she attended Wycliffe College, at the University of Toronto, to study theology. She was ordained to serve in the Anglican Church of Canada in 1998. More recently, Judy served for ten years as the pastor of Christ Memorial Church, Oshawa, where, in the spring of 2008, they began to get even messier than normal with the introduction of Messy Church. In 2012, Judy completed a Doctor of Ministry degree. Her research explored who was coming to Messy Church, why they came, and what effect their participation was having. Judy now serves in the urban parish of St Paul's, Bloor Street, in the heart of Toronto.

Growing disciples

Disciple-making has always depended on first connecting with people and then growing them spiritually. In a post-Christendom society, the ability to connect deeply with de-churched, non-churched and marginally churched people will be more and more important. Building these connections, and then growing people as disciples, is at the very heart of mission in all fresh expressions of Church, including Messy Church.

In the spring of 2011 I conducted a doctoral research study[24] to examine the missional connections being made as a result of

Messy Church as it occurs in the Anglican parish of Christ Church, Oshawa, located 40 miles to the east of Toronto. Among other questions, the research examined if the de-churched, non-churched and marginally churched people attending this Messy Church were growing as disciples. Seventeen families (including children), who had been participating in Messy Church for periods of time ranging from six months to three years, completed questionnaires together and underwent in-depth individual interviews. The results of this study were both encouraging and thought-provoking in relation to discipleship. This chapter offers a summary of the results, drawing on interview excerpts and noting some important implications for discipleship in a Messy Church setting.

To explore and assess discipleship, I examined what changes had occurred in the lives of those attending Messy Church, the majority of whom were de-churched, marginally churched and non-churched people. The changes explored were based on a model of conversion seen in the early church and described by Alan Kreider in his book, *The Change of Conversion and the Origin of Christendom*. This model includes changes in behaviour, belonging and belief.[25] Kreider argues that behavioural changes were assumed as one sign of authentic conversion in the early church (see 1 Thessalonians 4:1; Ephesians 4:25–32). Conversion also involved a new sense of belonging, as converts began to be incorporated into the Christian community (see Ephesians 2:11–22). Finally, beliefs too began to change as a result of rigorous catechesis (see Hebrews 5:12—6:2; Romans 12:2).

While baptisms and confirmations have long been seen as markers of Christian discipleship, they were not used as markers in this study. This was because the Messy Church in Oshawa was still in the early stages of development and the sacraments had not yet been incorporated into its regular life. Instead, applying Kreider's model of conversion, the research sought evidence among the participating families of three things: the development of basic Christian behaviour, a sense of belonging to the Christian community, and increased knowledge and acceptance of Christian beliefs.

Changes in behaviour

While there are many aspects of behaviour that could be associated with Christian conversion, five key ones were mentioned in the interview and questionnaire data of families participating in the Messy Church in Oshawa. These included knowledge of scripture (in either children or adults), talking with children about God, corporate worship, praying, and having fellowship with other Christians. The interview and questionnaires probed whether families experienced change in any of these ways of behaving and whether they attributed such changes to their involvement with Messy Church. Table 1 presents the percentage of families that reported such changes.

Table 1. Behavioural changes reported among families attending Oshawa Messy Church

Increased behaviour	Percentage of families reporting change
Knowledge of scripture	100
Talking about God with children	100
Attending corporate worship	82
Prayer	47
Christian fellowship	35

Knowledge of scripture

A key reason given by families for coming to Messy Church was their desire for their children and grandchildren to know the stories of the Bible and primary Christian teachings. As Table 1 reveals, the parents and grandparents in the study felt that this goal was being realised. Interview transcripts from every family contained comments about how being involved in Messy Church was increasing knowledge of Bible stories in their children, and in several cases it was increasing the biblical knowledge of parents as well.

Four excerpts from the interview transcripts of different families particularly reflect this increase, and demonstrate a variety of benefits. One mother, who attends Sunday church only marginally (no more than a few times a year), indicated that not only was her son learning the stories told at Messy Church but also that the stories were a topic of conversation afterwards.

We were just talking about this... last night when I was filling out the questionnaire. I did it with them at the table... and everything that he [her son] knew... I could name names that came up in the Bible stories that we were doing and he could name... well, not every one... But he knew every single story... It was amazing. It was like... wow, he's really remembering this.

A second marginally attending mother highlighted that not only was her child learning the Bible stories but that she was relearning them due to her child's participation.

And you know, even just review of the stories for my own self... Because where I learned them it was through Sunday school and after that through church... So even with me, it's refreshing my memory about a lot of things that I learned.

This comment that the stories were a good review for parents and an introduction for the children was echoed by others.

A grandmother highlighted that the learning of Bible stories was transferring into broader spiritual growth in her non-churched granddaughter. Having initially come just to Messy Church, this de-churched grandmother had now started bringing her grand-daughter regularly to Sunday church:

Yes, there's a big change [in their knowledge of the stories]… The kids knew nothing before… And what little I knew, it's expanded that… they're growing spiritually as well as socially… I said [to my granddaughter], 'When we go up and have the bread and wine, do you know what that's about?' And she's like, 'Oh yeah. Jesus' body and his blood.' And I was like, 'OK.' I didn't know what to say to her after that… I didn't know she'd know… but she does and she understands that… She really enjoys it here and she loves the stories.

The comments collectively suggest that this Messy Church's format of telling the Bible story via various media, followed by reinforcement of the story through songs, games, crafts and take-home activities, is helping its families to know key Bible stories. For many of the marginally churched and de-churched parents and grandparents, it reminds them of stories they once knew. For the predominantly non-churched children and grandchildren, it provides their first introduction to the great stories of the Christian faith.

Talking about God with children

Another change in behaviour reported by all the families in this study was that they talked to their children more about God since attending Messy Church. As families are experiencing it together and then taking home activities and books that they study together, more opportunities arise for them to talk about Bible stories and their meaning. Specific excerpts from interviews give examples of how attending Messy Church has resulted in families talking more about faith. The first comes from a mother who attends Sunday church only a few times a year.

Just to see them learning… I mean when we know what they've talked about… we usually have lunch after [Messy Church], and we go over it again with them. You know… 'What did you learn?' … To see what sunk in. You know, at lunchtime, us talking about it with them kind of brings the point home again. Sometimes when it's so busy at Messy Church, they're not necessarily getting the whole idea of it. And the activity sheets are good… [My son] did all of them this week. Yeah, he was pretty excited about them.

This comment highlights the parents' initiative in the process, following up on the story focused on at Messy Church. A second, from a de-churched mother, also comments on how the children's presence at Messy Church with both her and her own mother enables conversations with her children about faith.

We just really like it… Mom likes taking the kids too… we like having the kids there… I just love that they're learning through play and that the church is a fun building… the base is there… so it makes it easy for us to talk with them.

The third comment was made by a mother who was baptised as an infant and then never taken to church again. As an effectively non-churched person, she recognises that Messy Church now enables her to have conversations with her children that would not occur otherwise.

I would say we are talking more with them about God now… the first . part is, the children have questions now… so had we not started coming to Messy Church… and had their knowledge base not been increased… their minds would not be stimulated and they wouldn't be asking the questions… So because we're coming, it does evoke more thought and more questions from them, which we then have discussion on… And there are times, less with [my husband] but more with me, where we will engage in a conversation… depending on the situation… what they've seen or what is outside, and then we'll talk about it... Like maybe their grandmother who passed away... Like we believe she's up in heaven with God... And they're like, 'What does he look like?'... and I attribute that all to the fact that we come here.

The comments indicate that, by participating in Messy Church, these families are sharing an experience that, in turn, gives them a focus for discussion about God and about faith. Sometimes it is assumed that Christian belief precedes Christian behaviour, yet in the case of these families, the interview data suggests that Christian behaviour, such as participating in worship together, can lead parents to talk with children more about faith, which in turn can lead to deeper belief.

Attending corporate worship

A third change in behaviour reported by families was increased attendance at worship. The vast majority, 82 per cent, of the families mentioned that by participating in Messy Church they were worshipping God more. Several excerpts from the interviews with different families highlight this common theme.

One mother, whose husband's shiftwork affects their ability to attend Sunday church as a family, sees Messy Church as an opportunity for at least her and her daughter to attend a form of church together. Although they have moved to another nearby city and only attend Sunday church a few times a year, she continues to attend Messy Church almost every month.

Our schedule is pretty busy and [my husband] works odd hours, so going to church as a family on a regular basis is pretty difficult. He works with... [a local transit company], so they are a 24/7 operation... Their shift changes pretty much every six weeks, but... for him to get weekends off is like pretty difficult... so I find that Messy Church is really convenient, and it's a good way to have that time at church with [my daughter].

This understanding of Messy Church as authentic worship was echoed by another mother, who is non-churched.

We are worshipping more... especially with the struggle my husband and I have with 'how much and what elements'... Prior to coming here we were more opposing forces... I don't know that we would have introduced [teaching about faith]... so this has made a huge difference.

Here it seems that Messy Church provides a safe venue in which to explore faith as a family.

Finally, a further comment supports the idea that by offering a form of worship that is enjoyable for a variety of ages, Messy Church is encouraging families to be more regular in their attendance at worship. A de-churched mother offered this affirming feedback:

Yes, we are worshipping more... absolutely... And a big part of that is... we try to come on Sundays, but if it doesn't work out... It just wouldn't be happening... whereas [Messy Church]... it's once a month, and [my children] know that we're going... and so it's never an issue because they look forward to it and they're excited to go.

It is worth noting that these comments reflect the view that regular worship is something that can now happen just once a month. This understanding parallels that of Sunday church attenders, whose frequency of attendance at worship seems to be decreasing with increased demands on Sundays for such things as employment, child custody arrangements and organised sport schedules.

Prayer

The next most commonly reported change in the behaviour of the families attending Messy Church involved an increase in prayer, experienced by almost half (47 per cent) of the families. As in the first three reported areas of change, there was strong agreement between interview data and questionnaire data on this issue.

The following excerpts, from two different de-churched families, describe two of the ways in which prayer is increasing in the lives of these families.

Since coming, the kids are reminding me more about praying... They do remind me... [and] will say, 'Mommy, we haven't prayed in a while'... Or when Mom and I or the whole family is together, my son likes us all holding hands and praying together... It's a big thing.

Before I started taking her to Messy Church we didn't say grace [at meals]... I haven't been in the habit... Now we all hold hands and say, 'Thank you, God, for our food.' ... And the other day her father was over and... [she] was, like, bouncing all around and saying, 'Thank you, God.' And he said, 'What's she saying?' and he held hands too and joined in... and then he said, 'Oh, that's something I want to start at home too.'

Interestingly, both of the above comments refer to praying at meals. To many Christians, this may seem to be a small change, but all behaviour related to faith begins somewhere. If a family can begin to pray at meal times or at bedtime with their children, perhaps they will be more likely to begin to pray in times of need or of celebration.

Christian fellowship

The final change in behaviour noted by the families in the study related to Christian fellowship. Of the families in the study, 35 per cent mentioned this as something that had increased since attending Messy Church. All of these comments related to the fellowship they experienced at Messy Church with other families. They found encouragement simply from being around other parents and grandparents who wanted to teach their children about the Bible.

The following excerpts address different aspects of fellowship that are important to these families. The first shows how the fellowship of other Christians was important to a regularly attending grandmother who wanted her non-churched grandchildren to know that what she was teaching them was not just something she alone believed.

They get to socially interact with kids… who take the Bible seriously… Like, you don't hear, 'That's not true' or 'That couldn't happen.'… You don't hear that… and that's good for the kids because their father isn't a Christian… And so sometimes they pick up on the negative… like, 'The Bible isn't real'… or 'People just made it up.'… And so this is reinforcing to them that 'Oh, it's not just Grandma'… It's other people too.

For other families, the fellowship was important simply because it gave them a sense of encouragement to be with other young families their age who, like them, hoped to instil faith in their children. The following comment from a de-churched mother illustrates this.

It reaffirms, as a parent, 'Oh look, [other parents] have got the same struggles that you do… and want the same things for their kids… We're not there just to waste an hour… we're there to get something out of it… I enjoy that… just being with other families.

The above comments were positive ones about the opportunities for fellowship that Messy Church provided. However, not all families felt this to be the case. Interestingly, it was a non-churched family who sought for deeper relationships to grow among the families attending Messy Church. The non-churched mother explained the following:

If there was a little more social interaction between the adults and the children… like maybe if there was one day… [when] rather than focusing on any of the lessons or teachings we said, 'Let's just sit down and get the kids over here and talking about themselves, and just playing and interacting together'… and then the adults the same thing… 'This is who I am… this is what I do… this is where I live…' A little bit of family history… maybe not making it heavy in terms of faith and beliefs.

The above comment indicates that, just as it can be a challenge to build friendships at Sunday church, so it can be at Messy Church. This may be a particular challenge for Messy Church as it is experienced at Christ Church, Oshawa. Because several children have serious food allergies, no shared meal is included, as it is at many other Messy Church gatherings. This means there is less time for families to interact with one another. The fact that parents tend to be busy interacting with their children may preclude them from building meaningful relationships with other parents. For this to happen, an intentional restructuring of format or additional opportunities for fellowship may need to be offered.

In summary, based on the interview and questionnaire data, participation in Messy Church seems to be an important catalyst for behavioural change in families. Increased knowledge of scripture and talking about God together as families were the two primary changes noted by every family in the study. To a lesser degree, other noted changes included worshipping together, praying more and enjoying Christian fellowship.

Changes in belonging

In addition to examining increases in Christian behaviour, I also explored changes in each family's sense of belonging to the Christian community. Specifically, I examined their sense of belonging to the Messy Church community, to the parish of Christ Church, and to the broader church. Table 2 presents changes reported by families in the area of belonging.

Table 2. Changes in sense of belonging reported by families attending Oshawa Messy Church

Increased belonging to	Percentage of families reporting change
Messy Church community	59
Christ Church, Oshawa	53
Other church	0
Anglican Communion	6
Worldwide Christian faith	26

The Messy Church community

As Table 2 indicates, by participating in Messy Church, a number of families experienced an increased sense of belonging to the Messy Church community and/or Christ Church as a parish. Interestingly, the percentages of families reporting these two changes in belonging were remarkably close in number. It had been expected that participation at Messy Church would result in a widespread sense of belonging to this particular community of people, but that was not true of all those interviewed. Only 59 per cent of the families commented about an increased sense of belonging to the Messy Church community. This may have been because parents were still forming ties with other families. Three families mentioned that, while they felt connected to several members of the Messy Church leadership team, they did not yet feel very connected to other families attending.

Christ Church, Oshawa

The data showed that 53 per cent of the families reported having an increased sense of belonging to the parish of Christ Church.

This may have arisen simply because Messy Church gathers in the building of Christ Church, so families began to feel a greater affinity with the parish. It may have developed because they became aware of events, programmes and outreach ministries happening in the parish through the monthly update provided as a take-home resource. It may also have been that by coming to Messy Church, a form of worship offered by Christ Church, families were more open to being a part of the broader life of the parish and so sensed a deeper belonging to it. Several examples of increased ties with the parish have been seen in the lives of Messy Church families.

One de-churched grandmother, who had for the previous three decades had no church connection, now attends Sunday church on a regular basis with her two non-churched grandchildren. One of these grandchildren joined the Christ Church children's choir. Both grandchildren now attend Sunday school regularly, and their grandmother has joined Mosaic, a two-year discipleship training programme for adults. This de-churched grandmother made the following comment about her own recent involvement at Christ Church:

I've got more confidence in myself—as you can tell, because I get up and read scripture [on Sunday mornings at Christ Church]. That was a big one for me... and it was like, 'Oh, OK, this isn't so bad.' Because I'm a naturally shy person. So getting up in front of everybody and reading the first time was like... [sucks in breath].

In the case of another family, the non-churched parents have asked for information about baptism. They are considering this step for their two daughters because, in their words, they 'want them to belong to a faith community'. While it is uncertain whether the two parents will agree about this, they sought information about baptism and stated that if they did have their daughters baptised they would like it to happen at Christ Church. This raises interesting questions about how they view Messy Church. They do not appear to see it as a separate entity from Christ Church but as a sub-group of the parish.

One family, where the parents were initially classified as de-churched, has more recently been attending Sunday church several times a year. While they still would not meet this study's standards as regular Sunday attendees (that is, at least once a month), they have moved from de-churched status to marginal attendees. Similarly, another grandmother who was attending Sunday church on a marginal basis has increased her involvement in the broader parish by offering to help with the week-long Vacation Bible School that Christ Church offers to the neighbourhood each summer. In all of the above cases, participation at Messy Church seemed to increase various families' openness to and sense of belonging within the parish of Christ Church as a whole.

The wider church

Finally, several churched families in the study expressed the view that their involvement at Messy Church had deepened their sense of belonging to the worldwide church. One churched mother grew up in an Anglican home but was married to a Pentecostal and was attending a Pentecostal house church. She stated that it was important to her that, through Messy Church, her children were exposed to a different form of worship, taking place in an Anglican setting. She saw this as a way to reaffirm unity among Christians. Similarly, two Seventh-Day Adventist grandmothers commented that by participating in Messy Church they had a greater sense of the shared Christian faith across denominations.

Changes in beliefs

Just as the study was interested in exploring changes in behaviour and belonging, it also examined changes in beliefs reported by the participating families. Table 3 indicates the changes, and lack of changes, reported in beliefs.

Table 3. Changes in beliefs reported among families attending Oshawa Messy Church

Increased beliefs	Percentage of families reporting change
Reality of God	24
Eternal life	24
Applicability of Christian teachings	12
Overall strengthening of belief	35
No change among adults	47

No change

Perhaps the most striking finding listed in the above table is that while high percentages of families reported increases in Christian behaviour and in belonging to the Christian community, almost half of the participating adults (47 per cent) reported no change in their beliefs. This may be due to the fact that, by adulthood, beliefs are less changeable than behaviour and sense of belonging. It also may have to do with the majority of Messy Church activities being geared toward children. Perhaps the teaching at Messy Church is not adult-focused enough to bring about change in the beliefs of many adults. The lack of change in beliefs may also be attributed to these adults already having well-formed Christian beliefs, even though many of them participated in Sunday church only marginally or not at all.

Areas of change

As Table 3 indicates, those adults who did comment on changes in beliefs, either among their children or in themselves, reported these changes to have occurred in three areas: the reality of God (reported in 24 per cent of families), eternal life (24 per cent) and the applicability of Christian teachings to everyday life (12 per cent). The changes also encompassed an overall strengthening of their beliefs as Christians (35 per cent).

The following excerpts from various families' interview transcripts relate to one or more of these areas of belief. The first of these excerpts is from a mother with no church background.

A change in my beliefs? Hmm... I think so, for myself... in terms of being more open to religion and faith... Because I didn't have that when I was younger... so I'm more conscious of it... talk more of it... You know, the family is involved in it more... and it's engaging and opening... Because it engages conversation between us... it has evoked a change.

This comment suggests a very early stage of interest in faith. There is no indication that this person is a fully formed Christian. Nevertheless, she has expressed that a change has been occurring as a result of participating in Messy Church. The following comment from a de-churched mother relates to a particular situation in their family life when she noticed a change in the belief of her children:

I really noticed [a change] last summer when my uncle passed away... My cousin's little guy had a really hard time with it... but he doesn't go to church... He doesn't go to Messy Church... With our kids we could just explain where he was... he was with God... he's now up in heaven... and they just accepted it... To be selfish, it made it easy for us as parents... They were just so open, because they already had the concept of what heaven was... that there was more to life than this.

This comment reflects the mother's recognition that, by participating in the worshipping community of Messy Church, her children were enabled to grasp the concept of eternal life. She also recognised that when children learn key religious concepts, they have direct application to life situations. Interestingly, this same concept of life after death and the applicability of Christian teachings were echoed in a second interview transcript. One grandmother, who also attends Sunday church regularly, offered this comment:

My daughter, she knows the truth, but she doesn't go to church any more... and my son-in-law, he doesn't really know... but I noticed that when my grandkids [who attend Messy Church] were talking to their cousins, their cousin, who goes to church, said, 'You're going to see Grandpa again. You don't have to cry.' And then [the grandchildren who attend Messy Church] said... 'Well, at Messy Church we learned this'... and they were talking about the Bible... and it was real and they're getting that it's important for your own life and it helps you.

This grandmother's comment highlights the role that the community of faith can have in nurturing the development of beliefs and solidifying them.

A third comment reflected that grappling with faith questions was not just happening in the children attending Messy Church. A mother, who attends Sunday church only a few times a year, believes it is also being nurtured in at least some of the adults.

I guess I'm seeing it [faith] more as... not just a routine thing... It's a deeper thing... Now that the kids are coming with questions, I'm thinking there's more meaning to all this... and there's a deeper thought that goes into it.

A final comment related to developing or deepening beliefs was made by another mother, who is a regular attendee at Sunday church. This family initially attended Messy Church only, but then began attending regularly on Sundays as well. Her statement indicates the spiritual growth now taking place:

I guess I'm kind of waking up... spiritually, I guess... This whole thing of going to Messy Church... and now Christ Church on Sundays... is

showing me that there is something more than just sitting in the pew and
planning your week out… or saying, 'Shhhh, here's a red pencil for you.'
… This has been kind of like an awakening… and it's a bit destabilising.

The data indicate that although almost half of the families participating in Messy Church did not report any change in belief among the parents or grandparents, just over half the families did report changes in beliefs. These changes involved either an increase in a few specific Christian beliefs or a strengthening of their Christian beliefs overall. With so few key Christian beliefs mentioned in the interview data, further research into a wider range of beliefs, and changes to these beliefs, would be helpful. The open-ended nature of the interview questions may not have been the best device for eliciting comments related to a variety of Christian beliefs. Parents tended to speak about specific beliefs related to their children's understanding of the faith. When they spoke about their own beliefs, they tended to be more general in their responses.

Wider issues

Parents and grandparents as Christian educators

In addition to exploring family changes in behaving, belonging and believing, I sought to explore changes in the way parents and grandparents saw themselves as the Christian educators of their children and grandchildren. One question asked families to indicate factors that were 'quite important' in their wanting to be a part of Messy Church. One of the factors listed was an increased role for parents and grandparents in helping their children grow spiritually. Of the 17 families, 13 (76 per cent) answered positively. In the interview data, however, few families referred directly to this role. Instead, they spoke more indirectly of what they were providing for their children and grandchildren by bringing them to Messy Church.

One non-churched mother expressed contentment that 'my husband and I are giving our children something that we didn't have'. In a similar vein, a de-churched mother saw Messy Church as a way to provide something valuable that was also part of her childhood. She said, 'I give my children what I got at Sunday school and youth group.' Churched grandparents also seem to view Messy Church as a way for them to provide their non-churched grandchildren with spiritual nurture. Churched parents commented that Messy Church was a context and format that worked for all their children, regardless of their different levels of distractibility. A de-churched mother married to a non-Christian husband felt that, unlike Sunday church, Messy Church was a context to which she felt comfortable coming on her own with her children.

Related to the question of the adults' role as Christian educators of their children and grandchildren was the question of whether or not they were talking more about God with these children. In every case, families responded positively to this question. This shows that although they may not recognise that they are fulfilling the role of Christian educators, they certainly demonstrate important behaviour associated with teaching their children the Christian faith. In a reversal of the parent–child role, one grandmother shared how her granddaughter, in her own way, is educating her non-churched parents about the things she is learning at Messy Church.

We talk about what we do [at Messy Church] and, like, when they take the crafts home... the last time, I think it was Moses in the bulrushes... and so [my granddaughter] took it home and showed it to her mom and was talking about it... and her mom put it up on the fridge.

Implications for discipleship

My examination of Messy Church indicated several findings related to discipleship. The first and most obvious of these was that it is possible for an established traditional parish, using Messy Church, to connect with and begin to disciple marginally attending, de-churched and non-churched people. Based on a model of conversion that involves changes in behaviour, belonging and belief, I found changes in each of these areas. The primary implication is that even in a culture that is dismissive of or hostile to Christianity, there are still opportunities to nurture new people as followers of Jesus. The challenge will be for traditional churches to make the connections that will enable such discipleship training to occur. This is unlikely to happen if churches simply continue to do what always has been done. In the church's present context, all Christians will need to rediscover a passion to reach people with the Christian message. Without the conviction that this is at the very heart of the mission of the church, it is unlikely that established congregations will make the effort, pay the necessary cost and take the required risks inherent in establishing experimental forms of missional ministry.

A second finding was that discipling people takes time. While there were significant changes in behaviour, belonging and belief in the Messy Church families, these changes did not happen instantly. A key implication for future praxis is that discipleship must start with people as they are, and must be intentional in growing them over a period of years. As the families attended Messy Church together and learned more of the Bible, they began to talk more together about God. Prayer also increased in nearly half of these families, and even more attended regular worship and gained knowledge of scripture. Particularly in an increasingly secularised society, intentional discipleship will need to be at the heart of the mission of local congregations.

A third finding was that involvement in an experimental and innovative form of ministry can foster not only a sense of belonging to a new form of church but also to the broader parish. This indicates that established parishes should not fear that such new forms of church will drain people from their Sunday congregation. Rather, this finding implies that new forms may lead to growing connections and possible future involvement in the broader parish.

Generally, people coming to Sunday church do so because it works well for them. While some young families may find that Sunday worship does not work well for them, they may still feel a deeper sense of belonging to a parish that offers a form of worship in which they do feel they can participate.

A fourth finding was that growth in one area of faith can lead to changes in other areas. De-churched and non-churched parents and grandparents who attended Messy Church regularly found that both they and their children knew the Bible better and that they were talking more with their children about God. Although many of the marginally attending and de-churched adults in the study did not recognise changes in their beliefs, many reported a strengthening of belief. For several, this was related to being part of a worshipping and learning community of their peers. The implication is that churches need to move beyond the idea of discipleship as simply the acquisition of certain bits of knowledge. Rather, a threefold focus, on the development of Christian behaviour, a sense of belonging to the Christian community, and expanding and deepening faith in Christ, should form part of the intentional discipleship of followers of Jesus.

A fifth finding is that grandparents with faith are uniquely positioned to disciple their grandchildren, and that Messy Church can be an effective vehicle to encourage them in this role within the setting of a faith community.

Despite some evidence of growth in discipleship, there are several challenges that became evident in terms of discipleship in the Messy Church context. Each hour of Messy Church requires approximately 15 hours of preparation. It is therefore very difficult to offer this form of church more than once a month, which seems too infrequent to build substantive relationships or to offer adequate Christian teaching. The implication is that when a form of church is focused on connecting with a specific group or subculture through worship, it may be a challenge to meet discipleship training needs sufficiently in that context alone.

Implications for Christian education of children

There were five key findings related to the Christian education of children arising from examining Messy Church in Oshawa:

- Many parents and grandparents want to be involved in their children and grandchildren's spiritual development.
- By actively participating with their children at Messy Church, parents and grandparents are equipped with tools to serve as Christian educators for those children.
- By offering such experiences and providing additional resources to families, the church can support parents and grandparents in this key role.
- Christian grandparents are uniquely positioned to serve as Christian educators of their non-churched grandchildren.
- At least some non-churched parents want their children to learn about the Christian faith.

These findings have implications for future missional praxis. The church needs to examine its role in the area of the Christian education of children. Whenever possible, it should move to more of an equipping role to provide parents and grandparents with encouragement, resources and ongoing support to serve as spiritual educators within their families. With many societal factors working against people attending church even weekly, it will be crucial for the home to become again the primary place of spiritual nurture for children, as it was in the Judaism of Jesus' day.

While there is little evidence in the Gospels of Jesus having formal schooling outside his home, his extensive knowledge of the faith was evident to the religious teachers with whom he interacted at the temple when he was just twelve years old (Luke 2:46–47). This strongly suggests that Jesus had been taught the faith at home, as was normative. Such instruction of children in the home, paired with belonging to a faith community, is a long-standing pattern in

Jewish tradition. In the book of Deuteronomy, when the Israelites are reminded of the central commandments of God, they are instructed, 'You shall teach them diligently to your children, and shall talk of them when you sit in your house, and when you walk by the way, and when you lie down and when you rise' (6:4–7, ESV). This command is repeated almost verbatim in Deuteronomy 11:19–21.

It is clear from these passages that religious instruction of children is given as a task to parents as part of the patterns and rituals of the faith community. Churches need to recognise and celebrate parents' ability to influence their children's spiritual development every day. In addition to supporting parents in their role as Christian educators, the results of the present study suggest that grandparents also need to be recognised as key influencers in their grandchildren's spiritual development.

Another implication arising is that, through ministries such as Messy Church, congregations may be able to meet the needs of non-churched parents who want to offer their children some religious instruction. With non-churched people comprising an ever increasing percentage of society, there will be parents, like the non-churched parents coming to Messy Church in Oshawa, who feel ill-equipped to instruct their children about Christianity but want them to have a basic understanding of the faith. Even if such parents want it for literary or historical reasons, this desire provides an opportunity to reach both them and their children with the good news of the gospel, particularly through a low-threshold mode of church like Messy Church.

In conclusion, the results of this research suggest that Messy Church is indeed a setting in which discipleship is occurring. The challenge of the future will be to deepen the initial connections formed through such fresh expressions of Church. When this is done, the deep transformative power of the gospel, already in evidence, will fully bloom.

❖

Case study: Messy Church at St Christopher's

Alison Paginton

Alison Paginton is Regional Coordinator in the Bristol area.

Messy Church at St Christopher's, an Anglican church with a small parish on the Bath side of Bristol, did not begin with someone waking up one morning saying, 'I know, let's start Messy Church.' It began after a 'gifting' exercise, which the congregation started in 2008. The findings were presented to the Annual Meeting in 2009 and Messy Church began in February 2010. Quite a journey, before we had even started!

In December 2009, a mad month to ask anyone to do anything, we held a Messy Church taster evening for the congregation to let them know what we would be asking of them if we were to start Messy Church. Out of an average Sunday congregation of about 48, 32 people came along and 30 of them signed up to join either the craft, catering, setting-up, clearing-up or publicity team. Some signed up for more than one team. And so Messy Church at St Christopher's began.

Since that time, God has done so much that it is difficult to know where to begin. One thing for sure is that it is hard work— but so rewarding. It took some time for the Sunday congregation to understand that Messy Church *is* church—just church done in a different way from what they experience on Sunday. Gradually the cries of 'Why don't they come on a Sunday?' all but disappeared.

However, then the Messy Church congregation started to ask the leaders which Sunday service would be the best for them to attend. This presented the church leadership with an opportunity. Messy Church meets on the first Saturday of the month. Our family service was on the first Sunday of the month, and it was appreciated that asking people on the edge of the church to come along two days running was a step too far. We decided to accommodate the Messy congregation, so the family service was moved, renamed and relaunched.

In August 2011, the first 'All Together Worship!' service was held, on the third Sunday of the month. From the very start, a growing number of Messy Church families attended it and, subsequently, other services too. We have had a number of Messy Church children baptised or dedicated. Six adults have come on to the electoral roll and three are to be confirmed in September. A number of families help to supply cakes and prepare crafts for sessions and one mum has become a member of the craft team. I am told that Messy Church at St Christopher's gets talked about at the school gates even by those who don't (yet) attend.

While the Messy Church congregation has flourished, so has the Messy Church team. People who had 'known' each other for years are actually getting to know each other properly over glue pots and glitter or the washing-up. Some have confessed to having never read their Bibles as much as they do now as they prepare themselves for the 'table talk' with the craft activities.

The catering team is amazing. We have had soup made from scratch on the morning of Messy Church and delicious cottage pie, to name but two dishes. We never know how many people will turn up, and several times there have been over 100, but God has always provided and no one has gone without lunch. We have paid for two of the team to take their food-safety qualification and they all now wear their Messy Church aprons with pride. It always seems a miracle when the catering and clearing-up teams turn the hall, within 20 minutes, from a craft room to a café laid out for lunch. Two of our lay readers take turns to lead the worship, and we have first-aiders and Acorn Christian Listeners in our 'supporters' team.

Messy Church has been a real blessing to the whole church in the way it has enabled relationships to grow and blossom. Several times a year, the team meets for a time of sharing, learning and worship. When you are trying to blend together different personalities and gifts, there are sometimes issues that have to be worked out, but God has been gracious and so far there have been no difficulties that could not be resolved.

The families who attend have given us much joy, not only through their enthusiasm and willingness to get 'messy' but by giving us the privilege of sharing a small part of their lives with them. We have had one dad come with his son on his access day, as he had no money and nowhere else to go. We had one woman who came with her friend's disabled child, having found it hard to take her anywhere else. Another family who had not been welcomed in their local church came with their son in a wheelchair, and we have one interfaith family who regularly join us. We were asked by the community to make crowns for the Jubilee street party in 2012 and have been invited to do Messy Church in a tent in the park at a community event in September. We have also enjoyed welcoming a number of visitors from other churches who are thinking about starting Messy Church.

We have stuck as closely as possible to the blueprint that Lucy Moore presented in her first two books, although we have learned and changed things along the way and will continue to do so as the congregation grows older. Activities that suit three-year-olds will not keep them interested when they are, say, seven, especially if they are boys. Messy Church is not an easy option, a quick fix for getting children into the pews, and it does not work everywhere.

We started by listening to God, to hear what he wanted to do in our community with the gifts he has given us. I hope that we will always continue to do so. We have tried to stay faithful to this calling and, although it is hard work, the worshipping community of St Christopher's has been blessed in so many ways through Messy Church.

Messy foundations

❖

5

Messy theology

Paul Bayes

Paul Bayes is Bishop of Hertford. Before that he was the Church of England's National Mission and Evangelism Adviser, after 25 years as a parish priest, university chaplain and church planter. For six years he was involved in planting a cell church which included all-age cells, and he strongly recommends all-age small groups as the best way for adults to grow up in the church.

'Truly I tell you, whoever does not receive the kingdom of God as a little child will never enter it' (Mark 10:15, NRSV). What I want to say in this chapter is that theology, if it's not messy, is entirely incomplete. I also want to point to some of the things that Messy Church brings to theology or reminds theology of—things that the church forgets at its peril.

Theology's problems

By 'theology' in this chapter, I sometimes mean the thinking that we all do about God in the church. More often, though, I mean the thinking that specialists—theologians—help us to do by their work of researching and reflecting and writing. In both these arenas, doing theology (any kind of thinking about or talking about or writing about God) is tricky. If God exists, then God is the most important subject there is. So it's not surprising that we want to get our theology right and to reflect God's beauty and truth properly.

For this good reason, over many centuries, intellectual rigour and beauty have become something to aim at for theologians in the West, and so there is a great deal of rigorous, elegant and beautiful theology in the world. Sometimes it is so rigorous that few can understand it, and sometimes theologians do not seem to mind that as much as they should. Complaining about this is a familiar pastime for the wider church, and it's not at the heart of what I want to do here, although I recognise it as a problem and I wish we all cared about it more than we do.

But there is a further problem. Because theology has become an academic discipline, it is no longer expected that non-academic people should or can contribute to it at all, except as providers of raw material. This is understandable, and it need not always be exclusive. Of course it is open to many people to equip themselves with the tools they need to engage theologically. Much of the training for ordained and lay ministry in the church is designed to put some of these tools into people's hands. Nonetheless, there are some people groups who will never be able to use these tools. In particular, I think of children, or people with learning disabilities, or people who cannot speak any of the bare handful of languages in which almost all theology is done, as well as those whose way of thinking is mainly anecdotal, visual, narrative-based, intuitive or poetic. This restricts us badly.

The unavoidable remedy

For those of us who are Christians, there is a familiar medicine for this problem. We long for truth and beauty in our theology. But, for us, God is as he is in Jesus, and as far as the main thing he came to do is concerned, Jesus had no beauty and his truth was deeply concealed (see Isaiah 53:2).

Rowan Williams' first book starts by saying:

Christian faith has its beginnings in an experience of profound contra-dictoriness, an experience which so questioned the religious categories of its time that the resulting reorganisation of religious language was a centuries-long task.[26]

Of course he is speaking of the cross, the cross which tests everything, which has always been a stumbling block to those who value beauty and clear thinking, the cross without which we have no salvation.

Moreover, in his own teaching Jesus was consistently transgressive, contradictory and awkward. The Pharisees in particular would testify to this. Being awkward was central to how Jesus lived. As the Lutheran thinker Gordon Lathrop says, 'We are speaking of the biblical, historic Christ who eats with sinners and outsiders, who is made a curse and sin itself for us, who justifies the ungodly, *and who is himself the hole in any system.*'[27] So, if we are to catch something of God's truth and beauty, then alongside getting things right and doing things properly, it seems that we need other tools in our toolbox. Jesus himself gave us some clues as to where to find them. For example, he had an unusual amount of time and respect for children—time and respect which, I have to say, his followers have consistently failed to give them since. For this reason, I was glad to be asked to write about the messiness of theology in the context of a movement in the church that focuses on families and their children and has become remarkably popular, effective and helpful. Among many possible areas, I shall look at three: reframing, curiosity and truthfulness.

Reframing

'I like children, but I couldn't manage a whole one.'[28]

It's a Wednesday afternoon in 2011. I'm in the Church of England Diocese of St Albans, where my ministry is based. I have been invited to Messy Mass in Elstree, to share the life of this group and to preside at Holy Communion. We've reached a point in the afternoon when it's time to get creative. There are lots of creative choices today, and in one of them a group of young people is gathered round a table piled with potatoes, turnips, carrots, Brussels sprouts and cocktail sticks. They are following the suggestion (which seemed pretty clear to me), 'Why not make an animal out of these vegetables and cocktail sticks?'

A tall young person, eight years old or so, comes up to me with a potato into which four cocktail sticks have been inserted, two at each end, with two little carrots on one end and two Brussels sprouts on the other. He shows it to me proudly. I take it into my hands and turn it round. 'That's great,' I say. 'Er... what kind of animal is it?' The child looks at me incredulously, then looks back at what he has made, as if to make sure. He looks at me again. With reproach and pain in his voice, he says, slowly and patiently, 'It's a submarine.' There is a pause. I look again. 'Of course it is,' I say. 'And the engine is...' My pointing finger drifts towards the Brussels sprouts. The kid's eyes narrow. '... here', I say, pointing firmly to the carrots. The young designer nods and smiles approvingly.

To reframe a question unilaterally is a transgressive, contradictory and awkward act. How the blazes was I to know that it was a submarine? I'm an obedient adult. The rules said that it should have been an animal.

On the other hand, now you come to look at it, if it *were* a submarine, it is obvious that the engine would have to be where the carrots were, so that when they go around they can drive the thing along. And if you're going to have observation windows at the front of your submarine, and you've only got a limited number of vegetables to choose from, it's obvious that Brussels sprouts would do the job very well because they're more or less spherical and they look a bit like eyes. Once you've done the reframing, things begin to fall into place.

Incidentally, when it comes to potatoes, reframing can have all kinds of results, as author Charles Handy makes clear:

I remember the year when Britain was short of potatoes... A friend and I went shopping for potatoes to find there were none. Weeks later he asked me what I had done as a result.

'Bought rice instead,' I said. 'Why?'

'I rang a contact in India,' he said, 'bought one thousand tons of potatoes to be shipped to the UK at a landed cost of £130 a ton and sold them in advance for £250 a ton.'

'But, Percy,' I said, calculating quickly, 'that's…'

'Yes,' he interrupted, 'but don't worry, it didn't happen, the Indian Government refused an export permit.'

Still, his reframing nearly made him £120,000, while I bought rice.[29]

The point is that reframing opens possibilities that would not be apparent without the courage needed to refuse the frame you're given and create a new one. Recent theology has frequently been blessed by movements of reframing from the perspective of oppressed or ignored people: black theology, feminist theology, liberation theology, queer theology, Global-South Pentecostal theology, Asian theology, to name a handful. Each of these has been written by, and has learned from, groups of people whose insight and knowledge have previously been discounted and marginalised and have even led to persecution. An inclusive church will rightly want to see the truth precisely in places that were ignored before, and for Christian theology not to do this would be for us to ignore the methods of our founder, who was transgressive, contradictory and awkward.

In my view, though, the people group who have been theologically marginalised and ignored the longest and most consistently to the present day are children. Week by week in our churches we continue to patronise them, silence them and ignore their attempts at reframing our faith. If they are asked to share their thinking at the end of our Sunday worship, we applaud their insights into the holy scriptures rather than learning from them. And yet, if we will look and listen, the drawings and sculptures and ideas and thinking of children in every church can enormously enrich what we know about God.

Peter Harvey tells the story of a school lesson where, to test the children, the teacher said, 'Why didn't God create a perfect world?'

One of the children replied, puzzled but as quick as a flash, 'But I thought that's what he was doing.' The teacher learned a little, as I did when I heard the story. Indeed, I've been thinking about that child's reply for 35 years.

Faith is messy. Theology, as I have said, had better be messy if it's to be Christian. And church is messy. Messy Church has caught on all over the world and in many Christian denominations and streams. For a whole range of reasons, many of them explored in this book, it has become one of the flagships of the fresh expressions movement. Like the Trojan horse, it appears a harmless, innocuous-looking thing that conceals the means of revolution. This revolution extends to theology as well as to ecclesiology and church practice, and it can begin with reframing.

The church is the bearer and the vessel of the Christian revelation. At the Bible's command she guards the deposit of faith and hands it on, making suggestions up the generations as well as down them. What kind of animal is that faith? Sometimes it's a submarine.

Curiosity

'Dear God, how did you get invented?'[30]

A bishop goes to visit a vicar in the vicarage. The vicar goes to make the tea, and the bishop waits in the drawing-room. The vicar's little daughter comes in and says, 'Bishop, can you tell me something my daddy can't understand?' 'Of course,' says the bishop reassuringly, 'of course. What is it that your daddy can't understand?' The little girl says, 'My daddy can't understand how you ever became a bishop.'

This story is the only apocryphal one in this chapter and it has not, yet, happened to me, though hope springs eternal. But it does rather beautifully express the subversive curiosity of children.

When the Lord Jesus invited us to become as little children, what was in his mind? Was it the little, no-crying child of 'Away in a manger' or the weaned child of Psalm 131, calmly and uncomplainingly feeding or gurgling, quieting its soul with the food of the tradition? Or was it the children we actually know, with their endless questioning, squabbling, probing, shifting of the goalposts and refusing ever to take 'Just because!' for an answer? Ever since I was a curate, it has seemed to me that a way of being church that values and encourages playful questioning cannot be far from the kingdom of God. Theology begins with the incomprehensible mystery of the life of the triune God. In the face of this mystery we make our suggestions and we ask our questions.

This is, of course, the glory of nurturing new disciples with Alpha or Emmaus. They enter the family of God believing that it's OK (1) to listen to solid, good teaching and (2) to have a long and structured opportunity to question it. It took me a long time as a vicar to realise that our serial Alpha people, our 'Alphaholics', didn't ask to do Alpha over and over again because they hadn't understood what they'd been told. They simply saw that, in the church they were being invited to join, there was no more opportunity to keep on asking 'Why?' just a few minutes after the person at the front had told them something was true. In short, they were not really wanting to be grown-ups. The curious child in them was alive and well. Thank goodness.

'Messy Church' is a great name for lots of reasons, one of which is that it undercuts the kind-hearted view of adults that mess is a juvenile thing and that one day people will grow out of it. Playing with clay, teenage mess, the endlessly recursive 'Why?'—too often the church's 'elders' hope that all these are phases in a seamless transition to a blessed maturity where there is no mess at all and people just sit still and listen. In fact, though, the mess of God's creation has always been part of the deal. In the beginning, the earth was formless and void (Genesis 1:2). God lit up the void and gave it a pattern, but it's not evident from Genesis that he cleaned it up. Instead, he filled it with life. Then he made us, in such a way that we would be curious about all that.

My old teacher, Walter Hollenweger, would draw our attention to the marvellous phrase in 1 Corinthians 14:33: 'for God is a God not of disorder but of peace'.[31] He underlined the fact that Paul didn't say, '… a God not of disorder but of order'. Instead, Paul spoke of peace. Bishop David Pytches used to ask, 'Do we seek the order of the nursery or the order of the graveyard?'[32] The graveyard is where nothing moves because nothing can. The nursery is the place where entropy is constantly fought and defeated, where spills are wiped clean, scraped elbows are washed and sticking plaster is applied, squabbles are defused, people are reconciled, answers to questions are attempted and conversations are sustained—in short, where the kingdom is glimpsed.

So, reaching for peace—staying poised and open and calm—in the midst of disorder is a valued skill, although, for me, the professions that value it are not valued as highly as they should be. I think of the caring professions, of primary school teachers, of Messy Church helpers. The poet John Keats, however, valued the same skill most highly of all in the very greatest artists:

At once it struck me what quality went to form a Man of Achievement, especially in Literature, and which Shakespeare possessed so enormously —I mean Negative Capability, that is, when a man is capable of being in uncertainties, mysteries, doubts, without any irritable reaching after fact and reason.[33]

For Keats, curiosity simply involved a refusal to shut down the options too soon. The wisdom of the child is so often like this. I witnessed the theological opposite many years ago in a diocesan clergy conference, sitting next to a colleague and awaiting the beginning of a Bible study. The guy next to me opened his notebook and jotted down the three or four bullet points which, in his view, the speaker needed to cover. As the talk unfolded, he was clearly scandalised that the speaker was leading the conversation in completely different directions. At the end, he underlined his own bullet points and snapped his notebook shut, before grumbling about the decline in Bible teaching today. I wish that were a funny story, but I remember it too clearly to laugh.

In March 2011, Lulu asked, 'Dear God, how did you get invented?' Her father sent the question to a number of church leaders. Most did not reply, but Rowan Williams, then Archbishop of Canterbury, in an intervention that won him almost unanimous praise and respect when the family shared the story, wrote Lulu an email which included these words:

Dear Lulu,

Your dad has sent on your letter and asked if I have any answers. It's a difficult one! But I think God might reply a bit like this—

Dear Lulu—Nobody invented me—but lots of people discovered me and were quite surprised. They discovered me when they looked round at the world and thought it was really beautiful or really mysterious and wondered where it came from. They discovered me when they were very very quiet on their own and felt a sort of peace and love they hadn't expected.

Then they invented ideas about me—some of them sensible and some of them not very sensible. From time to time I sent them some hints— specially in the life of Jesus—to help them get closer to what I'm really like.

But there was nothing and nobody around before me to invent me. Rather like somebody who writes a story in a book, I started making up the story of the world and eventually invented human beings like you who could ask me awkward questions!

I continue to be moved by this reply, as many were, because it shows a working theologian of world class, seeking to say simple and true things as if at a Messy Church table. Usually the story ends there. In this context, however, we have to let Lulu herself have the last word. Her father reports:

She listened quietly as I read the Archbishop's letter and it went down well. What worked particularly was the idea of 'God's story'. 'Well?'

*I asked when we reached the end. 'What do you think?' She thought a
little. 'Well, I have very different ideas. But he has a good one.'*[34]

It seems to me that Lulu's response is not only the response of a
child who, of course, will one day put away childish things. It is also
the response of a person at ease in the garden of curiosity, 'without
any irritable reaching after fact and reason'. The Archbishop's good
idea does not drive out Lulu's own ideas, which are very different.
So the conversation continues.

As a bishop, I hope and pray and long for a church filled with
more people—of all ages—like that. Discipleship is so much more
than that, but discipleship without it is not messy enough to grow.
For me, that's at the heart of Lucy Moore and Jane Leadbetter's
words:

*The way you go about making disciples may involve horrifying amounts
of icing sugar and glitter glue, but it's always there, this priority that will
keep you all going through the hard times: we're here to make disciples,
not to try to get people coming to our church service or to give them a
Nice Time.*[35]

Truthfulness

Ten years ago, I was involved in cell-church planting in South
Hampshire.[36] One of our particular focuses was a number of all-age
small groups, meeting weekly and, as far as possible, with all ages
together for all or most of the time. Many of the children in our
groups were from lone-parent families, and they came with their
parent or carer each week.

Classical cell church structures its meetings round the four 'W's:
Welcome, Worship, Word and Witness. The Welcome session is
designed to be a more-or-less structured icebreaker, usually light-
hearted and light-touch, which gathers the group and helps it
reconnect. It's normally marked by laughter. These are the Welcome
rules, so long as no one reframes them.

So, in early December the icebreaker question is 'What would you like for Christmas?' Round the circle we go: a new pen, a new laptop, a new outfit, a new book. We come to a five-year-old boy who is always rather quiet and withdrawn. 'Well,' we encourage him, 'what would you like for Christmas?' 'A new daddy, please,' he says. There's a silence, then sobbing. The group moves into a new place in its life, as we comfort and help the sobbing child. The truth continues its work—to make us free as we know it.

Living untruthfully is the more common way for human beings, and of course the church has God's word of acceptance to speak there too. Rick Fabian points to the place where lies are transformed when he says:

Psychology Today *magazine has suggested that the average American tells over nine hundred lies a day. 'Lovely to see you!' 'I'm doing just great, thanks!' 'I'll be there in a minute!' At Jesus' table we sinners eat together, offering nothing. Not our repentance; not our frail New Year's resolutions, which… Jesus has never credited; not our little moral improvements; nothing. God does all that happens there.*[37]

Increasingly, though, we are learning to make spaces where truthfulness is OK and gets no one bothered. Here's a post from the Messy Church blog, in its entirety.[38]

This is a really interesting blog post from a parent who has just visited a Messy Church because of the fascinating reasons she gives for taking her child to church:

'In our village we have a church. Now I am not Christian, and I am not an atheist. I believe in people's beliefs. It was so beautiful being in the presence of God, their God—something I really want to expose Caleb to from an early age; also because the club is fun and everyone there is kind. But I think it's important that Caleb sees religion and understands it's about an individual's belief, not the actual God itself.

'Anyways, as you can see, the day was spent playing with toys. He loved them so much. He's too young for them, which of course got him even

more excited. After that we had a "Messy Olympics" with all the kids and parents. I did join in whilst Shelly sat with Caleb and watched. We then all went into the church to receive our medals. Caleb got one for just being cute I think! Everyone aw-ed and applauded him receiving his award. We then sang songs and Caleb fell fast asleep on me, so we had to take him home before sandwich and cake time!'

As it says itself, this is indeed a really interesting blog post, not least for what it says about being truthful and its place in the local church. The way we must teach is changing, in ways that many have noticed over the past 30 years.

In late Christendom, the leaders' guides for our nurture courses, like 'Saints Alive', would tell us to invite questions on doctrines of the faith, assuming (1) that people knew these doctrines and (2) that they would have a problem with them. That may have been the way to handle truthfulness at one time, but even in the 1980s, when I was a 'Saints Alive' leader, the fact is that these questions were not asked. No one seemed to mind about the empty tomb. They either accepted it uncritically or they saw it as wholly irrelevant—I was never sure which. But their unanimous focus, as theorists of evangelism have increasingly come to teach, was on the lived truth of the faith rather than the propositional truth of the course curriculum.

The woman quoted in the blog post above has not yet established any clarity about the faith, other than her clear belief that other people's beliefs are valuable, real and good. Not only was she welcomed with this belief alone, but she is still welcomed and not judged or commented on, even when her story is shared with other Messy Church practitioners. As Keats would say, there is no irritable reaching after fact and reason. Instead, the woman is free to look at the surface of things—and what she sees is Messy Olympics, the love shown to her son, and fun and kindness in action. And one more thing: 'It was so beautiful being in the presence of God, their God.'

When I worked as an adviser on evangelism, I was usually asked to talk and think about the shape of the church. That's a fact with many implications, by no means all good, which I have no space to discuss here. But on the rare occasions when I was asked for advice about evangelism, I would look to 1 Peter 3:15–16: 'Always be ready to make your defence to anyone who demands from you an account of the hope that is in you; yet do it with gentleness and reverence.'

It was so beautiful being in the presence of God, their God—something I really want to expose Caleb to from an early age; also because the club is fun and everyone there is kind.

Non-propositional truthfulness was made manifest in this Messy Church without reference to anything but play, welcome, enjoyment, hospitality—and the presence of God, which the writer wants to share with her son. How long will it be before the question comes about the hope that is in that church, that church which so clearly knows what gentleness and respect look like in its dealings with a seeker? How long before our words, too, will find their essential place? Not so long, I believe. Not so long at all.

Conclusion: uncontrolled eyebrows and messy theology

A fair bit of my present work involves interviewing clergy for jobs as vicars. At one such interview recently, one of the parish's lay representatives had a question for each of the candidates. It went like this: 'How do you see a future for the Church of England when its leader can't even control his own eyebrows?' He asked the question with a twinkle in his eye. It produced some great answers.

In my lifetime I have seen two Archbishops of Canterbury with eyebrow-control issues. The first was Michael Ramsey, a theologian of great clarity and organising intellect who was not afraid to glory in a messy church if he believed messy church to be the true church. His remarkable first book, *The Gospel and the Catholic Church*, was published amid the gathering storms in Europe in 1936. In it he wrote these very famous words, addressed to the Anglican family but not at all exclusive to them:

*While the Anglican Church is vindicated by its place in history, with a strikingly balanced witness to gospel and church and sound learning, its greater vindication lies in its pointing through its own history to something of which it is a fragment. Its credentials are its incompleteness, with the tension and travail in its soul. **It is clumsy and untidy, it baffles neatness and logic.** For it is sent not to commend itself as 'the best type of Christianity', but by its very brokenness to point to the universal church wherein all have died.*[39]

Not the 'best type of Christianity' but the broken community that points to the universal Church. It's not a bad vocation for a local church as well as for a world communion. What I have tried to say in this brief chapter is that we can only point with integrity to the universal Church if the voices in our community are as universal as possible. This is why any church and its theology have a lot to learn from its marginal voices, and, in the context of Messy Church, especially from the voice of the child in the family, whatever that family may be. I have pointed to just three areas—to reframing, to curiosity and to the truthfulness you need for both—where the gift of the marginal child can enrich any Christian thinker.

The other recent Archbishop with uncontrolled eyebrows has said almost the same thing:

We can meet [other Christian traditions than ours] in a spirit of rivalry and suspicion or else in a spirit of gratitude, and I want to put in my vote for a spirit of gratitude. That is part of what I mean by a Church both Catholic and Reformed, not eager to reconsolidate a smooth system, and prepared to live with plurality not because it is indifferent, but because it is in fear and trembling of the mysteriousness and richness of God which no system can manage for us.[40]

In the Athanasian Creed it is written, 'The Father incomprehensible, the Son incomprehensible, and the Holy Spirit incomprehensible... and yet they are not three incomprehensible, but one incomprehensible.'[41] That's pretty good, but it's as far as prose will get you. In the end, our theology is messy because no one understands God.

On the other hand, the task of theology is not hopeless. A young teenager wrote to me this year in readiness for her confirmation, saying, 'I was five when I began to realise everything about God,' and she was not wrong. That's the mystery of it: we'll never know, and at the same time by God's revelation we have the pearl of great price. The trick seems to be not to mind 'the mysteriousness and richness of God which no system can manage for us', but to love it dearly and bravely. The trick seems to be to keep the eyebrows growing, to make room for the mess; it's the only clear way.

✥

6

Messy disciples

John Drane

John Drane is Affiliate Professor of New Testament and Practical Theology at Fuller Seminary, and a Visiting Fellow of St John's College, Durham. He is the author of many books on church and culture, and is a member of the board of the Mission-Shaped Ministry *course as well as being co-chair of the Mission Theology Advisory Group.*

Discipleship and mess

Discipleship is messy because life is messy. If the call to follow Jesus is something that we are to contextualise into the whole of life, then the act of being a disciple will inevitably follow the contours of life. The way we celebrate success will be infused with gospel values, and when we confront life's challenges we will do so in the conscious knowledge that following Jesus is going to make a difference. It is, of course, possible to deny that life is messy, and some Christians do. Advocates of the 'prosperity gospel' insist that a life that is not characterised by money, success and power is not a life of true discipleship, because God allegedly wishes to bless us with these things in exchange for our obedience. At the same time, others recognise that life can be tough but argue that, through appropriate discipline and perseverance, Christians can expect to overcome, and our eventual outcomes can all be good.

In my experience, life is more complicated than either of those scenarios—and, I would suggest, that is how the journey of discipleship has always been. It may occasionally be uncomfortable or embarrassing to admit to our own struggles as we seek to follow Jesus, but I believe that openness and transparency are at the heart of any authentic discipleship. Furthermore, this is a missional issue. The journalist John Shore articulates what many outside the church think, when he provocatively asks:

Why are so many Christians so obnoxious and mean-spirited? It seems like Christianity's mostly about being judgmental, narrow-minded, and having an infuriatingly condescending attitude toward anyone who isn't a Christian. Christians are so busy being smug about being Christian that they forget to be kind.[42]

The complaint is a common one—that we Christians present ourselves as judgmental and critical of others, implying that we have our lives together and everybody else is in a mess. Not surprisingly, that is the source of one of the most common criticisms of Christians—that we are hypocrites. When people say that, they are not usually meaning to suggest that we are bad people or that we are either corrupt or dishonest. More often than not, it is a way of questioning what can come across as a superior attitude, as if we have our lives together just by virtue of being Christian, and, if other people would join us, then they too could enjoy a similarly charmed existence.

The truth is that being a Christian is not a free pass to a painless life, and if we are honest we know that we struggle with the same problems as everyone else: we are by no means immune to the existential breakdown that plagues so many in this 21st-century culture of insecurity and uncertainty. My understanding of mission starts and ends with that consciousness. To put it simply, if we have anything worthwhile to share with other people, it will not be because we are different from them but because we are no different. Our fears, hopes, tragedies, joys and triumphs are the same as everyone else's, and the good news in today's world is not 'We have it and you need it' but 'Life can be tough, and always unpredictable, yet in the midst of it all, following Jesus truly makes a difference'.

As I have reflected on the subject of this chapter, it seems to me that this missional perspective should form an important foundation for the discussion. Indeed, as I thought about the relationship between faith and mess, I began to wonder if all forms of church life ought not to be messier than they typically are, if they are truly to reflect a fully incarnational understanding of the gospel. Of course, the apostle Paul advised the church in Corinth that, far from being messy, in the community of God's people things should be done 'decently and in order' (1 Corinthians 14:40). Historically, that instruction has certainly been taken seriously in relation to institutional structures—perhaps more seriously than it deserves, given that it was recommended as a corrective to a very specific circumstance in mid-first-century Greece.

It has also contributed to an understanding of discipleship that can be described, at best, as quietist and passive—namely, the notion that faithfulness consists in attending church services, making a financial contribution to the running costs and trying hard to be nice to one another. I do not wish to suggest that church services are a bad thing, still less that they never sustain the faith of those who attend them. But the inherited emphasis on corporate worship of a certain kind being at the heart of authentic discipleship has had some unforeseen (and, no doubt, unintended) consequences.

Some Christians complain about the perceived marginalisation of their faith in civic life, but when secularists say that Christianity is something to be practised in private with other Christians, they are merely reflecting the way many believers have actually expressed their faith in the recent past. The idea that there might be regular practices—whether ethical, political, civic or ritual—that are intrinsic to discipleship and impinge on daily life is not a notion that, generally speaking, has characterised either the belief or the actual behaviour of most Christians.

This also is a missional concern, though not for the reasons adduced by those campaigners who wish to re-establish a privileged place for Christianity in the civic forum. I constantly meet people who say that if being a Christian is only concerned with attendance at a service once a week, then Christianity can hardly claim to be a serious spiritual pathway. Paradoxically, perhaps, these same people, who would struggle to make time in an already overcrowded weekly schedule for yet another 60-minute activity, would have little hesitation in committing themselves to something that will affect the whole of their lives. In a 24/7 culture, discipleship needs to be a 24/7 endeavour—and that means a pattern of discipleship that not only allows for, but intentionally connects with, the messiness of everyday life in all its diversity.

Jesus and the Twelve

In pursuing this theme, we can do no better than to start with Jesus himself and his own followers. Although disciples feature in the narratives of all four Gospels, we know remarkably little about most of them. The Twelve seem familiar but a majority of them are known to us only as names (Matthew 10:1–4; Mark 3:16–19; Luke 6:13–16), while the 70 are anonymous (Luke 10:1–12). Then there are others, notably women, who were clearly regarded as core disciples and may well have been included within the 70, although they are not clearly mentioned in that context (Mark 16:1–8; Luke 8:1–3; Acts 1:12–14).[43] This relative absence of specific personal information about the first generation of disciples probably explains why, in seeking to identify biblical models, we have often given Paul's dramatic experience precedence over the story of those who accompanied Jesus himself (Acts 9:1–9).

Especially in evangelical circles, this has tended to define the life of faith as something that stems from a dramatic life-changing episode, which engenders radical change and is initiated by praying 'the sinner's prayer', typically consisting of confession of sin along with acknowledgment of Jesus' divine status and, perhaps, other doctrinal formulations. This approach to discipleship first came to prominence among American revivalist preachers at the end of the 19th century, when it was arguably an appropriate contextualisation of the gospel in an emerging nation that, following the ravages of the Civil War, was making conscious choices about what sort of society it would become. Once it was removed from that context, however, this approach became formulaic and predictable in a way that, according to Richard Peace's magisterial study of the topic, is now unhelpful when sharing the gospel in today's world:

At this moment in history when so many people are interested in spirituality and open to Christianity, it behoves us to respond to their needs in ways that build upon this Spirit-driven desire to know God. We will not be able to help people if we insist that their experience must parallel the experience of St Paul.[44]

While acknowledging that some people do indeed have dramatic experiences that signal the start of their discipleship, Peace goes on to develop from the stories of Mark's Gospel a 'process-oriented paradigm for conversion' as 'a more holistic way of doing evangelism that yields in our generation the good fruit that Mark desired in his'.

In recognition of this—and inspired by empirical research on the ways in which people do actually become Christians[45]—it has become fashionable to think of discipleship as a three-stage linear process, often summarised as believing, belonging and behaving. On this understanding, believing the right things is foundational: once a person has done that, we allow them to belong to our churches and then we work on them to ensure that they will behave appropriately. Some add 'blessing' as a fourth element, while others have speculated that the order might be amended to place belonging first, followed in turn by believing and so on. This is not the place to engage in any further extensive discussion,[46] except to note that it is a model of faith that, in any case, only really works in the context of those who already have some form of prior commitment to or understanding of the gospel. Long before his Damascus road encounter, Paul himself was by no means an unbeliever, and his dramatic experience was less of a conversion from darkness to light and more a question of new light on an existing faith commitment.

While we cannot deny that some individuals do have sudden life-changing experiences, all the evidence suggests that these people are in a minority; most come to faith in a way that is not only more gradual but also tends not to follow any one prescribed pattern. Many people first encounter Christians through either blessing (which might take forms as various as engagement in community service or free hugs offered in the street) or behaving (a remarkable number want to change their lifestyle and are looking for others who will work alongside them on that transformation).

This should not surprise us, as most people today have no knowledge either of church or of Christian belief. One of the more surprising movie successes of 2012 was *Salmon Fishing in the Yemen*, in which, in an early scene, the leading characters arrive in the Middle East to embark upon the hopeless enterprise indicated by the film's title. One of the first things they see is a group of Muslim men praying, and, by way of comment on that, salmon expert Fred Jones says, 'I don't know anyone who goes to church any more. On Sundays we go to Tesco.'[47] All my intuition (and a good deal of empirical research) tells me that Fred speaks for most people in Britain today, and, at a time when a majority of the population never meet anybody with an active church connection, it is obvious that neither believing nor belonging will form much of an entry point into discipleship for them.

When we compare that reality with the way in which Jesus invited people into the new frame of reference which is God's kingdom (or, as veteran Scottish theologian Ian Fraser puts it, 'God's way of doing things'), it is striking how appropriate his appeal was, not just in his day but also in ours. His message was couched not in terms of theological ideas but in ways that his hearers could easily relate to in their everyday life: so he speaks with fishing communities about fish (Mark 1:16–20), while with rich people he speaks about money (Mark 10:17–22) and, with a woman by a well, the topic is water (John 4:7–15).

Peter the so-called Rock

Those episodes offer disconnected snapshots of the way the good news was communicated to particular individuals, but there is another follower of Jesus about whom we know rather more, who enables us to reflect meaningfully on the messy nature of discipleship. That individual is Peter. In an earlier book I explored his journey in some considerable detail, but, since that is now long out of print, it is worth briefly summarising the salient features here.[48]

Peter's faith journey was undoubtedly a messy one. He always believed in God, of course—something that might not be so far removed as it seems from the experience of people today. While strictly theistic beliefs might not be widespread, huge numbers still believe that there is 'something there' beyond ourselves. When Peter first met Jesus, he was working at his fishing business on the shore of Lake Galilee (Mark 1:14–20). This story is commonly regarded as Peter's call to discipleship, yet it was remarkably devoid of most of the elements that Christians have often equated with that concept. Jesus describes his vision of a better world, and (paraphrasing into 21st-century terminology) says something like, 'If this grabs you, then join me and we'll explore it together.' If Peter believed anything at all, it was just that whatever Jesus was promoting, his message was worth further reflection—and that Jesus himself was a person who could be trusted, so it was worth spending time with him to explore some more. Few would wish to deny that this was the point at which he became a disciple, but it is undeniable that it was more of a personal interaction than a theological conviction—something that is especially significant in the context of missional engagement with people today.

When compared with some commonly inherited understandings of discipleship, what is missing here is at least as significant as what is included, for there is no mention at all of personal guilt, confession of sin, prayers of commitment, forgiveness, acceptance of dogma or admission to the life of the church. Indeed, subsequent episodes highlight Peter's lack of theological awareness. It is not until we get to Mark 8:27–30 that he is able to affirm any sort of Christological orthodoxy. Even then, he is still struggling to make sense of it (v. 33).

Messiness and ambiguity were constant companions in his journey with Jesus. You might think that by the time he had been with Jesus for three years, Peter would have had most things sorted out into some form of definitive conviction, but the episode in the high priest's garden tells a different story (John 18:15–27). By this time, presumably his Christology was more or less settled, and, had the young servant asked him a question regarding Jesus' alleged status as Messiah, he might well have had a straightforward answer. But her question was more direct and personal and, for that reason, more threatening: 'You are one of this man's friends, aren't you?' (see Matthew 26:69–75; Mark 14:66–72; Luke 22:54–62; John 18:15–27). That brought to the surface all sorts of personal insecurities which, at the very least, suggest that if 'conversion' is about radical change, then Peter's underlying emotional commitments might at this point be regarded as unconverted. This is addressed later in the Johannine narrative by his post-resurrection encounter with Jesus (John 21:1–23) and, in Acts, through the events of the Day of Pentecost (Acts 2:1–42).

Whatever the locus of this new stage of discipleship, the next time he was similarly challenged, Peter was ready to go to prison for his allegiance to Jesus (Acts 3:1—4:4). Even then, he still had a way to go, as he discovered when he was summoned to the house of Cornelius, where his essentially racist worldview inhibited him from meeting with a Roman (Acts 10:1–48). It was understandable enough in the circumstances—which included the brutal suppression of his own people by the Romans—but, if he was to be a mission leader as well as a pastor, he needed to overcome his hang-ups about people who were different from him. Without the recognition that God is not limited by our self-determined categories, he would never fulfil all the world-changing potential of discipleship. In this particular episode, we might reasonably wonder who was the better disciple. Was it Cornelius, who was open to whatever God had for him, or Peter, who was so resistant to change?

Significantly, Peter was still arguing with Paul some years later over the same questions (Galatians 2:11–14), and as late as the mid-50s he was still sufficiently parochial in his outlook for some legalists in Corinth to claim him as their patron (1 Corinthians 1:12)—a reminder that following Jesus is a constant invitation to see the world and its people differently, and that this will be an ongoing challenge. Subsequently, Peter's commitment led to his untimely death at the hands of the Romans and secured his place in history as the foremost of Jesus' original disciples. But he is an inspirational role model for later generations not so much because of his martyrdom but because of the turmoil, the blind alleys and the mistakes that emerged from his willingness to give all that he had for the cause to which Jesus had called him. In short, he is a disciple with whom we easily identify because the messiness of his own faith journey is so frequently reflected in our own.

Discipleship and faith development

Not only is Peter a good biblical example of the messiness that characterises authentic discipleship, but his story also helps to identify some of the reasons why Messy Church connects so readily with today's people. Ever since James Fowler's groundbreaking work relating personal development to faith development, it has been taken for granted that discipleship is not something static that we receive (or accept) in a moment of time, but something that evolves and grows through the many ups and downs of life. Fowler's ideas stemmed from the research of developmental psychologists and provided him with a useful framework within which to express a concept of 'stages of faith' that, in some way, can run parallel to stages of life.[49] Using that model, he identified six stages of faith that he believed characterised the universal spiritual experience, and it is not difficult to offer correlations between Peter's experience and these stages.[50]

The understanding of faith as a journey is, of course, intrinsic to the biblical narrative and is central to the Old Testament as well as the New. The same understanding also features in the stories of notable Christians throughout history, whether ancient figures such as Augustine or Julian of Norwich or more recent individuals such as Søren Kierkegaard, Evelyn Underhill or M. Scott Peck, among many others.[51] In its original form, Fowler's understanding produced more questions than answers, not least because of the uninterrupted progressive linear view of faith that it seemed to envisage. Peter's eventual willingness to sacrifice himself for his faith undoubtedly correlates with Fowler's final and sixth stage ('universalising'), but the route by which he got there was much more like a spiral than a straight line, and there were many retrograde steps as well as much progression in his commitment to follow Jesus. It was more like the proverbial three steps forward and two steps back except that the steps were not always either forward or backward but quite often went sideways or even upside-down. To describe the life of faith adequately requires a more multidimensional model in which whatever stages we might identify have a more fluid relationship one with another, and a recognition that the relationship between them is not necessarily a cognitive one (as Fowler rather assumed) but reflects a more holistic understanding not only of the human psyche but also of the unpredictability and ambiguity of life itself.[52]

The understanding of discipleship as a series of linear stages has also been questioned on the basis of research into women's spirituality, where the evidence very much suggests that discipleship is neither a neat linear construct nor an exclusively cognitive affair. When we adopt an empirical and ethnographic approach rather than the somewhat theoretical understanding that inspired Fowler, it can be shown that women's spirituality tends to be expressed in more holistic ways—ways that, of course, Jesus himself advocated with his definition of discipleship as loving God with heart, soul, mind and strength and taking due care of the self as an essential aspect of being able to journey alongside others (Mark 12:28–31). When viewed from this angle, some less abstract and more humane qualities come to the fore—things like embodiment, interaction, mutuality, playfulness and story. All of this naturally leads to an assumption that, far from being an essentially rational or cognitive matter, the formal intellectual expression of faith may not be central to discipleship at all.[53] The suggestion is not that the notion of faith as a developmental process should be dismissed as an imaginary chimera, but that the process is infinitely more flexible and diverse than Fowler originally thought.

Discipleship and changing culture

It is not difficult to see a culturally determined pattern here, which not only sheds light on the apparent success of Messy Church but also establishes renewed connections with understandings of discipleship that are biblically based, as well as reflecting the experience of actual people in their following of Jesus in today's world. For the last few centuries, our models of Christian education and mission have been based on the philosophical foundations of the Enlightenment, using processes of teaching and learning that have their origins in the systematised world of the Industrial Revolution. They have tended to (indeed, were designed to) produce a standardised (McDonaldised) product, so that all disciples would look the same. Fowler's somewhat inflexible definition of faith development was born in a world that, even though things were changing, still operated under the influence of Christendom and, more broadly, a patriarchal culture that can only flourish in a culture of uniformity. That way of being is no longer dominant in Western culture, and its demise has made it possible for other voices to be heard. Increasingly, the voice of practical discipleship is challenging the rigid theories of the past. As David Bosch observed:

The Christian faith is intrinsically incarnational; therefore, unless the church chooses to remain a foreign entity, it will always enter into the context in which it happens to find itself.[54]

Messy Church, whether by design or happy coincidence, has recognised that reality by identifying one way in which faith can be incarnated in this emerging cultural context. As in many other aspects of church life, the experience of women has played a significant role in this realisation, although I remain to be convinced that the qualities and characteristics of discipleship that are identified in studies of women's spirituality are necessarily unique to the experience of women. My hesitation in making that identification is partly pragmatic: there are still churches that will happily regard any ministry that involves children or intergenerational activity as the appropriate place for women to operate, and will use that as a way of marginalising them from other aspects of church life that are regarded as more significant. But more than that, I would argue that most, if not all, of these characteristics are simply the way we now operate in a postmodern cultural context. This in turn no doubt reflects a growing appreciation for feminine insights and practices, so the two are not entirely unrelated. In addition, personality type and preferred learning styles feed into this discussion, and these not only transcend traditionally gendered roles but also are not limited by age or generation.

There can be no doubt that Messy Church in its pristine form operates with a different learning style from other more conventional forms of Christian gathering, and that may be one of the reasons for its wider appeal.[55] The same may well be true in relation to personality types. Although there has been plenty of research on the personality types most represented by existing church leaders and members, there is not—as far as I know—any comparable research specifically concerned with the personality types of those involved in Messy Church (or, indeed, any other fresh expressions of Church). It is, however, reasonable to wonder if there is a significant difference in terms of both learning styles and personality types, and if this might explain both the attraction of Messy Church and the reasons why those who come to faith in this environment are unlikely subsequently to transfer to a more traditional gathering.[56]

The growth of Messy Church mirrors the changing nature of society, which has created a prism through which we can now see aspects of Enlightenment-inspired culture that not only constrained the human spirit but were actually untrue and damaging to the Christian cause.[57] Through fresh expressions of Church, we are seeing a rediscovery of biblical values, where the diversity of discipleship was such an indispensable aspect of church life that Paul was able to make a virtue of it, with his many references to the 'body of Christ' as the quintessential expression of the multifaceted character of the people of God (Romans 12:4–8; 1 Corinthians 12:12–30; Ephesians 4:15–16; Colossians 1:18; 3:15).

Moreover, when we reflect on Jesus' own style, it has a good deal in common with patterns of worship and spiritual exploration that might seem to be recent innovations. He is constantly to be found in dialogue with people, creating spaces within their imagination to explore new possibilities, telling stories and asking questions to which there is quite often no real answer, but which make room for personal discovery. And how he loved to play! He certainly liked drawing and could use it to considerable effect when words were not the most useful medium (John 7:53—8:11), having fun with his interrogators in the process. In later centuries he was often depicted as a 'holy fool', not on some whimsical fancy but because so many of his antics reflect a pedagogical style focused on interaction and fun.[58] I find it impossible to read statements such as 'Many who are first will be last, and the last will be first' without also imagining him playing with a line of real people and physically rearranging them so that those who were at the end did indeed move up to the front and vice versa (Mark 10:31).[59] At least, that is what children would do, and at the heart of his call to discipleship was the insistence that it is only by becoming like children that anyone can truly understand what it means to follow him and 'enter the kingdom' (9:33–37, 10:13–16).

Creativity and spirituality

It is more than 20 years since George Land and Beth Jarman published their groundbreaking research on what they called 'divergent thinking', based on work that started in the late 1960s.[60] Influenced by NASA, which had devised ways of assessing the creative potential of its engineers and scientists, and recognising that in a world of ever-increasing complexity simple linear solutions were no longer adequate, they conducted a longitudinal study of some 1600 children. They discovered that, on the NASA scale, 98 per cent of these children were classified as genius level at three to five years old, but, by the time they hit adulthood, only two per cent were still capable of the sort of creative thinking required to resolve complex problems. Moreover, this had nothing to do with IQ but appeared to correlate with the ways in which these children had been socialised, in particular their educational socialisation. It was almost as if they had been born to be naturally bright and their socialisation was reducing their intelligence, not increasing it.

A key difference between toddlers and adults turned out to be their attitude towards working with others. When faced with a new challenge, children naturally seek the wisdom of others, but the prevailing educational paradigms regard such collaboration with suspicion and insist on individual problem-solving as the right way to go. This not only disables adults from seeing creative ways around complicated issues but also renders them less capable of working with others in many areas of life. We can see the consequences all around us today, whether in relation to the recent financial crash or the breakdown in personal relationships that have blighted so many families in Western cultures.

When we put this research alongside Jesus' teaching on the importance of disciples being and becoming children, some interesting correlations and possibilities start to emerge. Contrary to the opinions of most commentators, there is more to the childlike nature of discipleship than some romanticised notion about the innocence or openness of childhood (which, in any case, was not a category that would have been understood as such in the first-century Roman Empire). Could it be that Jesus is actually highlighting something intrinsic to the human condition—that true wisdom is not acquired by gaining illicit access to the tree of the knowledge of good and evil through our own carefully crafted systems and structures, but is part of the creativity at the heart of God, as evidenced on the very first page of the Bible, in which we share by virtue of being people made in the divine image, male and female (Genesis 1:26–27)?

At the core of that creativity lie qualities such as spontaneity, intuition, conversation, collaboration, fun, colour, sound and texture. These are all words that naturally spring to mind in describing how God is depicted in the first chapter of Genesis. They are also words that describe Messy Church at its best—a gloriously interactive and open-ended exploration of life, faith and God in partnership with others that, like the relationship between the primal couple and God in the garden, is in constant danger of being systematised so as to become the exact opposite. This has been one of the constant challenges throughout the centuries as Christians have sought ways of nurturing not only their own faith but also the faith of others, and it brings us back to our starting point here.

To be authentic, discipleship will always be a messy business. It is messy because true discipleship follows the contours of life, which is unpredictable and ambiguous while always holding out the possibility of new directions and discoveries, invariably in partnership with others, and often filled with fun as we are overtaken by the unexpected and grow into new dimensions of understanding God, and ourselves, in the grand scheme of things. And that, at its best, is the sort of discipleship that Messy Church engenders.

Case study: Messy Church Fiesta

Christine Barton

Christine Barton is the Messy Chuch Regional Coordinator for Shetland.

Our Messy Church Fiesta took place in Shetland in May 2010. Shetland, the most northerly point of the United Kingdom, is an archipelago of over 100 islands. It lies 200 miles north of Aberdeen, is reached by an overnight ferry or by aeroplane, and supports a population of around 22,000.

We had ventured to include elements of Messy Church in the occasional all-age services at Scalloway Methodist Church, one of eleven churches in the charge of our minister. We were fearful of naming a service Messy Church and of changing the order of service in such a radical way, but it was the initiative of Elinor Thompson, a church member and circuit steward, that resulted in a District Messy Church Fiesta. That weekend, Scalloway Methodist Church 'stepped out of the boat' and went 100 per cent for Messy Church services on a Sunday morning once a month.

The title 'Messy Church' has prompted many conversations. Most of us have been questioned in shops, been tapped on the shoulder when the name has been overheard, and seen interest generated in the workplace, when the regular question of 'What are you doing this weekend?' meets with enthusiastic responses describing the events and crafts that will be taking place. We are so thankful that we decided on the name of Messy Church, as it also enables us to explain that it is a service for everyone, no matter how messy their lives, because Jesus came into this messy world and lived, loved and worked with people who were in a mess one way or another.

The first Messy Church service attracted nearly 30 people. Since then, the numbers have settled at an average in the 60s, with people aged from newborn to 90, as well as whole family groups. The largest number of people attending has been over 90—far too many for our tiny building—and included quite a number of people from other churches who came to 'taste and see'. Last year we refurbished our hall, where Sunday lunch is served to over 40 people, so during this time we moved the venue to the village youth centre. Interestingly, a number of people came who have never been into the church building, but the acoustics were so bad in the large room that we required, and the dining area so small, that it was not possible to continue meeting there.

Scalloway Methodist Church is not a particularly attractive building and is situated within a conservation area. We have therefore sought to publicise the Messy Church service and topic by decorating the outside (and inside) of the building in an attractive and lively way. This has made use of various people's artistic skills in making props, artwork and balloon models. The local gala committee invited us to take part in the carnival and we were also asked to be involved in a marketplace event which was showcasing activities in Scalloway for children and youth.

A desire I have had for the church is to bring the inside of what happens at church to the world outside. At the youth centre, where we were able to showcase Messy Church, we had a display with colourful handouts explaining what happens at a typical Messy Church service. Crafts from past services were displayed and activities for anyone to participate in were also available. We included various methods used in teaching, including illusions, balloon modelling and puppets, with a section from *Messy Church: The DVD* running throughout the session. One woman said she had wondered what went on at Messy Church but had never dared to come in, and we were delighted when her daughter and granddaughter attended the service the following month. She also submitted an article to *The Shetland Times* in which the Messy Church stand took centre stage and was highly praised. As a result of the marketplace event, we were invited to an event the following week, attended by the Prime Minister of Norway, and all the children from the local school introduced him to the Messy Church stand.

Although Scalloway Methodist has a membership of fewer than 30 people, Messy Church has drawn out so much gifting that was not being used within the fellowship of the church. The planning and delivery of the service is a team effort, without which we would be exhausted by now. The services are run by church members and draw upon their organisational abilities, with practical people preparing and clearing up the rooms. Each craft is prepared by the person responsible for it. Some people only enjoy catering and cooking, while others are artistic and skilled in drama. We have discovered amazing teaching abilities and, most importantly, skills in getting alongside and relating to the people who attend. Our church has been very supportive financially and members have also been extremely generous with resources.

We call Messy Church a church service because it contains all the elements of a service, presented in different and more creative ways, and it has created a desire among some of the adults for more. These adults have not attended church but would like the opportunity to ask questions and learn more about the basics of the Christian faith. In September we are starting a monthly café church in the youth centre, hoping to meet the needs that have been generated. We are also going to run a parenting course, as well as a youth fellowship for the children emerging from the Sunday Club. Before Messy Church, the Sunday Club consisted of only three or occasionally six children. The numbers now average 15, and we find that they look forward to Messy Church more than Sunday Club, as it is rather different from any of their past experiences of all-age worship.

In the village of Vidlin, the Sunday school was just about to close, so they asked if we would go along and introduce Messy Church to the members there, to see if it was something they could do. Three of us went along and, helped by three people from the Vidlin church, we held a Sunday Messy Church service. We have found that people are initially reserved and embarrassed and frequently state that they are not artistic. It is not long, however, before they discover that artistic abilities are not necessary and then they relax into the experience. Activities are not all about being creative and artistic; we try to offer a mix of food, games, crafts, challenges and activities for young and older people too. The Vidlin church held its third Messy Church on an Olympic theme, culminating in a week of special Olympic activities. The older children have particularly appreciated these services and a group of eight young teens are now enjoying meeting together regularly in a youth fellowship.

Being a small team, the greatest challenge we have faced with Messy Church is how to cope when several leaders are away at the same time. We are trying not to make the event dependent on anyone specific and to allow people to have a rest. It is also important that we work with what we've got and keep encouraging good communication, forgiveness and prayer. We are now having regular update sessions delivered in the Sunday evening service to keep people informed of what is happening in other areas of the church. The church members have been very open to all the latest developments, but cautious as to why we plan to hold the café church in the youth centre, and so the theology of church has also been discussed. We hope that we will continue to enjoy Messy Church for many years to come, but we realise that it is important to be open to the Holy Spirit, the work he will do in this community and the way he would have it done.

✤

7

From Sunday school to Messy Church: a new movement for our age?

Bob Jackson

Bob Jackson was an economic adviser to the Government in the days before Mrs Thatcher. He then got ordained, enjoying parish ministry in his native Yorkshire for 20 years before working for the Archbishops as a Springboard Missioner. His job was 'to research and disseminate ways of turning round the numerical decline of the Church of England'. His new calling continued in his job as Archdeacon of Walsall and now as an independent church growth teacher, researcher, author and speaker. Bob lives in the village of Eyam in the Peak District with his wife Christine, and is currently failing to work out how to semi-retire. He is the Director of the Centre for Church Growth at St John's Nottingham and a Visiting Fellow at St John's Durham.

Changing methods but an unchanging calling

On holiday in one of the remoter Orkney Islands this summer, we passed a church advertising the Sunday service at 11.00am and Sunday school at 2.30pm. The memories of my afternoon Sunday school, in Sheffield in the early 1950s, came flooding back. During the 1950s and '60s, almost every other church in the country had moved its children's work to Sunday mornings to coincide with the church service, but here was one that never did.

There were good reasons for the change elsewhere: teachers didn't want to turn out twice on a Sunday, churchgoing parents struggled to know what to do with the children on Sunday mornings, and there was a desire for the whole family of God to come together for worship. Decisions to switch to Sunday mornings were made at denominational as well as local level. At first things went well—most of the children transferred to the new time, and life became easier for churchgoing families—but it became much harder to recruit new children on a Sunday morning than it had been in the afternoon. Sunday school began to seem part of an insiders' church event rather than a free-for-all to which parents could send children without the danger of entanglement with adult church. The dreaded rotas began to kick in, allowing teachers the chance to attend church themselves sometimes, and the continuity of relationships was lost. Also, of course, the world outside was changing fast. Within a generation, almost the only children attending church groups were the children of Christian parents.

It now looks as if this change of time contributed significantly to the long-term decline in Sunday school numbers, which accelerated hugely around 1960. Perhaps the good islanders of Westray in Orkney, immune to English fashion and nearer to the Arctic Circle than to London, had been right to stick with the old ways. For most churches, major periodic changes in the way they work with children and families are inevitable in a changing world. However, it is the method that changes, not the calling.

One of the recurring themes of the book of Deuteronomy is that the people are to remember for ever more how God took them out of Egypt and gave them his commandments in the wilderness. Their relationship with God and obedience to his way of life are to be sustained for ever, by teaching the children:

Do not forget the things your eyes have seen or let them fade from your heart as long as you live. Teach them to your children and to their children after them… These commandments that I give you today are to be on

your hearts. Impress them on your children. Talk about them when you sit
at home and when you walk along the road, when you lie down and when
you get up. (Deuteronomy 4:9; 6:6–7, NIV)

From the time of Moses onwards, the Old and New Testament
peoples of God have sustained their faith through its transmission to
the children. As the psalmist put it, 'He commanded our ancestors
to teach their children, so that the next generation would know [his
statutes], even the children yet to be born, and they in turn would
tell their children. Then they would put their trust in God and
would not forget his deeds but would keep his commands' (Psalm
78:5–7, NIV). Often, the main vehicle of transmission has been
family life—children learning and catching the faith of their own
parents. Sometimes it has been the more organised activities of the
church, perhaps through schools or monasteries.

I clearly remember the people who taught me the Christian faith
in Sunday school and Bible class 50 and 60 years ago. Doubtless,
they in turn remembered those who had shared it with them, and so
on back through the generations to Christ himself. Communicating
the experience and commandments of God to the next generation is
not an optional or peripheral activity for the Christian community.
It is one of the church's core functions to ensure the survival and
flourishing of its faith.

So the context for asking fundamental questions about Messy
Church is far wider than simply consideration of a specific tech-
nique. It is about how the church of today can best fulfil its eternal
calling to pass on its experience of God and obedience to his teaching to the young. In an era of ageing traditional congregations as
well as Messy Church, the faith often needs to be passed on to
parents as well as their children. The faith-transmission methods
will continue to change, but the calling remains the same. So, as
well as reviewing its methods, the church needs to keep renewing
its basic confidence and calling, in order to pass the torch of faith
on to the next generation. A church that simply embraces the latest

gimmick is likely to run into trouble, but a church that is motivated to re-energise its missional calling will always find new ways to meet changing times.

The rise and fall of Sunday school

In the 18th century, this calling was expected to be fulfilled through the catechism classes run by the clergy. Anglicans would use the Catechism from the Book of Common Prayer, and Dissenters the Westminster Shorter Catechism (which, of course, was anything but short). Children and young people would be gathered in groups, usually on Sundays during Lent or the summer months. In the Anglican Church, these classes might lead on to confirmation. Particularly in the Puritan tradition, it was expected that such teaching would be supplementary to the Christian education that all parents were expected to give to the children growing up in their Christian homes.

However, the classes tended to attract the respectable rather than the masses, and were held at the discretion of the clergy concerned, some of whom were 'too busy' to conduct them, and also of parents who might or might not send their children. They did not touch the increasing social needs of children growing up during the Industrial Revolution or meet the need for basic training and education for the new urban working classes.

The Sunday school movement initiated or popularised by the Gloucester newspaper publisher Robert Raikes began around 1780 and quickly spread around the country, aided by his published accounts in newspapers and magazines in the early to mid-1780s. Sunday schools, unlike catechism classes, were run by lay people, often paid. A mixture of motives and objectives was associated with them. Raikes observed that vandalism by boys was concentrated on Sundays—the devil finding work for idle hands to do. Early Sunday schools were not so much academies of faith as a mission to the poor, teaching basic reading skills and moral discipline, turning dangerous leisure time for children into the opportunity of a Christian education while getting vandals off the streets and creating positive citizens who would go on to create Victorian Britain: 'Start children off on the way they should go, and even when they are old they will not turn from it' (Proverbs 22:6, NIV).

However, children were also seen as sinners from birth, in need of spiritual as well as moral and social redemption. By 1786 the Manchester Sunday school charity had produced a prayer to be used at the start and end of every Sunday school day, illustrating that it saw its purpose as being about education and virtue, and about religious faith:

Almighty God, from whom all holy desires, all good counsels, and all just works do proceed, we bless thee for inclining the hearts of thy people to establish these Schools, for the instruction of the ignorant, and the advancement of thy true religion and virtue.

Advice on the setting up and running of Sunday schools in the *Evangelical Magazine* in 1798 suggested that schools should start with religious instruction, then move to reading and spelling before public worship, which was often an integral part of the Sunday school package. It was suggested that parents making application for their children to enter the Sunday school should be given tracts and be spoken to about the faith. Also, a team of visitors should be appointed to visit homes, especially those of absentee scholars. Raikes himself used to visit the homes of all his scholars and would talk with the parents about their children's welfare and upbringing.[61]

So, early Sunday schools:

- were run by a mix of paid and volunteer lay people.
- had a social and educational dimension, aiming to transform society, as well as a religious-conversion motivation.
- attempted to reach the mass of the people, not just a privileged class.

- attended to parents, home situations and some pastoral care as well as Sunday instruction.
- were transdenominational in form and organisation.
- became associated with one person but were primarily part of a movement springing up in many places, not a central 'command and control' organisation.
- crossed theological boundaries, meeting the aspirations of both social and conversion gospellers.
- started among the poor in the cities but quickly spread to all social groups, towns and rural areas.
- were integrated into the general worshipping rhythm of the churches.
- used dedicated buildings and private houses rather than church buildings for their classes.
- met on Sunday, partly because it was the sabbath but mainly because Sunday was the only day when most children, working in factories, on the land or at home, were available to attend.
- grew in numbers very rapidly once the concept was refined and publicised.
- became an international movement quite quickly. The first Sunday school in the USA was probably set up by Samuel Slater in the 1790s among the textile mills of Rhode Island.

Graph 1 charts the growth of Sunday schools in the UK from their beginnings up to their peak around 1910. The numbers should be taken as indicative rather than authoritative, for comparable numbers were not collected by different denominations in the same years as each other. They come from a variety of sources; for example, the 1787 figure of 250,000 was Raikes' own estimate.[62]

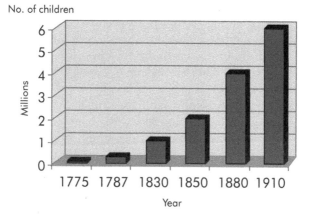

No. of children

Graph 1: Sunday school attendance in the UK

Graph 2 shows the breakdown between the major denominations. All were heavily involved in Sunday schools, although the majority of children attended either Anglican or Methodist schools.[63]

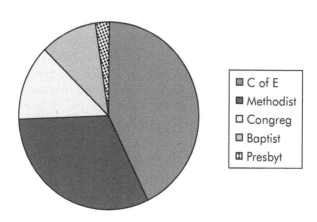

Graph 2: Sunday school rolls in England at their peak around 1910

By 1910, around 85 per cent of all the children in the UK attended Sunday school. This extraordinary growth, over a period of about 130 years, clearly had a profound impact both on the character of the nation and on the life of the churches. The country's self-understanding as a Christian nation was strengthened, and the religious and ethical beliefs of most people were mainly or partly forged in Sunday schools when they were children.

In the 20th century, Robin Gill showed from a survey of non-churchgoers how different were the beliefs and attitudes of adults with a childhood church experience. Although many children never made the transition to adult church and some were actively put off by their Sunday school experience, nevertheless the growth of the churches in the 19th century followed the growth in Sunday schools and was significantly fuelled by it. For the last 200 years, the majority of adult churchgoers in the UK have had a background in Sunday school, church children's groups or Bible class. When speaking with many groups of Christians at conferences and courses over the past 15 years, I have often asked those with a childhood church background to raise their hands, and almost always about 90 per cent of the group do so.

So it is that the decline of Sunday schools since 1910 has carried with it a time bomb in relation to adult church attendance. It is no coincidence that church attendance decline has followed on from Sunday school decline. Graph 3 charts the decline of child Sunday school membership in the 20th century. By 2000, Sunday schools were reaching no more than about five per cent of the population of children in the UK.[64]

No. of children

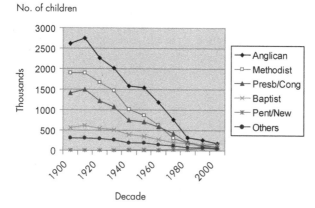

Graph 3: UK Sunday school attendance 1900–2000

The search for new ways to reach new generations

The decline of Sunday schools does not, however, tell the whole story, especially in the later years of the 20th century and the early years of the 21st. Churches have developed other ways of reaching children that do not necessarily appear in Sunday school statistics. After all, it was only the method that was getting dated, not the calling. The church has always taken Jesus' admonition about children to apply to every succeeding generation: 'Let the little children come to me, and do not hinder them, for the kingdom of heaven belongs to such as these' (Matthew 19:14, NIV).

New names, new styles

Most churches have abandoned the title 'Sunday school' and called their children's groups by other, more attractive names, such as the CPAS 'Scramblers–Climbers–Explorers–Pathfinders–CYFA' pro-gression. Some church children's groups now meet on weekdays.

More children may come as a result, but sometimes they are omitted from the official counts, so that actual growth in numbers looks like decline. In my own church in Eyam, many children attend three weekday evening Christian clubs for different age groups, but never come on a Sunday, so their existence is unreported. 'Average church attendance' trends, therefore, may not accurately reflect the actual involvement of children in church activities.

Although there may have been a decline in the numbers of children and young people attending traditional 'Bible classes' such as Urban Saints (Crusaders) and Covenanters, there has also been a growth in new-style children's outreach projects, with streams such as Metro Sunday school and Kids Klub. Many children and young people find their major Christian input in annual events and holidays such as Spring Harvest, New Wine and Soul Survivor. A very high proportion of fresh expressions of Church, not just Messy Church, are aimed at children, young people or families. The scene is complex and fast-moving.

Family services

In the last quarter of the 20th century, many churches invested in monthly all-age 'family services', through which children attend church but do not necessarily attend a Sunday school. They share the experience with their parents; in fact, often it is this appeal to whole families, rather than either children or adults, that attracts them into churchgoing. Invitations go out to people on the fringe, maybe those coming to the parent-and-toddler group in the church hall or attending the church school, or families who come for the Christingle service at Christmas. The family service is usually a once-a-month takeover of the main Sunday morning service, leaving the other weeks more or less unchanged. This has the advantages of mixing the new families with the existing congregation and of making it easier for them to 'progress' to regular weekly churchgoing. It also takes fewer resources to change the style at one existing service than to start something extra.

Finally, a major reason in many churches for starting a monthly all-age service has been to give the Sunday school teachers a rest or because the rota was too thinly stretched. This tended to make the family service not so much a shiny new strategy as a last resort to shore up the crumbling Sunday school model. Also, in some churches, the rise of the family service has led to conflict and compromise. Established regulars may not like their service being displaced once a month by what seems to them to be a shallow, noisy and alien event. Young families may still be a minority in their own service and so feel uncomfortable with it. The event may simply be too long for them, although the regulars would feel short-changed if it were briefer. The minister fields complaints about the music from both sides at once and feels pushed about. In addition, devising and leading a good-quality all-age service is difficult. Some churches have leaders who can do it well, but most do not, so weekly regulars begin to give the all-age service a miss. Older children and teenagers feel that they have grown out of those embarrassing action choruses and vote with their feet. Few families make the transition to the very different culture of the regular service, and few flourish spiritually on the fairly thin once-a-month all-age diet. In some places the monthly all-age service has worked well, but in others these flaws in the model have been too great.

Other churches have tried a weekly family service at a different time on Sunday morning from the traditional service, or sometimes in the church hall at the same time as the traditional service. This enables both services to have a consistent style and membership and enables community and faith to develop at the pace of a weekly service rather than the snail's pace of a monthly one. However, the resources and creativity needed to sustain a high-quality weekly all-age event are probably too great for most churches, and many parents do not want a weekly struggle with small children trapped in pews, paying little attention to what is happening half a mile away at the front of the church. They would much prefer someone to take the children away for a while, giving them a chance to relax and appreciate some adult input for themselves.

Increasingly, both the monthly and the weekly models have also suffered from their traditional timing on a Sunday morning. From the late 20th century onwards, an increasing number of children have become unavailable for churchgoing on a Sunday morning. Many schools and sports clubs have switched to Sunday morning activities. For many children, Sunday is 'Dad's day' until teatime; Mum may now be on the checkout at the supermarket on Sunday mornings, while many older children are spending Sunday morning in bed, recovering from their latest over-busy week.

So there is a move in the early 21st century for family services to be tried on Sunday at teatime, and with some success. These services tend to be quite short, to have none of the baggage that comes with trying to adapt an existing service, to involve activities more energetic than listening to a leader, to be associated with eating quite a lot of food, and to attract new churchgoers. If the church building itself is filled with pews, they may well meet in the church hall instead. These services are not 'Messy Church' clones but they may be its cousins.

Specialist paid staff

There has been a large increase in the numbers of paid and trained youth, children's and families ministers employed by denominations and individual churches. At first, most paid ministers worked with young people, and professional training was quickly developed for this work through the Centre for Youth Ministry. Children's workers followed, and professional training is now beginning to be offered for them, too. More recently there has been an increasing number of appointments for families workers, often older people, who are employed for mission and ministry among whole families.

In the Church of England, many of the new paid staff are partly financed through a specialist funding stream coming from the Church Commissioners, through dioceses, called 'Mission Development Funding'. In the Diocese of Lichfield, for example, around

50 new posts have been created with the help of this seed-corn funding. The numbers of children attending church services and events in churches that have a paid worker have gone up significantly, reversing a century of decline.

More emphasis on schools

Church of England and Roman Catholic dioceses have sought to increase the amount of Christian input offered to children in church schools. The Anglican Diocese of Blackburn, for example, has worked to increase the number of Church of England secondary schools and is sourcing finance for a full-time chaplain in each school. In many parishes, lay church members as well as the clergy are getting involved in primary school assemblies, Christian clubs and other support work. Judging by the annual 'Statistics for Mission' returns, there has probably been an increase in school services taking place in Anglican churches in recent years. Sometimes these are annual or one-off events, such as the school harvest service; sometimes they are weekly assemblies.

New ways of counting

Focusing on the average numbers attending Sunday worship or Sunday school has become an increasingly misleading way of counting the children. This is both because churchgoing children as well as adults now come to church much less often than in the past—on average, somewhere around one week in two—and because many worship events happen on weekdays or in fresh expressions of Church that slip under the statistical radar.

Since 2000, the Church of England has counted attendance on weekdays as well as Sundays for four weeks in October each year. Although child attendance on Sundays has continued to decline, there has been a corresponding increase in weekday attendance, so that reported all-week child attendance has stayed almost the same, at an average of around 220,000.

Most recently, one or two Church of England dioceses have begun to ask churches to report the total number of people who participate in church worship, plus the numbers of joiners and leavers. The overall number of joiners always seems to exceed the number of leavers, but this trend is especially marked among children. For example, churches in the Diocese of Leicester reported 139 children and young people leaving them in 2010 but 406 joining them, a net increase of 267, around seven per cent. The net increase reported in Lichfield Diocese in 2011 was around 1000 under-18-year-olds, a growth of about eight per cent in one year.

Although traditional measures of traditional activities may continue to go down, it is beginning to look as if new indicators, which capture more successfully the new life and complexity in church events for children, young people and families, may now be rising quite fast. It may be that the 100-year story of declining numbers of children in the churches is finally over and a new period of growth is in sight.

Perhaps the largest single component of this recent turnaround has been the rise of a new way of doing church for the whole family together—Messy Church. It is now time to focus on the increasing role of Messy Church in this resurgence of church among families.

The growth of Messy Church

The biggest single factor in the turnaround and new growth in the numbers of children and families participating in the life of churches in the last few years would appear, from looking at the figures for individual churches, to be the expansion of Messy Church. For example, by autumn 2012 the Diocese of Lichfield had 100 Messy Churches spread around its nearly 600 parish churches, accounting for around half of the extra children who were new to churchgoing in the diocese that year.

The first Messy Church, led by Lucy Moore, started in Portsmouth in 2004. Rather like Robert Raikes' first Sunday school in 1780, there were some similar formats already around, but the Messy Church name and format were quickly copied. Lucy Moore's books and the Messy Fiestas quickly helped to popularise the format in the same way that Robert Raikes' magazine and newspaper articles did in the 1780s, but it was impossible to get a handle on how many Messy Churches there might be until a registration website (the Messy Church Directory) was set up by BRF in February 2009. Numbers registered grew quickly from the original 99, reaching 1350 by July 2012. The number of registered churches has roughly doubled each year, as shown in Graph 4. A small proportion of registered churches are overseas: 42 out of 610 recent registrations (seven per cent) were churches in Australia, New Zealand and Canada, and 93 per cent were from the UK.

So far, not many Messy Churches known to the central organisation have ceased to function. It is early days yet, but it is clear that the vast majority are at least able to survive, and grow, for several years after inception.

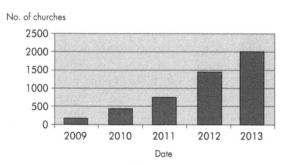

Graph 4: Registered Messy Churches (in August of each year)

Initially the denomination of the churches involved was not recorded, but this is now known for 568 of the more recent registrations. The denominational spread is shown in Graph 5, using as similar a definition as possible to the corresponding Edwardian Sunday school graph (Graph 2).

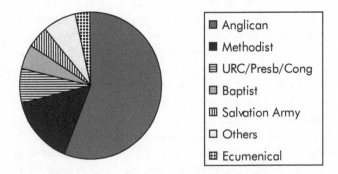

Graph 5: UK Messy Churches
registered between May 2011 and July 2012

It can be seen that the Anglican proportion (56 per cent) is greater
and the Methodist proportion (15 per cent) is smaller than for
Sunday schools in their heyday.

By pooling evidence from many churches and from the 47
regional coordinators, the Messy Church leaders estimate that
average attendance at a Messy Church is around 60, or perhaps
slightly more, including the leadership team. Roughly half are
adults and half are children. Estimating the August 2012 number
of UK-registered Messy Churches as 1400, this suggests an average attendance in the UK of around 85,000. However, as with
conventional church, not everyone comes every time. It seems
likely that average attendance frequency is of the order of two in
three, which yields an estimate of 130,000 members of registered
Messy Churches in the UK in August 2012. If church sizes are the
same across the denominations, this suggests a total membership of
around 73,000 in Anglican registered Messy Churches and around
20,000 in Methodist churches, with the remainder being spread
among other denominations.

However, it has proved difficult to persuade Messy Churches to register themselves on the Directory. Many churches known to the Messy Church regional coordinators have not registered. Others may have started up but not come to the attention of the Messy Church organisation at all. Many have the title of 'Messy Church' but some others have adopted local names. Some are only 'semi-Messy', so definitional problems arise. However, the best estimate, pooling evidence from around the country, from Messy Church regional coordinators, diocesan children's work advisers and Google alerts, is that the total number of Messy-style churches or events is around three times the number registered. This would therefore suggest around 4000 Messy-style churches in the UK in August 2012, of which probably around 56 per cent are Anglican. Their total average attendance is somewhere around 240,000 and membership somewhere around 360,000.

The number of Messy Churches is growing so fast that by the time these very rough estimates are published, they will already be seriously out of date. However, they are sufficient to demonstrate that the Messy Church movement has grown fast enough in its first eight years to bear comparison with the lightning-speed early growth of the Sunday school movement. Robert Raikes' own estimate of 250,000 scholars in 1787, seven years after his first Sunday school, bears a striking resemblance to our estimates of Messy Church membership eight years after the start of the first one. A small proportion (perhaps 15 per cent) of the Messy Church numbers are the planting and leadership team members, but the main difference when compared with the Sunday schools is that half of the new Messy Church members are adults, usually the parents of the children involved.

It is clear from much anecdotal evidence that the great majority of new Messy Church members are new to churchgoing, or at least returning after a break, rather than transferring from another form of church. The new 'joiners and leavers' questions being used by some dioceses are beginning to provide more systematic evidence of this fact. For example, of 1400 child 'joiners' to churches of all sorts in Lichfield Diocese in 2011, 20 per cent were newborns, 59 per cent were children attending for the first time, seven per cent were returning after a break and just 14 per cent were transferring from another church.

It is also clear from 'joiners and leavers' numbers that families form the great majority of the total church growth being recorded. Children appear to form about 40 per cent of the total number of joiners, suggesting that the bulk of adult joiners are their parents or carers joining with them. It would also seem that, as a result of all the developments in relation to families, children and young people discussed above, of which Messy Church is now numerically the largest, the average age of Anglican Church members across the country is once more coming down.

It is impossible to tell at this stage how much further scope there is in the Messy Church model for numerical expansion in the UK. However, the currently uneven spread of churches does suggest that there is much more potential yet. For example, so far, there are hardly any examples of Messy Church in the Roman Catholic Church, yet Catholicism accounts for around a third of all UK churchgoing. The Diocese of Lichfield has actively promoted Messy Church and therefore has several times the number of churchgoers found in the average Anglican diocese. At the very least, it will be possible for others to catch up. There appears to be no let-up in the appetite for Messy Church training events around the country.

So we can expect the number of Messy Churches to keep on rising strongly in this country for some time to come. A million participants in a few years' time looks possible on present trends. The similarities between Messy Church and the early Sunday school movement are also quite striking; most of the 13 characteristics of early Sunday schools listed on pages 135–136 also seem to apply to Messy Church. However, whether it can ever reach the dimensions of the Sunday school movement and so become a mainstream majority culture for UK family life is somewhat further off and remains to be seen.

The depth of the impact made by Messy Church

The breadth of Messy Church's impact is already great and becoming greater—but how deep will be the impact of Messy Church on individual lives, on the Christian church and on society as a whole? As Paul indicated to Timothy, Christians have high ambitions for the influence of the faith on children: 'From infancy you have known the Holy Scriptures, which are able to make you wise for salvation through faith in Christ Jesus' (2 Timothy 3:15, NIV).

The rise of Messy Church has taken us by surprise. A format that was tried out to see if it would work, born out of frustration with formats that didn't, has so rapidly become a significant church stream that it has left those involved breathlessly trying to catch up with what God seems to be doing. We see today something of the same mix of theology, muddled purpose and sketchy strategy that was seen in the early Sunday school movement. While this is understandable, and while we must trust that the Holy Spirit knows what he is doing, the impact made by Messy Church may only become deep and long-lasting if matters of purpose and strategy are clarified and pursued. Three questions in particular suggest themselves.

- Is Messy Church about Christian conversion?
- Is Messy Church for the whole of life?
- Is Messy Church about making Christian disciples?

Is Messy Church about Christian conversion?

Historians argue about the extent to which the early Sunday school movement was about 'reading and writing' education, morality and getting vandals off the street on the one hand, and Christian faith and conversion on the other. That mix or muddle of purpose and motives continued throughout the Sunday school era. As far as I remember, my Sunday school made no attempt to convert me or even to explain the cross and resurrection to me, but it did give me, every Sunday, a temperance leaflet to take home and solemnly hand over to my dad once he had returned from the pub. Many Christians began to expect children to leave once they had 'grown out of' church or Sunday school, consoling themselves with the thought that they might return when older and, even if they didn't, they would be better people for their Sunday school training.

If both those consolations were true to an extent in relation to Sunday schools, there are weaker grounds for thinking they might be true in relation to Messy Church. Many Messy Churches are reluctant to push a strong Christian message for fear of putting parents off. Sunday school took place every week; Messy Church is monthly. Sunday school was part of a Christendom framework of life, but Messy Church is up against a strong secular post-Christian culture. And will there be a Messy Church to return to once a 'Messy' child has children of their own?

So, in the 21st-century world, in which the distinction between a Christian and others is sharper and clearer than in the Christendom world we have left, unless Messy Church is about helping people to develop a genuine Christian faith it is hard to see it having a deep and lasting impact either on individuals or on society as a whole.

Is Messy Church for the whole of life?

The expectation in churches that children would leave at a certain age has been, in many ways, self-fulfilling. In the pure form of Messy Church, parents are also expected to leave when their children 'grow out of it'. This problem of 'stage of life' church is, therefore, even more acute than in traditional church. Messy Churches need to decide whether they are a 'stage of life' format, like toddler groups, or a 'whole of life' Christian church.

Typically, it is taking years for most people today to move fully into Christian faith, even with weekly church involvement. Most people tend to belong before they believe. Messy Church as a 'stage of family life' format may not offer enough depth and length of exposure to the faith to enable a change in belief, and there is little evidence that people easily switch to other forms of church once their 'Messy' stage is over. If Messy Church is to fulfil its potential and have a deep and lasting impact on people's lives, it has to become a 'whole of life' church, appropriate for teens and young adults as well as children, and welcoming adults whose children have grown up. This links to the third question.

Is Messy Church about making Christian disciples?

Unless there are opportunities to go deeper into the faith, apart from the monthly family time, Messy Church may make few Christian disciples in the end. There is an urgent need for nurture materials in a 'Messy' style that both adults and children can access in order to explore their own faith further. The sacraments of baptism and Communion need to be incorporated. Small groups need to be developed. Christian festivals need to be celebrated. Families becoming Christian need help to develop and sustain Christian family life in the home. At least some of the adults and children who have started attending Messy Church need to be brought into leadership and discipled through being part of the leadership team, as quickly as possible.

Learning from the past

If Messy Church is to have any depth of impact, therefore, it needs to broaden its offer and content into whole-of-life discipleship. This is exactly what Sunday schools and Bible classes were unable to do. By their very nature, they were temporary and partial church, and most people were lost when the time came for transition to another form of church for another stage of life. Attempts were made to retain some young people by turning them into assistant

Sunday school teachers, but in most cases this only delayed the inevitable loss. Messy Church has the opportunity to make whole-of-life disciples without handing people over to another form of church because of its basic format: it already includes adults along with the children.

In other words, Messy Church would seem to have the potential to transcend the fundamental problem of Sunday schools—that they were not, in themselves, fully church. When Messy Church becomes full church, encouraging conversion, available for the whole of life, and growing disciples as well as adherents, the depth of its impact will be incalculable.

Learning from Messy Church

Is Messy Church a 'one off' or the first of many success stories? The Christian church should not be surprised by the rapid rise of a new and creative form of church, because God has been in the business of renewing the life of his people for thousands of years: 'Forget the former things; do not dwell on the past. See, I am doing a new thing! Now it springs up; do you not perceive it?' (Isaiah 43:18–19, NIV). This book is by various authors who are trying to perceive the new thing that God is doing with Messy Church, but they are writing in the wider context of a God who is always doing new things.

Messy Church is proving that the Christian church in Britain today can reinvent itself in ways that appeal to a mass market of younger generations with no previous church background. Some of the secrets of success can be discerned. For example, good 'double listening' to the Holy Spirit on one hand and contemporary society on the other has been essential. A lot of listening, thought and discussion, over a period of several years, went into the creation of the first Messy Church in 2004. There was a step of faith in declaring that this new creation was 'proper' church, not just a feeder or children's activity club. There was a financial step of faith from the backers at BRF, and there has been a generosity of spirit in encouraging all-comers to have a go with no attempt at control. There has also been a determination to fit in with, support and be part of church as a whole rather than hiving off as a separate organisation. There is also a sense of catching the zeitgeist of the age and the wind of the Spirit at the same time.

The point is that if this growth can happen with Messy Church, it can also happen with other new models, forms and visions of Church. Out of all the experimentation and fresh expressions of Church that we are seeing today, it is likely that other new and unexpected successes will emerge. With the confidence of seeing what God is already starting to do with one form of Christian community, the UK church should be keenly on the lookout for what next will help to draw the nation to know and worship Jesus Christ.

8

What is the DNA of Messy Church?

George Lings

Since 1997, through Church Army, George Lings has been researching fresh expressions of Church from their beginning. His background was parochial ministry and a vocation to study church planting. He has chronicled some of the stories of fresh expressions and commented on their dynamics and wider significance. He first met Messy Church through a DVD clip about the Portsmouth story in 2006. Since then, Lucy Moore has been a welcome visitor to the research team. George wrote up an example of Messy Church in Liverpool, in No. 46 of the Encounters on the Edge *booklet series, and has written about a derivative called Sweaty Church in No. 56 of the same series.*

It is relatively simple to ask whether Messy Church has a 'DNA', but we must consciously realise that this is to use an analogy. That is not unusual, for much of theological discourse does the same, drawing on very familiar words and their associated meanings, such as 'father', 'covenant' or 'body'. In this chapter, I explore how the DNA analogy can be used in three ways. Two of these, I think, are helpful and illuminating; however, one is a dead end, which is itself an ironic but not inappropriate application of the DNA analogy.

'Having a DNA' has become a shorthand phrase. In the literature that deals generally with fresh expressions of Church, as opposed to Messy Church in particular (although it is perhaps the most rapidly multiplying kind of fresh expression of Church), DNA is an analogy to which a number of authors resort.[65] However, they are usually referring to DNA in one specific sense, and this is the first use that I will now unpack.

DNA as shorthand for an essence

The first and most common use of the analogy refers to the search to identify underlying values—the pursuit of a definitive list by which to identify something and also thereby to assess it. This search is closely related to the quest for a deep inner reality. Other equally analogical terms, such as 'heart', 'essence' or 'core', have also been used. Some of these words, not least 'heart', suggest that there may even be a single diagnostic factor to be identified. The phrase 'God is love' would be an example of one such statement. Terms such as 'heart', 'core', 'essence' and 'DNA' also carry a recognition that a search is going on beneath external forms to discover internal dynamics. The 'something' being sought is not immediately visible, and yet what it *is* leads to what is manifest. We talk about the heart of the matter, the core of an argument, or the essence of an idea. All these images convey latent energy and the potential to shape what grows from them. Similarly, values themselves cannot be seen, although they can be written down; to become visible, they must be allowed to determine choices about practice and be enacted or demonstrated. There is thus a complex relationship between theory and practice, which is more like a dance between the two than like a linear progression; processes such as the pastoral cycle or theological reflection have teased out this relationship.

Is it, then, possible to identify the heart, core, essence or DNA—whatever analogy of inner reality we use—of Messy Church? Just as the Bible offers a better guide to theology than do the vagaries of church history, so in search of the inner Messy Church DNA, I turn to an examination of the values written down by its founder, Lucy Moore, rather than the very variable practice of local Messy Churches. I do not imply that Lucy has any revelatory infallibility, much less divine identity, but she has laid down what she believes Messy Church is about. That deserves to be taken seriously and ought to be the primary way by which the DNA, as core question, is evaluated.

Messy Church DNA identified

Messy Church has core values, or a DNA, which are clear and defining. When lived true to its source, its literature and its informed advocates, there is something visible, very close to 'pure' Messy Church, that can be observed (although I shall argue later that this means something different from cloning). The values are sharp, persuasive and counter-cultural. Within the short life of the Messy Church movement since 2004, I suggest that the values have not fundamentally changed, but they have become more sharply defined and even reordered. I note that the New Testament itself witnesses to the gradual distillation over time of understandings of the Trinity, Christology and atonement, so I trust that it is legitimate also to take time to discover an understanding of Messy Church.

Shake up a bottle containing liquid and solids and it will take time before the liquid becomes clear and the heavier material settles. It may be that only through longer local experience, or observing diversity of practice and regretting distortions elsewhere, will aspirant aims and provisional principles become clear values. The stories from newer monastic communities, crystallising their values, demonstrate a similar process.

Tracing the development from 2006, the first *Messy Church* book talked of 'our principles, in no particular order' and a slightly religious list followed. It began by naming an opportunity for worship and for people of all ages to belong to a church. It went on to name the following: having fun, God-given creativity, experiencing Christian community, and introducing people to Jesus through hospitality, friendship, stories and worship.[66] At first glance, this looks rather like what most churches do, although the words 'fun' and 'creativity' are not the most obvious descriptors of most pew-sitters.

The list resonates with oneness, holiness and being apostolic; it is short on catholicity. In Chapter 3, on the Messy Church aims, the order and even content changes, although worship is still the first category discussed, followed by all age, Christ-centred, hospitable, and creative.[67] I still wonder in retrospect whether this order, which places worship first, was chosen partly to persuade those with a traditional mindset of Messy Church's claim that it is church.

At meetings in 2010 with regional coordinators, and in personal interview with Lucy Moore about the DNA of Messy Church, it became clear to me that the values had settled: hospitality, creativity, celebration and all-age. Distillation has produced a list that is briefer than the original. This in turn gives pegs on which to hang any Messy Church presentation and advocacy. Each value influences the others and also leads to the usual shape and order. In keeping with the DNA analogy, the four bases of hospitality, creativity, all-age and celebration could be drawn as a double helix with all the elements interacting with each other.

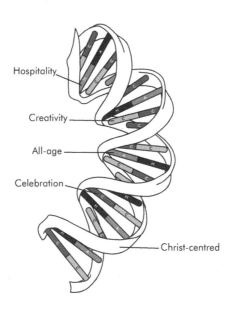

I think it is essential and legitimate to make explicit a fifth value—'Christ-centred', partly because Lucy Moore includes it in her original account of Messy Church.[68] It is also needed because, although the other values are heart-warming and, importantly, evocative of what it is to be human, they might be espoused by a secular group or another world faith. They are not necessarily Christian. With Christ at the centre, then, rightly understood, the hospitality is derived from God's hospitality shown to us in Christ, and the creativity reflects the joyous riot of God's untidy but deliberate creation. All-age springs in part from God's image being found in all people as well as the body of Christ, including all kinds of people and all stages of being human; and, lastly, celebration is rooted in the virtues of praise and thanksgiving that will be completed at the return of Christ and the realisation of a new heaven and earth.

In writing this, I sense a link to creedal thinking. I do not mean that people should proclaim, 'I believe in Messy Church.' What I mean is that to examine the DNA of something is to embark on a process of deciding more carefully what it is and what it isn't. Creeds also have had this double character, in that, by implication, they anathematise views that are contrary to their content. Similarly, distinct values imply a 'but not this' feeling.

Thus, Messy Church values can be boiled down to a few state-ments, each of which contains both an affirmation and a denial.

- Messy Church is for all ages; it is not merely a children's activity.
- Messy Church is about creativity; it is not narrowly about craft.[69]
- Messy Church is about worship and community; it is not a bridge back to 'real church'.
- Messy Church aims for transformation of family life; it is not simply fun for kids.
- Messy Church hospitality is a conscious missional value; it is not merely easy access.

Some values are counter-cultural

My own experience of congregational life reveals a spectrum of attitudes to children and young people. I recall attending traditional parish Communion with my parents, where children were expected to turn up and keep quiet, pacified if need be by discreet distractions in the pews. The strongest contrast would be with my curacies, with their weekly family services and, later, early experimentation with all-age worship, which took the need still more seriously for a variety of both educational inputs and worship styles.

Perhaps these latter ways, which I thought more sensible and more normal, had dulled my perception of how counter-cultural Messy Church seeks to be. I knew how often church services send the children out as soon as decently possible, but had not picked up on how society at large can do the same. It was Lucy Moore's colleague Jane Leadbetter who pointed out to me how advertisements for some holidays present images of the parents enjoying peace and quiet while their children are being entertained in a separate programme. The large annual Christian gatherings follow a similar pattern, and the government creates a comparable dynamic by wanting to have both parents in work, encouraging childcare as soon as possible. 24/7 patterns of life and shiftwork also militate against families having time together. The TV left constantly on and computer games played by individuals alone are a very poor substitute for quality time together. Those in such family groups merely coexist without communing. Others have written about concerns that children are being made to grow up more quickly than may be wise, becoming both economically and sexually active at an early age.

Messy Church has set its face against this trend. There is a strong belief that the church has the opportunity to show a better way. Rather than pontificating about what is wrong with society, how much better to embody, in Christian communities, what could be done that is preferable. So, quite deliberately, with a light touch, the first book made clear the stance: 'Messy Church is a once-monthly time when *families come together*, to enjoy being together, making things together, eating together and celebrating God together.'[70] The word most emphasised here is 'together'. The order may be significant, too: there is 'coming', 'being', 'making' and 'eating', out of which 'celebrating' God becomes more natural because there has been space to notice what can be celebrated. There is symbiosis when worship enriches life because it springs out of life.

Unpacking the four 'bases' of DNA

Lucy Moore's 2010 list gives a helpful order. Any Messy Church gathering begins with *hospitality*, and this runs through the entire event, just as it does with Alpha. I think it no accident that the second *Messy Church* book makes much of this value found in scripture as well as in creating a counter-cultural take on life. It celebrates the role of food and the welcome of strangers as honoured guests, creating an oasis amid the arid nature of busyness and a place of healing laughter.[71] Notice, too, how this picks up the early key verbs, 'coming' and 'being', in the first *Messy Church* book. However, it is not the case that Messy Church hospitality is reduced to a professionalised welcome, as is done superbly by good hotels—after which they forget you as soon as you check out. There is hospitality in the way a nervous adult is welcomed to a craft table, in the whole process by which a non-churched person is helped to cross the threshold to the alien world of church, and in the shared meal. Lucy's honesty, and careful reading, reveals that the meal began in Portsmouth as a practical gift to the Thursday afternoon helpers, but it has become 'one of the main aspects'.[72]

I wish there was space to unpack how much has been lost to church identity by the exclusion of a meal from its normal gatherings, to which 1 Corinthians testifies. There is an attendant loss of a quasi-domestic context for church in which to experience community. If Messy Church is tapping back into that, then it is they who are raising questions for the wider church, not the other way around.

Then comes *creativity*, which links to the verb 'making' in the first *Messy Church* book. What a change this is from much of church! At worst, the expectation of children in church is that they should not make a noise—or, in a family service, they may make a guess at the speaker's question or 'become stooges up at the front, holding up visual aids'.[73] Frankly, do attending adults 'make' anything by their own choice in church? Sometimes there is space for private inner responses to God, but much else has been precisely choreographed for them in printed texts and now, even more closely, through pre-chosen PowerPoint slides. With PowerPoint, you can't even flick your eyes back up the page to the previous verse of a song to be reminded of the nudge from God that it contained.

In Messy Church, however, 'making' is not a matter of pre-determined responses but of taking initiatives and working together at the tables. I remember learning that the much-derided word 'fellowship' need not mean bad coffee and artificial conversations but, at root, means being people who have a partnership or a share —for example, in a fishing business or a eucharistic meal (Luke 5:10; 1 Corinthians 10:16). 'Participation' is one good translation. Turning church back into a creative, participatory, communal hive of spiritual life is a worthy goal that critiques much existing church practice.

Through true hospitality and creativity, those who come to us move from being clients, for whom we provide pre-cooked liturgical dishes,[74] to being guests for whom we care. They also become co-creators with whom we are fellow artists, and co-workers with whom we are partners. In the end, even the distinction between host and guest dissolves, and so all-age, Christ-centred community emerges. The unintentional lack of 'making' in many churches is a denial of our being made in the image of God. If passivity, which is highly diagnostic of pew-fillers in churches, is the result, it is deeply regrettable and fundamentally damaging. Any fresh expression of

Church that seeks to reverse this process has spotted something in church DNA that has been locked away.

Only then in Messy Church does the *celebration* occur, and it is relatively short. I note links from this pattern, which comes from expressing the four DNA values, to my own thinking on seven sacred spaces.[75] How intriguing that hospitality and the 'refectory' are clear and primary, and that the craft echoes both 'garden' and 'scriptorium', making both of them prominent, not merely useful. People walk along 'cloisters' to move to further places, having time to change gear between the various strands of an overall Messy Church gathering. They then come and go from a brief time in 'chapel'. Once more, 'chapel' (or so-called church) grows out of the other functions, rather than defining them all. The team meet to pray and to plan at another time, expressing 'chapter', and so only 'cell' is not obvious. Messy Church thinkers are already exploring how to provide a quiet zone, with a prayer table, during Messy Church, and some ongoing stories have begun to offer it. They are also pursuing how to do Messy discipleship at home, which would be another intuitive response to the omission of an equivalent of 'cell'.[76]

The DNA diagram makes being *all-age* intrinsic to Messy Church: it applies to everything else that happens in Messy Church. The case for all-age church is made by various groups.[77] In a book devoted to the subject, Lucy Moore deals with the principle at more length than the first two *Messy Church* volumes would allow.[78] I agree that the past exclusion in practice of children from much of the life of the worshipping community is problematic and unacceptable. I accept that adults have much to learn from children as well as vice versa. I concur that, too often, the dominant learning style in church teaching has been cerebral, and the effects on discipleship have not been impressive. Endeavours based on liturgical, musical high culture, I suspect, have fared even worse. Beneath this tactical case is a legitimate theological one—that diversity within the Trinity and in the resultant creation demands the kind of unity that holds diversity together. The reconciling work of Christ is the other great plank of the case that, in Jesus, divisions have been broken down and unity across ages is the only way forward.

I am less sure that it works so comprehensively. Can all kinds of people be together in one local manifestation of Church? The same arguments are aired in connection with race and with language. Here, real hesitation about, and often open disagreement with, the homogeneous-unit principle usually emerges. Yet even this area is not straightforward. Generally we are careful to avoid potential charges of apartheid, arguing that different races should be able to gather together to be church. However, at the same time, provision of services in different languages for some such groups is represented as acceptable. So, for example, it can be deemed wrong to exclude a Nigerian but fine to provide linguistic difference for a Pole. What seem to be lost in this emotive argument are effective ways to model both diversity and unity. That presents a different challenge from the one that arises when we bring everyone together and look for ways to make it work reasonably—although learning patience and tolerance in dealing with difference are worthwhile elements of discipleship.

Sometimes this unity-and-diversity issue is fudged by the use of eschatological texts, such as the vision of Zechariah 8:4–5. The all-age concept is there, but the text is about the streets of Jerusalem, not about what happens in the temple. All-age advocates have confused what needs to be true of community with what happens in worship, or they have elided, as do many, the complexity of the seven spaces of monastery and the simplicity of chapel. I am not arguing that children should never be allowed into adult worship—rather, that we need not assume that they should always be there.

Consider the parallel with a family that includes parents and children of any age before they leave home. There are indeed important times when they are together in one space: hanging around in the kitchen, sitting down for a meal, playing a game, watching family TV or going on holiday. But equally important are occasions for individuals to be in their bedrooms or studying, bonding time between siblings, and vital time for the parents when the kids are in bed or have gone to their grandparents. The rhythm of this community includes a mixture of times for all-age and times for children and adults to have space from one another. While it is entertaining to know that not everything children readily perceive can be understood by adults, it is also true that not everything adults must know should be disclosed to children. Here, unity and diversity are expressed through the dynamics of being separate *and* being together. To be all-age, all the time, would be appalling. I think we need the same in church communities, so I doubt that all worship should always be all-age and, equally, that none should.[79]

This, then, is the DNA (understood as something like essence) of Messy Church. There is a list of values—hospitality, creativity, celebration and all-age, all with theological roots—that connect being ecclesial with being human, held together by being Christ-centred.

DNA and the way reproduction occurs

The second factor that the DNA analogy inherently offers, which terms like 'heart', 'essence' and 'core' do not inherently convey, is that DNA is an understanding of the inner capacity of an organism to reproduce, and explains the processes by which that reproduction happens. The DNA analogy therefore refers not only to what is essential but also to what is transmitted. Thus it is a particularly dynamic image.

The suggestion that Messy Church has a clear and describable DNA leads quite quickly to the thought that this is partly what helps it to reproduce. I use the term 'DNA' here not to suggest a precise scientific mechanism but as an analogical way of speaking about the means by which an enduring identity continues to be carried forward into further expressions of Messy Church, which will have both family likeness and individual identity because they grow in different cultures and places.[80]

Therefore, this analogy could both humorously and seriously be described as 'fertile'. The linkage between essence and transmission is a serious issue in relation to the wider term 'fresh expressions of Church' and the way those fresh expressions of Church come into being. Those in favour of them argue that, at best, they are both faithful to the ecclesial past and creative in the way they are inculturated in the context to which they are called and sent. Those doubtful about or opposed to them are genuinely concerned that mere relevance is being sought at the cost of the loss of true ecclesial identity. I believe this latter nervousness leads to an over-reaction and engages with a third way to look at DNA.

Retaining the fullness of Church

For some, DNA can mean the search for a full code, carrying all the signals of what an embryonic ecclesial organism will and should become. Thus, discussion of its content opens up all the historical complexities of church: its precise doctrinal positions, governmental peculiarities, liturgical subtleties, ministerial protocols and anathemas of those who disagree. While this way of thinking is not unfair to the analogy, many would see it as of limited value in the search for ways forward to grow inculturated churches in a post-Christendom context.[81] For opponents of this third usage, smuggling in all the past baggage will not enable us to travel light. Those who operate easily with the other two convictions about DNA would broadly support that critique. They argue that our mission context has profoundly changed and, even more importantly, a shift in mission context does legitimate a shift in Church expression, because of incarnational understanding. Various sources concur with this thinking.[82] For them, the need to be nimble is legitimate, as is the search for differentiation between form and essence. Retrenching within what we already have is not the most pressing need.

Not all would agree; for example, Martyn Percy urges the need to hold our nerve in offering soft-edged traditional pastoral ministry and argues that an apathetic response to God has been characteristic of most past generations.[83] Davison and Milbank, in *For the Parish*, have argued for the centrality of practices, as transmission of the faith is like language immersion. (The values of Messy Church do operate in a similar way: by being exposed to its values, people begin to get it.) Some take refuge in the fifth-century Vincentian Canon to buttress ecclesiological immutability: *quod ubique, quod semper, quod ab omnibus credituni est* ('What has been believed everywhere, always, and by all'). It is, however, easier to say that than to agree on its contents. Proponents of fixed content, from Forward in Faith, Reform, New Wine and post-liberal theology, do not agree with one another, which makes for a significant difficulty. We can be sure that they cannot all be right.

Readers will discern that I include myself among the group who do not favour the dominance of this application of the analogy. The expectations are too controlling, the baggage is too heavy, and the witness to the approach is too divided. This danger is manifested by a recent report, with its list of eight factors called 'the defining set of ecclesial elements' for something 'to constitute a church'.[84] If strictly applied, I wonder how many existing congregations would be declared 'not church'.

Church reproduction should be non-identical

The DNA analogy has another contribution to offer to the above debate, relating to the second way in which I suggest it can be understood (in terms of reproduction). This is particularly true when applied to higher-level species, all of which reproduce non-identically. In such cases, it is axiomatic that both inheritance and individuality are present. With human beings, wise parents know that while their children are theirs, their children are not them. Another related feature is that, in families, members may share a surname but have individual first names. Each person's identity consists of both features, and to remove either would be to do violence to the person's identity. I see this played out unnoticed across a diocese, where each parish has a saint name and a diocesan identity. Again, to remove either feature would be a serious loss.

Use of the DNA analogy helps to explain features that we are seeing in practice. As healthy fresh expressions of Church are born and mature, they exhibit continuity with the past as well as contextual change. The analogy encourages the placing of trust, which will allow for unforeseen emergence in the next generation of churches. It also strongly underlines that a bipartite process is at work. It is beyond the scope of this chapter to argue in detail that the mission of God, through a bipartite process of partnership, is a deep, enduring, biblical theme. Strands of that case include humanity formed of dust and breath, the two-party nature of covenants, the incarnation by the Spirit in cooperation with Mary, Christ's identity as God the Son and son of Mary, and the partnership of the Spirit and the Church.

Thus the DNA analogy, when combined with the idea of life in higher-species reproduction, expects and explains why 'fresh expressions of Church' should be equally serious about having the surname of 'Church' and a first name that is 'fresh'—and, indeed, are inherently not identical to the past. It also encourages legitimate concern for what should not be lost, for, if something essential is lost, then the quality of what comes into being is fatally compromised. The debate about what is essential is not yet concluded, but perhaps the DNA analogy and its use show why there is bound to be a debate, because both essence and transmission are involved. Moreover, DNA is an inner feature; it is not the totality of the resultant form, let alone fully controlling how that form will grow and mature through both nurture and nature.

This may be the best place to insist that the DNA analogy should not be used to justify or embody a missional Pelagianism. What is spiritually alive, and also life-giving, is never the product of solely human endeavour. Grace and the involvement of the Spirit are essential. The Spirit hovered over the face of the waters; the Spirit came upon the young woman, Mary; the Spirit disturbs the church into mission and grows the character of Christ within us. Clarity about the values, and even accurate understanding of the non-identical reproduction of churches, must not be separated from reliance on the Spirit who guides, inspires and brings life. The balance is well struck by Paul, noting that he planted the seed, Apollos watered it, and God made it grow (see 1 Corinthians 3:6). Careful human understanding and intentional spiritual reliance on God should remain partners.

In relation to Messy Church DNA, it is now possible to note variants in the second generation of its family, beginning to be reproduced. We have the entertainingly named Sweaty Church in York[85] and Trashy Church in Kent. The first takes creativity seriously but links it to the competitive edge and energetic nature of both boys and girls, as well as offering something that the dads can revel in. Trashy Church noticed that teenagers were energised by concern for the environment and the creativity associated with recycling, so they take trash and do something constructive with it. Both are examples that good ecclesial reproduction is bipartite, drawing on inner enduring Christian values and the specific context, just as *Mission-Shaped Church* advocated a listening that is deliberately double. One word for this kind of process is 'incarnational', and a more exact one is 'inculturation'.

I do not suggest that Messy Church perfectly models or trans-mits everything that is desirable about church, or that humans can map the entire ecclesial genome. I welcome the language of Avery Dulles and Vatican II, saying that the Church's identity is bound in mystery, because of 'the most important thing about the Church: the presence in it of the God who called the members to himself'.[86] As Dulles continues, 'There is something of a consensus today that the innermost reality of the Church—the most important con-stituent of its being—is the divine self-gift.'[87] Despite this proper caveat, it seems to me that there is something within this mystery that can be likened to an ecclesial capacity for reproduction. Messy Church demonstrates that capacity well. Within the ecclesial DNA of the Church catholic, this genetic message is carried faithfully and so continues to reproduce in all as yet unborn expressions of church. Thus, something rather small, which does not claim to explain everything else, is nevertheless rather significant, both for the church's continued existence and its own self-identity.[88]

A limitation of the analogy

Replication of DNA is a biochemical process in which there can be a reasonable degree of certainty that the internal messages will be passed on. Cats breed cats, and carrot seed yields carrots. However, when DNA is used analogically, we are forced to admit that the process of transmission is affected by a variety of social, educational and presuppositional factors that considerably reduce any inherent ability to transmit that DNA with commendable accuracy. In some cases, the connection between centrally held values and local examples looks slight. It may be that we can identify what Messy Church DNA consists of and produce a coherent and credible list of its values. However, despite that, and despite the attempts of Lucy Moore and BRF to make clear what Messy Church is about, it is not guaranteed that other people will even grasp those values, let alone faithfully follow them.

Shapes are not the DNA itself

It is true that Messy Church has an advised shape:[89]

- 3.30: A period of welcome, games and light refreshment
- 4.00: Craft time in families
- 5.00: Celebration service in church
- 5.15: Hot meal together
- 5.45: Time to go home

However, these are only derived features, not its essence. Far more important are the underlying values. Just as has happened with cell church, punters and critics can be deceived into thinking that the shape of the event is the diagnostic feature. Offer 'welcome, worship, word and witness', and some people think they are doing cell church. Provide 'welcome, craft, celebration and meal', and it must be Messy Church. In both cases, the error is in confusing activity with purpose, and shape with values—and practitioners can fall into it. I have been saddened on several occasions, when I have talked with a Messy Church leader or heard them talking about Messy Church to the wider church, that the content was functional. One said, 'I take a theme, find some crafts, fit it to some songs and a talk and we lay on a meal.' Another tried to get the existing church congregation to attend the Messy Church, as if it was an entertainment to enjoy or a charity to support.

The consequence of such distortion puts a ceiling on what can be achieved. The more sublime aims and counter-cultural values are lost and the pressure of maintaining the activities takes over. Just doing the shape opens the door to dumbing down the potential for transformed families and Christ-centred community. It begins a degeneration that settles for the fun and loses the wisdom. It also colludes with our entertainment-based society and fails to build relationships. A previous critique of the unthinking copying of church plants called it 'cloning'. At least they had some DNA, even if it was fatally one-sourced and so often failed to sustain itself. The process of reproducing the shape of Messy Church seems to me more like inventing robots that look like humans. On the outside the shapes are the same, but cut into them and inside you find metal, not flesh, blood and spirit. No wonder they may struggle to bring life.

This is a risk that everyone involved in fresh expressions of Church needs to be aware of and steer away from. It manifests itself when a church becomes desperate to do something to attract the young, meets a model that becomes popular and so copies the externals without understanding the internals. Then, good ways to work become both trivialised and blunted. Careful engagement with context is reduced. Once more, the worst of church, done in attractional, client-provider mode, rears its head, and counter-cultural impact and (equally important) spiritual transformation are lost.

Can there be pure Messy Church?

With Messy Church, and with cell church years earlier, the word 'pure' has been used by their teachers and advocates. This may be dynamic equivalence for faithfulness to the founder[90] and his or her writing. What does this mean? Lucy Moore is passionate about the values and about addressing the limitations in churches through these values. Yet her books make very clear that best practice continued to emerge as they were being written and that Messy Church is 'not meant... to be copied slavishly... but an example to learn from'.[91] So is 'pure' desirable or possible?

The words 'pure' and 'messy' are a paradoxical conjunction. Yet it is desirable and possible that all of the above DNA components should be intended, and to some extent operative, for a venture to deserve the name of Messy Church. Otherwise, something occurs, comparable to the ridiculous situation in which people say, 'We are doing Alpha without the food or groups.' Using some similar presentational content, but without the diagnostic parts of the process, means that it isn't Alpha.[92]

This approach is radically different from proper inculturation. A few examples illustrate the point. Lucy Moore does Messy Church in Portsmouth on a Thursday, but only a small minority of other examples choose that day. Other days are equally valid. More serious variants include a Messy Church in Liverpool that chose to meet on a Saturday at 4.00pm. Because the meeting is not held straight after school, so there is no need or desire for immediate refreshment, they have dispensed with a stated component of the shape—the initial half hour of arrival and drinks. Other places have found that their accommodation doesn't allow them to cook a hot meal, so they run 'bring-and-share' or serve drinks and sand-wiches—a kind of English tea. Are these still 'pure' Messy Church? I believe you can tell by the values and, if in doubt, by the presence of relationship to, and consultation with, the founder. Thus it is clear that the time, day, venue and even shape can vary. As explained already, even 'craft' is not necessarily diagnostic. I believe that Lucy Moore is right to stress that the value beneath is creativity, because that reflects the *imago Dei*, rather than insisting on just one manifestation of it through craft. Maybe mess is inherent, too, because neither creativity nor humans are neat, simple or flawless.

This relative simplicity is awkward now that the Messy Church 'brand' is part of its identity. Identity is part of what holds a move-ment together. So now there is a registered trademark within BRF and a defined legal logo. Here, quality control and local freedom sit rather uncomfortably. If Messy Church commends creativity and also mess, how tight should control be? Yet if there is no control, how are the borders of true Messy Church maintained and not diluted or, worse, corrupted? One example is where Messy Church has gone into a secular school, drawing pupils from many faiths and none. The school welcomed its exploration of community, creativity and spirituality, but has to opt for a pluralist stance, ruling that although talk of God is allowed, reference to Jesus must be limited to his birthday. So is this Messy Church? Not being Christ-centred, either in language or intention, it cannot be, and so is called Messy Families.

What have we learnt?

Messy Church has a DNA in the sense of discernible values. It serves as a working example of the issues that always arise in transmission by DNA as a fresh expression of Church is born. These issues are typical of non-identical reproduction, which is inherent in the nature of Church, and they surface most acutely because of the birth of its young ones. I am fortified by the realisation that this complexity is related to similar patterns in Christology. The paradox of Christ is that the eternal Word speaks only in local dialects,[93] and that the universal Christ is most visible when embodied locally. We follow Jesus as closely as possible, but that doesn't mean women become men, or Gentiles become Jews. We cannot escape from the call to double listening;[94] it is inherent in being Christian and being missional. Then the only healthy option is to faithfully improvise, using DNA. Messy Church, at its best, is doing exactly this.

Case study: Messy Church @ Christ Church Primacy

Kevin Metcalfe

Kevin Metcalfe was Regional Coordinator in Northern Ireland and is a Church Army Evangelist.

Christ Church Primacy began its journey along the road of Messy Church in September 2009. Once a month on a Sunday afternoon, families have been coming to Christ Church Primacy to explore faith and life. It arose from a process in which the local church was exploring how to connect with the families of children with whom we had built up good relations. It has been a pioneering venture, as the first Messy Church in Northern Ireland, and more have been springing up as a result of hearing what God is doing with us.

For the first 18 months of the life of our Messy Church, it felt like a process of growing together in community. The families who attend have a wide range of backgrounds and faith perspectives, and the team has had to learn how the 'model' best fits our context. While following the ethos of Messy Church, we have found a greater Christian knowledge in our Northern Ireland culture, which does differ significantly from that of the rest of the UK. Over the past six months, a real sense of community has developed, exemplified by some of the parents and some of the teenagers becoming volunteers.

One of the most memorable moments of the last two years of Messy Church came at Easter time. We were focusing on the Easter story, and, as part of the gathering, we did a simple family format of the Jewish Passover meal. It involved the different foods used to represent the exodus of God's people from Egypt symbolically, together with a short liturgy. It also involved drawing out the parallels between the exodus and Jesus' death on the cross. As we moved through the story of the exodus, there was a noticeable stillness and a sense of God's presence settling on us as we remembered the story and thought about what Jesus did at Easter. Afterwards a number of parents commented about how 'special' it had felt for them to do the Passover together and how some of them recognised that God had been present.

In many ways, as I reflected on this experience, for me it felt like 'church'. The presence of God was among us as a community as we relived the story of God at work with his people. The questions that arose were: why couldn't this be church, and why should that act of eating bread and drinking wine (or grape juice) together be any less significant than the first Communion, Jesus' last supper? We didn't have an official minister presiding, but we did have Jesus present. On the counter-side, I was amazed one day to hear from one of the volunteers that a mum had said she didn't see it as 'real' church, despite the name of Messy Church. For her, what we were doing couldn't be proper church like that on a Sunday morning.

Now we are exploring the question of how we go deeper in discipleship with the families who attend. The process began with some inspiration from Peter Farmer, co-author of *Pioneer Mission*, on ways of making disciples and discipling people in the way of faith. From this we used a short survey as an 'excuse' to see where the parents were spiritually and to discover whether they wanted to be part of something that was more intentionally focused on discipleship. The response from some families was that they were happy with where they were and didn't want anything more. In other families, the mums were keen to attend something else for them, and one family wanted something else for all of them. At the time of writing, we have been using the summer to experiment with what the 'something else' might look like.

Reflecting on this process and experiment, it seems to me that, for our Messy Church, discipleship will look a bit messy, with some tailored formats for individual families to suit them where they are.

This particularly strikes me with some of the mums who have an obvious spiritual hunger, but whose husbands have shown no real interest. It is an exciting phase for us as we see people wanting more of Jesus while we continue to love and be alongside those for whom that hunger has not yet awoken in their lives.

While we explore this new opportunity, the ups and downs of maintaining a good team has become one of our biggest challenges. Although we have a fantastic core of volunteers who make Messy Church happen, a lot of volunteers who have been with us for a while have had to step back from involvement because of their life circumstances. So far, we have been able to work round this or recruit new volunteers, but it is an ongoing issue that has occasionally threatened the viability of the team.

In pioneering Messy Church in Northern Ireland, it has been really useful to me to have the role of Regional Coordinator. It has been invaluable in helping me to reflect on how Messy Church, and fresh expressions of Church generally, will look in this culture. My initial thoughts are that there is still a stronger Christian heritage in Northern Ireland than in other parts of the UK. This is part of the reason why there are relatively few fresh expressions of Church. The impact of this on Messy Churches is that many churches are more likely to be engaging people on the fringes and less likely to be connecting with people beyond. There has also been a tendency for a number of churches either to focus solely on fringe 'de-churched' members or to see them as their starting point, perhaps with a desire to reach beyond the fringe afterwards.

Just two years on, the most important principle I recognise in our Messy Church experience is that it's a journey. It feels as if we are only just beginning on this journey. I'm not sure whether I will really be able to say when we have 'arrived' as a Messy Church, as families are a continually changing dynamic. Families don't show us a blueprint of what they will be like in five years' time, so maybe many Messy Churches will live in a shifting dynamic of relational and developmental change that does not reach a point of arrival.

Messy practicalities

9

Messy maturity: paradox, contradiction or perfect match?

Beth Barnett

Beth Barnett is currently the Children's and Families' Facilitator for the Baptist Union of Victoria in Australia. For many years she has been a passionate champion of multi-age/multi-sensory Bible engagement as the foundation of inclusive, creative and adventurous worship and mission. From a background in music and education, Beth has trained and resourced those who serve children and families for the past two decades. She loves to engage in the godly art of risk-taking and to encourage others in doing the same—in their families, in their worship, in their mission and in their personal healing. Beth is the author of eight books of integrated resources and theological frameworks for Bible-centred mission in churches, communities and the home.

A question has been preoccupying my mind for quite some time. When Jesus calls us to become disciples, to follow along, what is meant to happen? Within that broad question, further ones arise. Do disciples become mature and, if they do, what does that maturity look like? Is maturity inherent to the discipleship deal? Or, like wealth, position, power, privilege and status, is 'Western maturity' something that the gospel frees us from? Is there such a thing as spiritual maturity?

I have been around the church all my life, which is long enough to have gained a strong sense that I should be growing in my faith— or is it in *the* faith? Whichever it is, I am constantly hearing that I should be growing and maturing. Sometimes people even say that I have a 'mature' faith, as if that were a compliment.

The language of 'maturity'

What are we talking about when we speak of 'maturity'? It is a term that is open to euphemistic misuse. Some examples include the following: a twelve-year-old's body is not yet fully mature, a 35-year-old's body is fully mature, and a 75-year-old's body is past maturity and has begun a process of degeneration. Often we use the word 'mature' in order to say 'old' politely. We speak of films with strong sexual violence as being suitable for 'mature' audiences, but one wonders whether a person with an appetite for sexually explicit violence warrants the term 'mature'.

In a church setting, sermons are often delivered as pre-packaged thoughts with three key points and an application—a fairly thin communication form, yet this is said to be teaching for 'mature' Christians. By contrast, children are typically engaged in multi-sensory, interactive learning that challenges them to wonder, imagine and formulate their own theories and requires an integrated action of some kind. I do not necessarily doubt that 'mature' people can engage fully and critically with monological sermons, but I am suspicious of claims that rank a controlled monologue as a more 'mature' form of thinking or communicating.

In this chapter I explore the idea of maturity from a theological perspective. To do this means to submit the ideas and ideologies of maturity to scrutiny and criteria that ask major questions, such as the following:

- Who is God?
- Who are humans in relation to God?
- How does the cosmos work?

- What is the large story of God that we are in?
- What does all this tell us about our questions of maturity?

I also examine the models of the Messy Church movement to evaluate the capacities and culpabilities of such communities in relation to the agendas of personal, communal and institutional maturity. However, my deepest consideration focuses on whether Messy Churches sustain disciples of Jesus in fruitful missional community. I hope that this is, in fact, a more pressing biblical question than the issue of maturity.

Discourses of maturity, development and growth

Where does this ideal of maturity come from? What drives us to include such a topic in a theological discussion?

In Western culture, the word 'development' is loaded with a positive charge. If something is developing, we usually see this as a good thing. It is an assumed criterion as we divide nations into categories of 'developed' and 'developing'. It seems that no one wants to be an 'undeveloped' nation. In Australia, children are routinely assessed in terms of 'normal' or 'delayed' or perhaps 'accelerated' development against a set of normative milestones, which are mapped out on government-issued charts and given to every new parent. This phenomenon of growth and change is, on the one hand, assumed and might be considered unremarkable, and yet 'developmental progress' has become a value-laden system by which we assess success and ascribe status.

Thus, in the public consciousness and in discourses of everything from the individual person to organisations, ideas, economies and nations, scales of development and progress have become our norm. This forms a double standard. Along with the assumption of growth as 'normal', markers of growth are offered as cause for honour and pride.

Many people have heard of the idea of 'stages of faith'.[95] Even if they haven't heard of it directly, they have acquired the idea that people go through maturing stages in their faith. This vision is conceived individualistically, from conversion, through early discipleship, into leadership or serving, and perhaps then on to a mentoring role. Or, thinking of it less actively and more devotionally, people begin trusting Jesus for salvation, and then gradually submit more and more areas of life to Christ, becoming more indwelt by the Holy Spirit and theoretically more like Jesus.

These are prevalent assumptions, but unfortunately they lack substantial biblical models. The great characters of faith (including Noah, Abraham, Samson and David) in the Old Testament seem as prone to weakness, sin, foolishness, pride and destructive behaviour in their latter years as in their youth. The New Testament communities to which Paul writes can barely have been shaped by the gospel for more than a decade at the very outside. None of them has had time to do much maturing. They live in eschatological expectation of Jesus' return at any tick of the clock, so it doesn't seem to be much on their minds that maturity is important. They have a 'hold steady while you wait' policy.

Leaping forward to the contemporary church, after my 45 years in various denominations, I've seen plenty of immature behaviour from people who claim to be elders in the faith, through manipulating meetings, dominating conversations and holding pastors and congregations to ransom with the budget. I have also seen some delightful old saints who are marked by their risk-taking, their capacity for change and their enthusiasm for another faith adventure with Jesus, who hold everything they have thought in the past lightly and are ready for the Holy Spirit to blow them in a whole new direction.

As we consider the idea of maturity, we must be conscious not to impose on our lives of discipleship an imperative that is no concern of God's. Yes, we are to imitate Jesus. Yes, we are to seek wisdom. Yes, we are to keep the faith. Yes, we are to live in the Spirit. But we are called as much to inhabit the kingdom as a child

(Matthew 18:3), to be made a new creation (2 Corinthians 5:17), to be born again, again and again (John 3:3; 1 Peter 1:23) and, in Old Testament terms, to receive the mercies of the steadfast love of the Lord, new every morning (Lamentations 3:22).

These are terms that sit strangely with the language of maturity. So while we address this topic to wring from it every good thing that God might have us consider in it, we hold it lightly, mindful that it is a preoccupation of Western, Enlightenment, developmentalist, progress-oriented culture, while the gospel is concerned with God reconciling all things in Christ (Colossians 1:20).

Some helpful biblical images

Sorting through all of these voices and agendas, I find it refreshing to return to the voices of the Bible. Although they have their own complexities and challenges, they are the place where I find clarity and freedom.

Paul

Paul constantly used images of vulnerability to frame his own participation in the life of Christ. Most of the occurrences of the word 'mature' in the New Testament can be found in Paul's epistles, and the word itself is not straightforward. The same word, *teleios*, and related grammatical forms, is in some places translated as 'perfect' or 'complete', but on a few occasions translators have opted for 'mature'. The actual word 'mature', then, is not certain in the vision of Paul, and there are good reasons to prefer the idea of perfection/ completion in the few cases where 'mature' appears in our English translations.

These translation issues may seem to muddy the waters at first. However, to engage in this challenge is to remember that the Bible didn't come to us prepackaged, leather-bound, in the King's

English, but through the living words that came from the mouths and into the ears of real live followers of Jesus, in a particular place and time. This recognition helps me to shed some of the cultural layers that have encrusted the text, and to allow my suspicion that the way we think of 'spiritual maturity' might not be as embedded in the Bible as it is in our cultural imaginations.

No one in the New Testament was baptised into an established parish church and brought up going to Sunday school; no one went to youth discipleship camps, did a leadership training course or went to theological college and got ordained. So this kind of progressive structure can be set to one side. Those to whom Paul wrote had only recently received the gospel; the Corinthians, for example, may have had seven years of gospel influence at the most. None of them was a long-term Christian. More than this, the early apostles had a strong expectation that Jesus would be coming back soon—within their lifetime—so the aim of developing into a 'mature' Christian didn't figure as strongly as the aim of being ready for Jesus' imminent return.

To be reminded of the historical dimensions of the biblical text releases us from all kinds of expectations and patterns that might prevent us from recognising the fresh call of a radical gospel mission in our days. If Paul could establish 'churches' based on households, without trained pastors and mature leaders, what might be possible, in the power of the word and the Spirit, in our time? If you raise your eyebrows, is it because you know about the tensions and pretensions of the Corinthian church? It was beset with all of the same issues of selfishness, status-seeking and conflict that are typical of most churches I know—but Paul simply calls them to love. He sets the example of the crucified, weak, vulnerable, humble Christ in their midst to imitate—not greatness but lowliness. It seems that his great development strategy was something in which the smallest child and the frailest grandparent could take the lead.

Jesus

Jesus is silent on maturity—or is he? He doesn't speak of becoming mature. He especially doesn't speak of becoming great. Jesus nowhere tells his disciples to go and make mature people, not even mature disciples. He speaks of becoming like a child—'growing young', as G.K. Chesterton called it. Jesus gives thanks that truth has been hidden from the wise and given to the young. A radical reworking of the expectation of honour through maturity is found in the teaching of Jesus, who placed a child in the midst of adult disciples as a model of the kingdom (Matthew 18:1–4). Jesus did this not to advocate for children but for the sake of adults whose grasping for power was crippling their discipleship.

Thus, a radical reworking of the expectation of honour through maturity is also found in the life of Jesus, who eschewed 'grasping equality with God' (see Philippians 2:6, NIV 1984). At least as far as Paul understands it, Jesus distances himself from spiritual strength and capacity (see also Luke 4:1–13).

Thinking absolutely literally about maturity, Jesus himself lived a short human life. Reaching an advanced age seems not to have been as significant in the project of incarnation as infancy, childhood and adolescence.

So, if not by using the language of maturity, and if not by embracing it in his human life, how does Jesus address the issue of maturity? Beyond the use of the actual word 'mature', Jesus uses images and metaphors that reveal his kingdom thinking on growth and maturity.

Messy Jesus: stories of maturity

Jesus uses lots of stories and word pictures about growth. He draws on the seeds that sprout, the vines that bear fruit, the fields of wheat and weeds, and the farmer who builds barns and tears them down to build bigger barns. Another farmer plants seeds, which grow while he sleeps, without any effort from himself. Growth—

at least, economic and agricultural growth—is not all sketched in bright colours.

What does Jesus say? Yes, be growing; be a vine that is alive, connected, growing and bearing fruit. But you will be pruned: you won't get too big for your boots. The prodigious field bears grain in measures of thirty, sixty or one hundredfold, but it is ripe for harvesting. So here we have growing, abundance and fruitfulness, which result in an image of cutting.

This is an upfront cue for us not to equate maturity and growth with bigness—not with numerical bigness, but also not with prominence or notability and not even with honour. If we are growing and fruitful, we will become less. We will give away our produce and be renewed in smallness. It sounds both strange and familiar, doesn't it? Followers of Christ empty themselves and become nothing; the one who is great is the one who serves.

I have enjoyed thinking about the association of the two words 'messy' and 'maturity'. The agricultural, fruit-bearing images have rung true. I grew up in a typical Australian suburb with the legendary 'quarter-acre block' that was the epitome of the Australian dream. The land of our suburb had, in the early days of settlement, held rolling orchards, and most blocks had at least a few fruit trees left on them, probably self-seeded after clearing, all quite established and mature.

Our block had a couple of varieties of plum tree, a fig tree, an apricot tree, a nectarine tree, a lemon tree, and a couple of apple trees that had been pruned with an axe at one stage and were grotesquely disfigured. I was moved with pity for them, sensitive child that I was, and would tentatively, gently and inquisitively touch their gnarled scars as my vivid childhood imagination wondered about their lives. But Dad coaxed them back to fruitfulness. Our summers were marked by bumper crops and the heavy smell of fruit filling the house. We tripped over buckets of produce everywhere, and my mum worked like a Trojan over the steaming Fowlers-Vacola bottling unit through the hottest part of the Australian summer to fill the shelves of our shed with preserves and cut fruit that we would eat right through to the next season. So here is my sweet, heavy-scented, sweat-inducing, delicious image of maturity, which is bound up in fruitfulness.

This image seems to fit with the experience of Messy Churches and Messy mission. Perhaps it can help us to understand what maturity looks like in any church, and can particularly encourage us to have confidence in the capacity for maturity in Messy Churches.

Maturity just happens

Jesus spoke of the seed that is planted in a field and grows while the farmer sleeps. This growth is nothing to be proud of. It just happens. Kingdom communities, it seems, will grow, all by themselves (Mark 4:26–29). The growth sketched in Jesus' parables highlights the fact that organic growth to maturity in agriculture involves multiple processes of change (v. 28), in fact, almost constant change. This all occurs out in the elements, exposed to predators and nourishments alike, and alongside competitors and threats (4:3–9). Growth and maturity are cyclical and seasonal, not linear and progressive, and, if truly 'successful', a plant sheds leaves, dies and disappears (John 12:24). The organic growth images that Jesus uses point not to cumulative improvement but positively to seasonal death. This is a somewhat arresting image for those of us interested in planting and growing. We need to be ready for death.

Let's go back to the grape on the vine, or the apricot on the tree. While it is still growing, it has only one thing to do—hang on. If it doesn't do this, and does anything else, it's all over. The growing fruit needs to be completely connected to and integrated with the life of a fruit-growing system. But once it is ripe, there are lots of things that might happen to that fruit in its mature fruitiness. The grape might be pressed for wine or eaten fresh or sundried in oil as a raisin. These are all very decent destinies for a humble grape. The apricot might end up as sauce for chicken or as jam for toast or (and this is my favourite) as a frosty serving of sorbet. All of these destinies, though, are messy and involve giving up life as a whole piece of fruit.

The plant, if fruitful, will be pruned or slashed or beaten as a result of harvesting. It will be reduced. As we consider the long-term life of communities of faith, including Messy Churches, this theology of death and new growth must be central to our vision of maturity. In some ways, the phrase 'messy maturity' is neither a contradiction nor a paradox, but a perfect match.

Messy maturity and the child

To a certain extent, we need to be wary of our own desire to be mature. Why is there a chapter in this book on maturity? Why are we concerned that Messy Churches should become mature or produce mature people when the language of maturity in Jesus' teaching is, at best, obscure?

Before exploring positively the shape of maturity in Messy Church, I want to sound this warning very clearly. We have noted above how the notion of maturity, in Western culture at least, is heavily burdened with pride, false gravitas and status. In following a faith that is based on becoming empty, not great, on service, not strength, and on love, not success, we should not be too preoccupied with concerns about maturity. It is not in Jesus' vocabulary. Jesus directly asks us to become like children. He calls us into downward mobility for the sake of others.

Messy Church models, and other fresh expressions of Church and missional initiatives like it, offer great ways for people to come as children. To be deliberately blunt, we must be careful not to damage or deplete a theological strength that is inherent in Messy Churches, for the sake of our pride.

If we are concerned that our Messy Churches are not making mature people, we are not asking the same questions as Jesus did. If we are concerned that our Messy Churches are not making converts and committed or confirmed church members, we are not asking the same questions as Jesus did. If we are concerned that Messy Church is not a financially sustainable model of church with appropriate fiscal growth strategies, we are not asking the same questions as Jesus did. If we are concerned that Messy Church doesn't feed people who have been followers of Jesus for 30 years already, we are still not asking the same questions as Jesus did.

Messy Church's models, which are intrinsically multigenerational in design, have been strongly associated with children. The presence of children in a service of worship should be as normal and straightforward as having children around the meal table. Dinner time with children can be a messy affair, but there is no question that children need to be at dinner, actually eating and drinking, and that they need to do it with adults. There are situations (and I'm sure you can think of them) that are exceptions to this rule, but the places in which children are routinely absent from meal times become sterile and artificial. It's not good for children to eat only among other children, and it's not good for adults to edit children out of their meals, either.

The meal table keeps a certain tension. Questions arise. We are reminded why we are eating. The bigger story of food production and consumption that we sustain and draw from is invoked and rehearsed. Where does cheese come from? Why can't we eat just chocolate? Who is not eating today in our world? Why is using a fork a good idea and why do we wash our hands? How do we handle leftovers? We are less likely to overindulge if our children are present, and conversation over food holds a strong connection as it becomes linked to physical and emotional, not just verbal, experience.

Children are an essential part of a whole and healthy community, and, if our congregations lack children entirely, they might well be diagnosed as lacking maturity. It is, sadly, often the case that a congregation lacks children because the older members are not willing to be generous enough to participate in ways that aren't quite their 'cup of tea' in order to allow accessibility and affirmation for children. Clearly this is a failure of a community to embrace the selflessness that is part of growing up. Many churches require greater flexibility, tolerance and convenience from their children than from their adults. A messy theology of maturity may need to speak with prophetic grit, as it articulates the mission and vision of Messy Church. We need to speak plainly about the role of children in the midst of a community.

The insights of the Child Theology Movement focus attention on the action of Jesus in placing the child in the midst of the disciples for the sake of helping the disciples, and not so much for the sake of the child. The movement also works from a multidimensional rubric of understanding children, recognising the varying nuances of how they are imaged in the Bible, not just as developing beings needing nurture but also as carriers of wisdom and revealers of the kingdom, prophetic voices and bearers of the *imago Dei*.[96]

Maturity is messy

In 2006, before Messy Church had reached Australia, we planted a strange Sunday afternoon congregation called 'Family Spirit'. It varied in some ways from Messy Church but shared some of the important elements—especially that of messiness. It was a huge experiment for us. We had no idea what we were doing, and I'm sure we made lots of mistakes, but we learnt lots.

One of the most important things we discovered was the non-negotiability of allowing those who came from the community to serve alongside those who came from the church. When the church people tried to 'serve' the community exclusively, community people became uncomfortable. They wanted to be a part of the Family Spirit community and pull their weight. Someone wanted to bring the milk each week for the coffee, someone else the cordial for the kids. We had to accept this and put aside the small issues of what to do when they didn't turn up, which, of course, happened sometimes. We had to learn that it was no big drama. Someone would rush home to get some milk or do a quick run to the shop to get some cordial, or we stole some from the cupboard and fixed it up later. (Don't tell the playgroup!)

It was fine. I think this was part of the maturing process for those of us who thought we were God's special missionaries, there to serve the lost. Maturity meant being willing to be served, being willing to be let down, and being willing not to have things running perfectly smoothly and 'keeping face'. Looking competent and well organised is not the same as maturity.

When it came to opening the Bible together, we had to accept the same protocols. We had to trust the process of reading and incarnating and exploring together. Children shaped our time as much as adults did with their insights, questions and actions. Some things were a roaring success and others were spectacular debacles, but neither of these were the centre of attention. Seeking the kingdom in our relationships, our ethics and our words and deeds in the world through our engagement with the Bible was the focus. Thus, it wasn't just our understanding of the content of scripture that shaped us, but the narrative of what the Bible actually is—the journey that the text has taken through the hands and minds and mouths of many to reach us and invite us to be part of its story too.

As responsible exegetes of scripture, we need to recognise the way in which texts bear the marks of their time. Some of our Gospels and Pauline letters were written earlier and some later than others; and across the decades the tone of the text gets less edgy, less radical, more conventional and in line with culture. Is this drift, evident in the writings from the early communities of the gospel, a sign of a church 'maturing' or of a wildly radical movement gradually being tamed?

This might point to a reflection that your Messy Church needs to consider as time passes. Do you see a taming of your adventurous spirit? Are you becoming more like... something else? This, and the questions below, are good ones to ask yourselves. There are no right or wrong answers; they are simply ways of provoking reflection and discernment for your Messy Church.

- What did we start doing and what have we stopped doing?
- What are we still doing but slightly differently?
- Are we feeling things getting harder or easier?
- Who is here that was here at the start?
- Who has gone and who has arrived?
- How often are we surprised?

Sustaining Messy Church maturity

How can the Messy Church model move into the strange, counter-cultural kind of biblical maturity that Jesus envisages in his parables and Paul models in his cruciform life? There is no rocket science here. It will be in the same way as for any church that allows constant renewal and transformation as well as growth and maturity. The sustaining, maturing and renewing source for any community of faith will be found in constant engagement with the Bible.

This is where I think Messy Churches have a great advantage over many traditional churches. A breakdown of the time a person spends reading and engaging with the Bible during an average service will come to less than 10 per cent of the time they have spent in the church. You'll note that I don't count the sermon in this calculation, because sermons are mostly second- or even third-hand thinking for passive listeners. They haven't had a great track record of bearing fruit, and it's easy to see why. In the Messy Church model, in its best expressions, the biblical text is worked over and over in multisensory and incarnate ways, for perhaps an hour or more.

Perhaps this is the place to sound a prophetic warning to Messy Churches that may be tempted to degenerate into models that view the 'celebration' time as the 'God time' or 'Bible time', and miss the true fertility of the model in which we roll our sleeves up and work the text together. We don't let armchair theologians do our thinking for us (and I say this as a theologian myself). We trust the power of the Bible to speak as we let it impact us sensorially, relationally and communally. We trust the power of the Bible to form and transform us as disciples, not through trite, three-point talks of any length but through the strong weaving of story and community and senses. Our model invests in the simple art of hearing and doing the biblical text, and because we want all of our senses to be open to the text, this takes repetition.

We hear the text with focus on *action* as the community physically 'rehearses' the actions/verbs of the text. We hear the text with focus on *place* as the community observes or constructs or investigates the context of the world of the text and the community's own context. We hear the text with focus on *power and politics* as the community simulates and articulates the 'systems' in the text— economics, customs of honour, hierarchies, rules or governments.

We hear the text with focus on *materials* as a community handles, touches, builds and processs the material objects of the text— foods, animals, plants, buildings, things made of stone, wood, fibre or metal. We hear the text with focus on *vocabulary and poetry* as a community vocalises the text, rehearsing the patterns, the pauses, and the rise and fall of tension and tone. We hear the text with focus on *emotion* as the community identifies and validates, through expression, creativity and the arts, the heart language and affective drama of the narrative.

With these multiple readings of the text (and I hope you will find others to add to this repertoire), the community of faith is exposed to the powerful realities of the text, with attention to the historical context, genre, form, language devices, imagery and structure.

I offer these suggestions, which give both too much and not enough detail, to help identify the dimensions of the scope and depth, complexity and vibrancy of biblical exegesis. There is no need to compromise the quality of scholarship available to our communities. There is no need to reduce the complexity of exploration. There is no need to mute the pastoral or prophetic poignancy of the Bible. There is no need to water down the application in our lives for younger or older members of the faith community.

By the time we have read with attention using all of these multiple methods, and listened together, our apprehension of the text is conceptually broad and concretely incarnational. Many wonderful resources for this process have already been published in the Messy Church materials.

Readiness, thoughtfulness and risk

You will realise that I am not convinced that 'Western maturity' supplies the most helpful categories for evaluating the viability and vitality of Messy Church. There are three characteristics of discipleship, which I think can form a useful rubric for considering the structures and strategies of good news discipleship communities.

The dynamics of readiness, thoughtfulness and risk can be encouraged at any age and for any activity or task, in learning, in praying, in compassion, in service and in leading. Think of your cook at Messy Church—ready, thoughtful and open to risk-taking, not knowing how many people will come. This is a posture towards God and towards one another that can be cultivated in all kinds of ways. Think of your woodworker at Messy Church—ready for God, thinking of God, open to the risks of God; ready for people, thinking of people, open to the risk of loving people.

Readiness

Readiness expands in several directions. It means being ready in the sense of prepared with an activity, materials and instructions, but also being ready in the sense of being alert, with our antennae up for what's happening next. It means being ready for change, because if Messy Church is what we are going to run with, it will change and it will change us. On a wider scale, this readiness calls our whole ecclesiology to 'prepare the way of the Lord'. Our denominations, academies and colleges will need to embrace a 'readiness' for leaders who are preparing for Messy Church mission. They will need to be ready for students who have been nurtured in Messy Churches and have perhaps come with an alternative biblical methodology, different expectations of agency in their own formation, and a vision of the gospel that doesn't necessitate many of the accoutrements that are large features in our current traditions and are reinscribed in the formation of clergy.

Thoughtfulness

The posture of thoughtfulness aligns with the best tradition of Christian theological reflection. Followers of Jesus are learners: we act and live, but we don't disengage from the structures of belief and the intellectual architecture that inform our practices. This is a discipleship pedagogy, a serving pedagogy, a gospel-centred pedagogy.

Beyond asking either 'How will Messy Church "mature" as a movement?' or 'How will Messy Church mature its participants?' we also must ask, 'How will Messy Church have a "maturing" (in the best sense of this word as explored above) effect on the church as a whole, including our theological and academic cultures?'

Messy Church has much to offer, including challenges to our theological colleges. For centuries now, our clergy have been consistently trained in the one monophonic expectation. The basic mechanism of communication in churches, for which clergy are trained, is monologue. This, we know, in our visual and mostly literate society, is a very poor means of communication and an even poorer means of transformation. Messy Church helps us to stop pretending otherwise. If the academy takes the past paths and potential of Messy Church seriously, applying its best theological reflection and critical skills from biblical scholarship, there is opportunity to develop a vibrant culture of biblical and theological methodologies that equip all in the community to minister with one another.

In speaking of maturity, I would hope that our academics and scholars find this idea challenging and exciting, not threatening and alienating. Messy Church methodologies give great room for questions, for multiple readings, employing the thoughtfulness that genre, form, redaction, reader response and many other tools bring.

Further than this, Messy Church operates on the premise that what we do each day in our households and neighbourhoods, living ordinary lives in the ways of Jesus and power of the Spirit, is how faith is formed and informed, tested and proved. An intentional gathering once a month acts as a place of expression and resourcing for the life of faith. To view the monthly gathering of Messy Church as the 'source' for maturing would be to depend on a very thin thread indeed, and this has nothing to do with the format or 'depth' of Messy Church gatherings.

To view the weekly gathering of traditional or contemporary church as the 'source' for maturing would be to depend, equally, on a very thin thread indeed. To name it bluntly, many people do operate as if this were the idea of attending a weekly gathering of worship. There is a background assumption that the church service somehow 'delivers' the substance of maturity. This idea takes a few different forms. Sometimes it is seen in the access to 'teaching' via a sermon. In other traditions it is seen in the performance of sacraments. Other ecclesial cultures articulate the value of a weekly worship service as an opportunity to meet with God, to be in the presence of the Lord, to be ushered into the presence of Jesus and, in doing so, somehow to improve or at least sustain one's faith or spiritual life.

These are all variations that are vulnerable to the same heresy—the heresy that we have a spirituality that is contained, a 'thing' that can be added to or diminished, and that needs 'topping up'. A further vulnerability related to our dependence on a weekly church service is the sense that God's presence is 'stronger' or 'more available' in some places, or, as we often hear said, that 'God rocks up there'—as if God's presence in the universe were limited to some localities.

These heresies are seductive. Followers of Jesus are easily tempted to think of church in these ways and to envisage their own 'spiritual development' in relation to the participation in and performance of certain ecclesial acts. A weekly worship service has become a cultural mainstay of Christendom. We do well to remember that this phenomenon is not historically consistent or inherent to the practice of faith. Messy Church, then, helps to break the nexus of expectations that have congealed around this practice and provokes us to consider how faith persists and is expressed in other patterns—domestic, voluntary, informal, relational, public, hourly, daily, seasonal patterns of practice. The monthly rhythm of Messy Church may lead us to recover spiritual disciplines that connect us to patterns of imitation of Christ, and mindfulness of the call to serve neighbour and love enemy.

The practices of simplicity can be helpful—eating simply, with perhaps no meat or dairy, or dressing simply by wearing black or brown or green. The practices of celebration can be helpful—daily lighting candles for the small good news stories that friends share, or holding brief moments of song and dance. Messy Church provides an impetus and a framework for exploring the value of daily and (at the other end of the time spectrum) seasonal or episodic practices.

Openness to risk

The posture of openness as an expression of maturity in Messy Church takes us beyond the idea of our own doors being open and returns us to the call to missional adventure. When I was little I was mostly housebound, visiting the chicken house, the grass lawn and the veggie patch; Dad's shed and the gravel driveway were the regular limits of my cosmos. To venture further, I needed older travelling companions.

Interestingly, my grandma was also mostly housebound, although she was physically quite fit. The horses in the back paddock, the rose garden and the front-gate letterbox were her limits. But there was a sense that this was not quite right. Even as a child, I could see that her isolation, her lack of connection beyond the domestic patch, and the anxiety associated with 'outside' meant that something was amiss in her grown-up status. There was no risk.

Thinking, then, of our Messy Church communities, an openness, an adventurous spirit, the capacity for risk, a willingness to go out as well as come home, will characterise a healthy 'maturity'. We are, after all, a community of faith. Faith involves doubts and risks and uncertainties. If we are sure, there is no space for faith. How ironic that the church has acquired a reputation for conservatism! Of all people, we should be those most willing to risk everything and lose everything, even our very selves—or, as radically as the New Testament writer Paul put it, our own salvation that others might be saved (Romans 9:3).

This idea might need to be articulated in your church community. I don't know that I've ever heard a sermon unpack that radical part of Paul's faith seriously. Much of the preaching I have heard directs us to strengthen ourselves and improve our own piety. Paul's letters to his gospel communities, by contrast, spoke of dying to self, of becoming empty for the sake of others—that those who were strong should give up their strength and become as the weak are. His ideas, unsurprisingly, are similar to Jesus' call to become like a child or a slave in service of others.

Paul laid his bets on the idea that to try to grasp God and accumulate spirituality will leave us impoverished and devoid of the Spirit (1 Corinthians 13:1–3). To live in faith is, in Paul's words, to be grasped by God, to be taken hold of, which means being out of our own control (Philippians 3:12). In C.S. Lewis's *Prince Caspian*, there is a beautiful scene in which the cynical, careful, canny and conservative dwarf Trumpkin finally meets Aslan. When confronted by the mighty lion of whom he had been so dismissive, he bows. A bow is a very controlled and contained posture. But, to his fear and delight, he finds himself tossed in the air—flailing but flying free. Lewis is a clever and subtle writer. He is offering us an image of what it is to be confronted by the reality of Jesus—a wild and risky ride—and he is showing our false attempts at reverence and dignity to be not so much futile as simply not what God is interested in.

Think of Noah adrift on floodwaters, or Jonah thrown in at the deep end, or Abraham on the road to nowhere, or the disciples following a renegade rabbi whose actions were often unreasonable, moving beyond risky towards downright ridiculous. It is not just that we might be called to actions that seem foolish, rash, immature or undignified. The disciples witnessed Jesus feeding 5000 families, interrupting funerals and rioting in the temple courts. Embarrassingly, it is God whose actions are foolish, rash, immature and undignified, seeming to fly in the face of the established order and collective wisdom of 'how religion is done'. We do not worship a wise old sage. We follow a young man whose ministry lasted barely three years.

When we established our missional community, Family Spirit, which ran on a Sunday afternoon, there were some wonderful families from established congregations who formed the core team. They were truly servant-hearted and regularly went the extra mile. Some of them would lead a Sunday club group in our morning congregation and still have energy to bring resources and engage in the afternoon. Some played in bands that provided music for two morning family services and then came faithfully in the afternoon as well. I was at full tilt at all three services, but that was as a member of pastoral staff; these families were pulling the double shift voluntarily. I was staggered by their commitment and energy.

However, this extraordinary commitment had an unfortunate side effect. Those who came from the community to Family Spirit soon realised that we were double-dipping, and, although we always had a wonderful time and everyone was fully engaged, it ate away at the integrity of Family Spirit as 'church'. A couple of the families who came to faith through Family Spirit eventually decided to come to our earlier services as well. Although I was fully convinced that Family Spirit, with all its interactive mess and engaging chaos, was a rich and enriching, sustaining and sustainable ecology for faith, in order to demonstrate this, we needed to stop looking as if we still depended on and invested in the morning service as a 'back-up'.

Similarly, a Messy Church will need to cut the umbilical cord if it has been born out of a mother congregation, in order to become a place in which faith that is ready, thoughtful and open to risk can flourish and be tested. While the participants, including the team, in a Messy Church maintain their ongoing regular attendance at another congregation, the integrity of the Messy Church model will be compromised. A messy theology of readiness, thoughtfulness and openness to risk is most vitally expressed in the everyday.

Messy and mature: contradiction or paradox?

I have considered whether 'maturity' is a helpful idea to connect with life in the Spirit as a follower of Jesus. I have noted the scant biblical basis for pursuing the idea of maturity in relation to faith and examined the phenomenon of maturity in agriculture, exploring the metaphorical ideas that Jesus referenced in many of his parables. This meant attending to the seasonality, fruitfulness, shedding and diverse transformations that are theologised in these biblical images, which liberate us from the oppression of constant, consistent, cumulative compulsions for growth.

I have shown how notions of 'development', 'progress', 'growth' and 'maturity' carry strong cultural overlays in the legacy of Western Enlightenment modernity, which are not necessarily in alignment with Jesus' vision of the kingdom as heard in the Beatitudes and seen in the cross, or emerging across the Roman empire through the lens of Paul's epistles to fledgling communities, which were endeavouring to shake off other systems of status and embody the self-giving and self-emptying model of Christ.

I have considered a vision of 'mature' community and posted warnings of the lure of status, position, pride and conservatism, which have come to distort the patterns of vulnerability, mutuality and childlikeness with which Jesus challenged his disciples. I have suggested that the postures of readiness, thoughtfulness and openness to risk might be seen as congruent values with the life of discipleship and the gospel of Jesus. These characteristics may provide a more dynamic rubric for energising, encouraging and evaluating the communal life of a Messy Church and the life of each participant.

I have affirmed the centrality and exclusivity of word and Spirit, understood as inspired scripture, as the formative and normative agent in Messy Church. It will be the corporate reading and appropriation of the Bible together in the midst of our local and global context that shapes us and becomes our centring, from which we take our vocabulary and materiality, our structure and ethics for gathering.

Messy Churches, which are multigenerational and participatory, call each person to mutual service, stretch our engagement in the form and content of scripture, and are aptly conditioned for the discipleship of readiness, thoughtfulness and openness to risk, which, I suggest, characterise the life of maturing, fruit-producing, giving, shedding, dying and renewing faith.

✤

10

Messy Church: how far can you go before reaching the limit?

Tim G. Waghorn

Tim Waghorn was born in Akaroa, New Zealand. He was raised on a sheep farm, later becoming a wool classer and buyer. He and his wife, Gail, and family made the move to Australia and now reside in Mont Albert North, a suburb of Melbourne, where Tim is vicar of the local Anglican church. He introduced Messy Church to his parish about two years ago. Tim has a love for movies, rugby (All Blacks), steampunk and '80s music. He hopes to visit the UK in the near future.

In our Messy Church, we think our role is to provide pathways and portals to mend the breaches between Jesus and our broken world. As we do so, God cements new relationships and souls are saved. Messy Church is a pathway that we delight in, bringing new families into God's greater family.

In this chapter I engage with the following subjects:

- Frequency of Messy Church
- Lay leadership and Messy Church
- What's next when people outgrow Messy Church?
- Liturgy in the light of Messy Church

Different perspectives on Messy Church

When is a church service not a church service? Where are the boundaries that separate an event from a service, or worship from activity? Has the word 'service' become outdated in today's environment? These questions relate to the definition of the body of Christ in the form of the gathered congregation. How we answer them will determine how we communicate 'worship' to the world around us.

The name 'Messy Church' itself says a lot about what it is. How does a postmodern society of generally unchurched people correlate with Messy Church? They know that church is not an event but something that's available all year round, for when they have a desire to engage with it. That's OK, as long as we are available when they are seeking. For centuries, church services have provided opportunities for people to gather, learn, grow, experience and come to knowledge and salvation. With movements such as fresh expressions, we continue to look at renewed ways of taking the gospel to the world around us.

Messy Church is, in our view, a beautifully simple model of Church. It has a name that breaks down barriers. When we began Messy Church, it was the name that struck a chord with our community. A number of families who flinched at a traditional form of worship were surprised by the name. For them, it spoke of a church that warmly welcomes all ages, allowing them to discover God in a way that is unique to their time in life. Messy Church has shown itself to be a brilliantly fresh style of church service to engage a new generation of seeking families.

What we are witnessing is one type of fresh expression of Church, increasing in diversity. Historically, we have been separated into denominations connected to issues of doctrine and the ways in which we express our biblical understanding. I believe we are seeing the diversity that began with denominational separation happening within the Messy Church movement, for good or otherwise, as it is done differently in different places. We need to be mindful, however, of who is at the core of Messy Church or any church, for that matter—Jesus Christ. Certainly there are enticing factors that make Messy Church unique—for instance, craft, food, games and, of course, mess—but they are peripheral to the nucleus of church in any format, style or setting.

Frequency of Messy Church

At our place of worship, Messy Church takes place weekly during school terms. Let me explain why.

In our local community, anything that occurs less often than weekly is labelled an event. Jesus' death was an event; his resurrection was an event. Our fair is an event. Christmas celebrations are an event because they are aligned with the seasonal calendar.

Families map out their timetables around dropping children off to school or kindergarten. For others, it is about fitting in activities for young children, ranging from playgroup to swimming and everything in between. Thursday might be library day followed by kids' gym; Tuesday is playgroup day or Mainly Music,[97] and the list goes on. Our aim is to provide an opportunity for families to include being part of church on that list. We discovered that the adults are reluctant to do that for themselves but will make exceptions for their children.

Conditioning over centuries has created the model of church taking place weekly on a Sunday. Even to the unchurched, this is still perceived to be the model. We utilise this approach with Messy Church, building on the concept of celebrating each week under Christ and seeking his blessing for the week ahead. As people of God, we need to prioritise worship and time with him. Children note the value of regular structure in their lives. These patterns sustain us in our home environment and also in the workplace. Our planet operates according to days, seasons and years, and so should church.

Messy Church fits into our weekly timetable. The first challenge is to take the message for the week and format it accordingly to suit the congregation. That already happens in most churches with dynamically different services. The format of one service is best suited to a traditionally structured sermon and is thus presented in a traditional manner. The second service allows for significant freedom in presentation, yet utilises the same biblical passages as the first. Messy Church follows the same line of preparation. I see a comparison here with the process of distillation. A liquid to be purified is evaporated via boiling and then collected in its pure form after the vapour has condensed. Distillation is used to separate fresh water from a salt solution and gasoline from petroleum. The condensed vapour, which is the purified liquid, is called the distillate. We think that the message presented at Messy Church is the distillate of the morning message, purified and directed in such a way that children and adults alike have access to its meaning and relevancy.

I believe that Jesus used a similar process, taking the Old Testament text and preaching it through parables, which were aligned with the comprehension of his audience. Jesus may have had the ability to produce the best sermon ever, right there on the spot. For us, Messy Church takes additional time to prepare, as our set-up and operation are more media-driven. Through images, music and sensory engagement, the message of Christ is brought to the gathered congregation. From the leadership perspective, it is more effective to redistribute a weekly message than to try to create something fresh on a monthly basis.

We needed to find a way of making a weekly service sustainable. Certain key elements assisted in this process, one of which was presentation. We did not have a music team that could or would commit to Messy Church. We wanted something that would be visual and engaging to all senses. Our service thus begins with a time of greeting and settling in, followed by a lively time of worship, using music video clips with lyrics. We soon discovered which music worked, and dropped any that didn't. We needed to find a presentation format that was simple to operate, yet relevant and appealing to new Christians of all ages. We also needed to streamline the service, because we have a small team. We rely on multimedia because this is the platform on which the world functions. Children know how to scan an iPad before they can walk these days. The more we can make use of common technology, the better we can engage our communities with the gospel in familiar ways.

The second challenging key component of running Messy Church on a weekly basis was planning the activity session. Those who spend time planning just one Messy Church activity based on scripture may find it daunting enough. Because of this challenge, we ran the risk of defaulting to well-worn paths of 'easy scripture'— that is, Bible stories that are well loved with a multitude of activities around them. But would we, then, be creating something simple for us at the expense of those we were trying to reach? Did we run the risk of presenting a tame gospel and biblical principles that lacked challenge? The goal for all Messy Church teams is to provide sound teaching from all perspectives of scripture. There are amazing stories in the Bible, and just as riveting principles.

For our Messy Church, the Bible passage accompanied by the teaching is the crucial element. If God's word were not our major reason for meeting in the first place, it simply would not be church but, rather, an afternoon activity for young families. As we see it, all other facets of Messy Church reinforce the gospel message, enhancing God's word through action, community and activity.

Lay leadership and Messy Church

Lay leadership, in my view, is advocated in the book of Exodus, beginning at chapter 36, where God commands all the skilled workers to build the tabernacle under Moses' leadership. The Lord equipped the general public with relevant gifts and talents to be used for his glory.

Often the church overlooks the fact that 'Moses summoned Bezalel and Oholiab and every skilled person to whom the Lord had given ability and who was willing to come and do the work' (Exodus 32:6, NIV). They were gifted in specific areas and were to focus on the region of their gifting. I note that they were also willing to come and do the work. They did not have to be coerced into serving the Lord. There is nothing more edifying before the Lord than when gifted lay people operate within their gifts, willing to serve the Lord and grow the kingdom. When laity assume roles outside their gifting, or are not willing to come and work, or lack vision, ministry will be shallow and empty. Equally, clergy should seek to discern the limit of their gifting.

The simple concept of focusing on our gifting and being willing to contribute within that role continues to work in the church as we know it today. Messy Church, drawing on many people's gifts, is a perfect example of giftedness being used to build the kingdom of God.

The upside of lay leadership in Messy Church

When lay leaders are involved in the life of the church, dynamics change. The church suddenly becomes more attractive to the outside world. When people from outside the church see people they know being involved in the life of the church, it brings them a step closer. By working with lay leaders, the clergy can lead more efficiently and provide the necessary pathways for church attendees to engage in life- and faith-building programmes. As a pastor myself, I am lost without lay leadership in various ministries that take place in our church. We are currently planning a new outreach mission service, which, by the time you read this book, will be up and running. It would not have been possible without the valuable gifting and dedication of lay leaders. The same passion and gifting allow us to take Messy Church to our community on a weekly basis.

We have seen lay leaders come and go. A number of them were

simply filling a gap. Some were clearly out of their gifting range, which had an impact on those receiving their ministry. Some of them did not grasp the missiology behind Messy Church but were there to find self-fulfilment in their own Christian walk.

Understanding missiology is an important aspect of successful lay involvement. Clergy are trained theologically and (we hope) in the field of local mission. Messy Church relies on the basics of loving God and neighbour. In Matthew 22:36–40, Jesus reminded the Pharisees that the laws from the Levitical days (see Leviticus 19:18)[98] were still relevant to the new covenant. This displays the timelessness of God and his love for his children. As we continue to share this love with our neighbours, they will be looking for the genuineness and unity that come from walking with Christ. When a church advances in unity, it becomes more appealing to the community.

Messy Church is rapidly becoming a neighbourhood-based out-reach service. Neighbour begins to recognise neighbour in the role of leadership as well as friendship. From this, a wider sense of family begins to form, something that is difficult for trained clergy alone to accomplish.

The downside of lay leadership in Messy Church

This heading may sound negative, but it needs to be explored. Denomination, location and beliefs will determine how each reader engages with this topic. Without lay leadership, the church (and especially Messy Church) would struggle at best, but there are times when the same can be said about the absence of clergy. Whether you call your leader Pastor, Vicar, Father or Minister, it doesn't change the fact that they are the appointed and anointed leader. In some denominations, there is a process of ordination whereby a person, through the process of discernment, biblical training and mentoring, is prepared for a life of ministry within their appointed denomination. An example can be taken from the Anglican Church of Australia, to which I am an ordained clergy person.

The priest is ordained following a period as a deacon and is authorised to baptise, be solely responsible for Holy Communion, to pronounce the Absolution, and give the blessing. Priests may be placed in charge of parishes or undertake other forms of ministry such as chaplaincy. Women can be ordained as priests in most dioceses within Australia—with the exception of Ballarat, North West Australia, Sydney, The Murray and Wangaratta.[99]

While this is only a brief summary, it indicates the role required of ordained clergy. The role is not simply limited to Holy Communion, pronouncing the Absolution and the blessing, for clergy must meet the following vocational criteria:

A person must exhibit a 'passion' for 'God in Christ' and his Church [and] show evidence of a desire to minister Christ and to talk about 'God in Christ' to others.

There must be evidence of capacity and desire to lead communities of faith and love. The person will need to possess people and community life skills and sensitivities [and] realise simply to have a desire to be a minister or 'attraction to spiritual life' is not necessarily a call to ordination. God's call must be tested by the Church.[100]

There is within every denomination a need for structure, leadership and accountability. Few Sunday services take place without clergy or assigned leadership being involved at one level or another. However, what seems to be quite normal is for Messy Church to function purely with lay leadership.

One of the factors that has assisted in Messy Church's engagement with young families in our area is that the church leader runs the service. The families involved sense that they are valued and cared for enough to have the church's top local representative educating them. I also run the preschool music programme because of this concept. It is a fast-track means of breaking down preconceived barriers—the belief that clergy are unapproachable, inaccessible or, dare I say, dry and out of touch with the real world.

There is widening debate in Australia about the line between laity and clergy when it comes to Messy Church. There are those who state that the lay people are rightfully building the church through this model and require minimal clergy input. Personally, I would love to hear of church pastors and ministers being directly involved in Messy Church, actively participating in every service as the ordained representatives of Jesus Christ. Nobody is above taking the gospel message to young or old. We may have our comfort zones in church style, whether traditional or contemporary. However, Jesus taught both in the synagogue and to crowds on a mountainside.

What's next when people outgrow Messy Church?

While most churches running Messy Church on a monthly basis will take six years to reach 70 services, we have reached this figure in two years. Because of this, we have fast-tracked many of the issues that I believe Messy Churches will face in years to come. Messy Church for us today is quite different from its beginnings. We have learnt much about our community through the service. We have made mistakes along the way. Some were easily rectified, while others came at great cost—but we didn't throw in the towel when the going got tough. As we pushed through hard barriers, stories from Messy Church members gave us encouragement. We saw differences in the lives of our newfound brothers and sisters. Through prayer and faith, we have continued to shape Messy Church into a model that, we believe, is right for our neighbourhood. This model won't necessarily be right for all; each must pray and trust God for the wisdom to shape a service that is right for their own part of the world.

A report on 'Churchgoing in the UK' was published by Tearfund in April 2007. It revealed that 15 per cent of the UK population go to church at least once a month.[101] The same report stated that, in the same year, 58 per cent of the population claimed to be Christian. What these figures show is the rapidly expanding gap between Christians who attend church and those who don't. Messy Church is beginning to make inroads with this missing 43 per cent and beyond. We find that, although the unchurched people around us do not know the finer details of doctrine relating to salvation and redemption, they do have expectations about what a church does and what they can learn. The 'message' or 'sermon' still ranks as the number one reason for people to attend a church service.[102]

The role of the Church is to grow and mature disciples in Christ. Church is not a spectator sport like rugby or football. People don't turn up at church to be entertained or simply to kill some time. We think that one of the big questions for Messy Church is 'what's next?' for people who outgrow this model of Church. All churches have a 'back door' by which people leave. This cliché relates to the 'flow-through' pattern of newcomers who enter the church and, when dissatisfied for one reason or another, leave again. We run the risk of losing large numbers of people from Messy Church unless we understand the needs of newcomers entering church for the first time.

I have been asking myself for months if our Messy Church is providing enough teaching content to keep the regulars attending. As a church, we have a commitment to the proclamation of the word, including expounding scripture with application for today's society. We grew our Messy Church from families connecting with our church through preschool playgroups. It is tempting to pitch the Messy Church theme towards children as, in our area, parents want to fill their children's week with many activities. We chose to focus on building into the lives of children, parents and grandparents alike, bringing Christ to the fore. We have seen family members maturing in faith, which is the very core of the church's role.

We are now wrestling with the 'Where to next?' question. As I've explained, because we run Messy Church weekly, we have accelerated the maturation process for new Christians and have essentially hit the ceiling of that growth within the Messy Church construct. In short, we are planning a contemporary service that will take these new Christians to the levels they seek and need. For us, to reformat Messy Church to cater for this spiritual growth is not practical without losing its essence.

This issue has come to our attention after some 80 Messy services. We have gone through a refining process during the past two years, which has seen the activity side of the service dwarfed by the teaching and biblical component. This has brought about the spiritual growth we have witnessed. People come to church knowing that it is going to present material about God. They come to a Christian church with the anticipation of hearing something to do with Jesus Christ.

The model of Messy Church that we have developed may very well become our Sunday school programme during our planned contemporary service. For us, Messy Church is a pathway to growing mature Christians. It provides a unique style of worship that brings people back to the attention of the mainstream church in a fresh way. However, having only monthly attendance is a hard road to building the body of Christ. In ways such as Paul mentioned in 1 Corinthians 3:6, Messy Church may plant or even water the seed, but it is God who makes it grow. Is the soil of Messy Church rich enough to sustain a seed to maturity? After two years of weekly Messy Church, I have reached the conclusion that it is a wonderful environment for Christians to begin the growing process of faith. It has brought the name of Jesus Christ to a world bombarded by secularist values and concepts of life. It allows families to begin the process of faith exploration together, while most other church services send the children out for separate biblical education. Messy Church removes preconceived barriers to worship—for example, the idea that children should not run around.

What we find that Messy Church does not do is to take the knowledge-seeking attendee to the next level; it keeps them in a holding pattern of craft, food and fun with a Bible message. Messy Church needs something else to feed into. It has to be something comparatively contemporary or the gap is too great. The warmth, energy and vibrancy must be present, having their source in the Holy Spirit.

Liturgy in the light of Messy Church

There are many reasons why families come to Messy Church. One of the main factors is to do with assumed boundaries. We live in a world where people hold to expectations. For example, you visit a doctor, you wait in the waiting room and you read outdated magazines until your appointment is announced. From there you enter the doctor's room for your consultation, for which, in Australia, you either pay at reception or book it against your health insurance cover.

There are many unchurched people who believe that a church service is that predictable. They assume that books will be brought out, one for the service, the other to sing from. There will be a great deal of standing, sitting and reading aloud. In some churches, there is that awkward moment when everyone has to say the Peace to each other.

Messy Church offers the opportunity to debunk the myths conjured up by public negativity. These foreign practices are removed and replaced with contemporary music and activities. If we were to put the Prayer of Humble Access before a Messy Bible talk on Holy Communion, it would be a challenge to bridge the gap between the two. I am always in favour of liturgy because of the richness and time-proven content that allows a service to flow towards being renewed in Christ. I am also a firm believer in contemporary formats and modification of liturgy. Liturgy has a valuable place in the life of the church. Through careful adaptation, I believe that liturgy can be transformed to a Messy model.

The document *Liturgy and Anglican Identity* produced by the International Anglican Liturgical Consultation of 2005 put it this way:

We believe that Anglican identity is expressed and formed through our liturgical tradition of corporate worship and private prayer, holding in balance both word and sacramental celebration. Specifically, our tradition is located within the broad and largely western stream of Christian liturgical development but has been influenced by eastern liturgical forms as well.[103]

This paper provides four illustrations of differing church services to display varying approaches to worship. While fictional illustrations are used, the described format of each service can be found in churches all around Australia. I do not claim to be a spokesperson for liturgy within the Anglican denomination; however, as a pastor/minister I do recognise the pastoral value of liturgy. I also note the need for a greater freedom when it comes to creative church ministry and acknowledge that this is a worldwide concern.

In his research paper for a Master's thesis, John Hebenton wrestles with this topic of freedom:

A questionnaire was run in two dioceses, a large urban diocese and a smaller provincial diocese... Four in-depth case studies were carefully selected... The case studies validated the findings of the questionnaires. They found the three main influences on those organising worship were their previous experience, the priority of mission over formation, and the desire to offer something different.[104]

Furthermore, the author was able to identify areas that are in need of future research:

The most pressing is to research what is understood by worship, and in particular the relationship between worship and mission. This is made

*more urgent by the growing adoption of Mission-shaped Church and
Fresh Expression ideology from the Church of England... this focus on
mission is largely understood in terms of offering new ways to engage non-
believers in worship.* [105]

Here is some evidence of a sense of urgency in bringing this issue
to the greater round table. Worship is shaped by liturgy more often
than we give credit for, but how much of liturgy actually shapes
mission? I have personally been involved in situations where liturgy
has created a tripping hazard for the unchurched. It is one thing
to respond corporately to written liturgy when the worshipper
has a theological understanding of the words they are saying. For
example, someone saying a standard prayer of confession will offer
up repentance to God—who is both merciful and our judge—
for sins committed, and seek his forgiveness. In a service setting
such as Messy Church, such words can very well stand out as too
confrontational. I have seen this kind of liturgy creating questions
rather than bringing peace. We live in a time when the unchurched
do not recognise the need for forgiveness from sin, because they
do not understand the theological concept of redemption and
retribution. Our role is to love and teach. It is when the lessons are
taught well that the Holy Spirit can bring the fullness of truth to the
lives of his children.

Conclusion

The world is becoming a better place because of Messy Church.
There are more than 1400 registered Messy Church expressions
around the world, listed on the Messy Church Directory, each
bringing all ages together to find out what it means to be a Christian
in their own contexts. [106] Churches all around the world are reaching
people of all ages in a fresh and unique way. Yet we must not deviate
from the purpose of the Church as found in Matthew 28:18–20:

Then Jesus came to them and said, 'All authority in heaven and on earth has been given to me. Therefore go and make disciples of all nations, baptising them in the name of the Father and of the Son and of the Holy Spirit, and teaching them to obey everything I have commanded you. And surely I am with you always, to the very end of the age.'

Recognising the authority of Christ, we have the responsibility of teaching and growing the body of Christ. This too is the ultimate responsibility of all of us who are teachers and leaders in the Messy Church environment. Activities and games may bring excitement and engage Messy Church-goers but will not change their lives. While wonderful fellowship around a meal is great for communities, it will not transform those communities. Only Christ can do that. While it is less challenging to tell the well-loved and familiar Bible stories, people only really grow when their understanding or notions are challenged.

We must never forget that Messy Church is more than a catchy name that makes church sound fun and exciting. Yes, church can be fun and exciting, but church, messy or otherwise, has the responsibility of bringing people to maturity in Christ. In his letter to the Galatians, Paul declared, 'It is fine to be zealous, provided the purpose is good, and to be so always, not just when I am with you. My dear children, for whom I am again in the pains of childbirth until Christ is formed in you...' (4:18–19, NIV).

A modern application of this passage is relevant to our approach to Messy Church. It is difficult to state the driving force behind Messy Church as being anything other than good, but in our zeal we need to be mindful to ensure that Jesus is at the core. If he isn't, we risk being just another church activity, such as a fête, but on a more regular basis. While fêtes bring people to the church property and lead them to interact with church people, the visitors leave with something from the church that is of their own choosing. Paul stated to the Galatians that they ran the risk of being zealous for the 'purpose of good' primarily when he was with them: they were in danger of pleasing human beings, not God. We have a clear directive that pleasing God is mandatory.

Paul expresses his desire to see people become mature in Christ. He knows that it will take time but it will happen. In a similar way, we see families and individuals entering Messy Church with the best intentions but, more often than not, little knowledge of the process of salvation. Salvation is a process of moving from a state of unawareness of God's grace and love to a place of redemption. The more families hear of God's love, the more complete the picture becomes, until the time arrives for a commitment to be made. It is also our responsibility to recognise those in Messy Churches who need more meat in their spiritual sandwich.

What will our pathways for spiritual development look like? Is there another level to Messy Church for which we need to start thinking and planning, before we are caught short? In my church, we are doing just that. We believe that there is a much-needed 'next step' for our Messy Church families, alongside the wider community, who are looking for a church that is relevant, honest and true to biblical truth and principles. There is anticipation for this next phase of church life for the Messy Church families to whom we have ministered. It is for such a time as this that we are here.

Messy Church can create the opportunity to take the good news of Christ to people who would never enter a church. The opportunity will bear fruit only if we are prepared to plant seeds and tend the soil. It saddens me when I read of Messy Churches that promote everything other than the reason for church to exist—Jesus Christ. Sometimes the only difference between their offering and any secular programme is the word 'Church' in Messy Church.

We encourage people to come to church, and yet some Messy Churches limit attendance. I think of the account in Mark 2:1–12, where a crippled man was lowered through the roof because the house was full of people gathered to hear Christ. Are our churches so full that we have to limit the number who can attend? What does this say to the lost who are seeking answers?

Messy Church has proven itself as a fresh expression of Church. It has transformed families in our neighbourhood. May we continue to see lives transformed for Christ, not be afraid to get a little bit messy in the process, and find the right steps beyond it for those who are ready.

Case study: the story of the 'Messy angels'

Sharon Pritchard

Sharon Pritchard is Regional Coordinator in County Durham and Adviser for Children's Ministry for the Diocese of Durham.

A couple of years ago, I had a call from a woman who was part of a group thinking about starting a Messy Church. They wanted a way of engaging with their local community—a former pit village with its fair share of socio-economic problems—and they felt that a Messy Church in the local school would be a good idea. Would I be able to come along to their next meeting to help them?

I dutifully went along to meet them one cold winter evening, finding my way in the dark to the house, which was right next door to a funeral parlour. I saw a light through a window and knocked on the door. What met me inside couldn't have been more different from the cold winter night: a group of twelve or so women, sitting expectantly in a small living-room with a roaring fire. The armchair next to the fire was empty, reserved for me as their guest. I sat down and knew straight away that these ladies meant business! After going through the basics, it became clear that they were already prepared: the headteacher at the school welcomed the idea and they just needed an extra bit of motivation and encouragement to go for it. We talked about the usual things—funding, budget, planning, crafts, worship, helpers—and within a couple of weeks they were off.

We managed to get our then bishop, Tom Wright, to pop into their first Messy Church, as he just happened to be visiting our deanery that afternoon, which proved a huge encouragement to everyone. With lots of extra hands and two of the clergy helping out, it became a great success, and today it is still going well. It is based at Sherburn Hill Primary School and is run by women from Shadforth village—'Team 1'. It happens once a month in school, with around 30 children attending and some of their mums helping out.

About a year after that first Messy Church started, the vicar, Eileen, felt it would be a good idea to run another Messy Church, but this time in the church building itself, St Mary's in Sherburn village. The parish is made up of four villages—Sherburn, Sherburn Hill, Shadforth and Ludworth—and, as in many such situations, although the school was not too far away, it was far enough to mean that the second Messy Church had a different core of people coming. This time, families were specifically encouraged to come along, and the same group of women worked together to open their doors to more people, once a month, with around 30 attending.

The vicar asked me if I would be able to meet with the team again, to evaluate and do some planning for the next term, and she said that they had an idea they wanted to share with me. One spring morning, I went along to the church in the village and sat round the table with the volunteers while we chatted about the things we were learning from the two Messy Churches they were running. We worked through some of the points raised, and planned and plotted what was next on the agenda for the coming months. Then came the 'idea'. There was another school, just down the road in Ludworth, a very deprived area. This village had once had a small wooden church, but it had been demolished approximately 40 years before. The clergy who had lived there previously had not been welcomed, and no clergy lived in the village any more. Eileen had felt for some time that there must be something she could do, something that was non-threatening, something that came from the church but was for that village, with all its problems. She had seen just how effective Messy Church had been in the Sherburn Hill school and indeed in her own church building, and she was determined to be a witness in the Ludworth school. She was planning Messy Church 3.

Eileen knew it wouldn't be easy and that the road was rocky, but she also knew that we serve a big God who loves all his children, wherever they may be, and blesses the work of those who serve him. She had decided to go and see the headteacher and talk about how the church and the school could work together more. God was already at work, and the headteacher welcomed the idea.

With the first hurdle cleared, next came the planning, funding, budget and helpers—the list went on. The group had already accessed all the available funds and grants from the diocese, and their Messy Churches were not generating any income to keep them going, which made some of the practicalities more difficult, but the joy in the faces of those women as we sat round the table is something I often think about. They were thrilled that the school had said 'yes', and what really spoke to me was that in their twilight years, this group was making such a difference not only in their own village but in the next village too, and that Messy Church had offered them a way of doing it.

The vicar walked me to my car and said that she had something to tell me. Not wanting to embarrass the team from Sherburn, she shared with me privately how they had decided to raise the money to start Messy Church 3. They had gathered all their old pieces of gold jewellery, as well as some from friends and family, and had sold it to one of the shops in town that buys gold and silver. They had raised £200, which was enough to get them started. As Eileen told me what they had done, I was fit to burst. The fact that this group was so committed, so dedicated, so devoted to what they were doing that they were willing to sell off their gold jewellery to bring Messy Church to a group of children in a small village school is one of the most inspiring stories I have ever been told. I know that as they have honoured God in setting up these Messy Churches and enabling the work to begin in a new place, God will honour them.

When I tell this story to others, I call the Sherburn team our 'Messy angels'. Their love for children and their passion for sharing the gospel with them through Messy Church inspires me to keep going when things get tough. I hope it will inspire you too.

✤

11

Some frameworks to explore Messy Church and discipleship

Bob Hopkins

Bob Hopkins and his wife Mary lead Anglican Church Planting Initiatives, a small team working in the UK and Europe. For eight years until 2005, they were also on the leadership team of St Thomas Sheffield, where they continue to serve. Bob and Mary have a wide ministry of consultation and training. Since 2005, they have been on the Archbishops' Fresh Expressions team and are partnering with CMS for a mission movement.

Our colleague Mike Breen often says, 'If you focus on making church, you won't necessarily end up with disciples, whereas if you focus on making disciples of Jesus, you are bound to end up with church.' The observation has also been made that Jesus said, 'I will build my church' (Matthew 16:18) but commissioned us to 'go and make disciples' (28:19). So the focus of this chapter explores Messy Church as church through seeking to understand discipleship better.

I start with one of Lucy Moore's statements in the Messy Church segment of the first Fresh Expressions DVD, made in 2005. In recognising the challenge of whether 'Messy Church' was fully church, she said:

I don't see it as a stepping stone into Sunday services, because I think that for a lot of people Sunday isn't an easy day to get to church on. To have something once a month which is always there is very important, and also, if it is not a valid service in its own right, then it is not worth doing. We do struggle with the fact that we get a lot of people here who are at different stages of faith development. Obviously in ten minutes you can't give a fully worked-out biblical exposition which is going to challenge people and take them a lot further, as you would like to, in their discipleship. But like a Sunday congregation, you're trying to take everybody on from where they're at so their faith journey progresses.

This statement gives away our tendency in the Western church to equate discipleship with communicating information and the sermon as its chief vehicle. I know that Lucy's and the Messy Church team's thinking on discipleship has always been wider than that, and has become ever wider as they have wrestled with this challenge. However, it forms an interesting starting point for the reflections that I explore, through two lenses. Firstly, I show how some biblical and holistic perspectives on discipleship enable us to see that more discipleship may be happening in Messy Church than we might at first think. This is encouraging, but then I take a second lens to explore how we could make more of these discipleship elements. How can we see ways in which much deeper discipleship could happen as Messy Churches become more intentional, and how can we consciously develop these aspects further and consider adding others?

At the outset, we should note that there are two significant limitations already mentioned in the literature. The first limiting factor is that Messy Church is an event and usually happens only monthly. The second is the scarcity of time that the team and volunteers are able to give, above and beyond the already demanding event. Many of them, although Messy Church is a high priority, do not see it as their church (which is a serious issue in itself), so it competes for limited spare time with their other church involvement. This, in turn, can also be seen as restricting either of the two broad options that I identified to enrich nurture and discipleship in Messy Church in my October 2011 web paper on this subject.[107]

The first option is to add to discipleship within the Messy Church event. I see this being done either by increasing Messy Church's frequency or by enriching the content of some of the events, while preserving the ethos and respecting the expectations and trust of those invited. The second option is to complement the Messy Church events with other activities and groups. This has the advantage that only those participants who are ready to go deeper will respond and it is not imposed on the rest. I explore here how these extra elements can be resourced either by the existing team or the invitees themselves, or through partnerships with other parts of the wider church, embodying mixed-economy thinking.

The way that I want to take the two lenses is to use a number of frameworks or analytical tools to seek a wider and deeper understanding of discipleship and church as they are happening and could perhaps happen more in Messy Church. Most of these frameworks or tools can be represented with diagrams or shapes. I offer four such frameworks and their shapes. I am aware that this is only one way of thinking, but in a visual culture it can be helpful. I also recognise that the categorisation implicit in these frameworks is over-simplistic and that reality is more complex, with overlaps and fuzzy edges—in fact, much more 'messy' and more like a spectrum. But, with this proviso, I hope they prove helpful.

Some of these frameworks and diagrams are explored in greater depth in the literature cited, but relating them to what is happening and could happen in Messy Church may be new. To try to understand the insights of the frameworks, I first summarise each one, keeping Messy Church in mind behind the ideas and analysis. Readers may make other connections to their Messy Church event, its key constituents and its DNA or foundational values. I show, too, how they expand our view of Messy Church.

The structure of culture and Kwast's visualisation of its interrelated areas

The first framework is of culture itself. Since we are in a missionary situation in Britain, we should learn from good mission practice and start with an analysis of culture to see how Messy Church is responding.

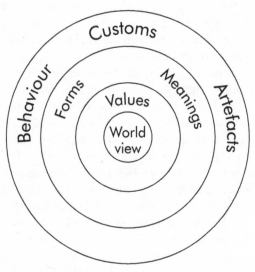

Figure 1. Culture and the 'Onion Rings' model of Lloyd Kwast[108]

While Kwast himself asserts that culture is complex, multifaceted and not neatly or uniformly organised, nonetheless I find his framework helpful. It proposes a measure of order and structure, like 'onion rings'. What we experience and observe in everyday life is the outer ring of behaviour, customs and artefacts. The way these observable aspects are understood is based on the relationship between forms and meanings. Every culture has its conventions and traditions about how these are understood. At the most evident level, language itself is a form (sounds) to which we attribute agreed meanings. Here we note that while the idea and concepts of Messy Church are travelling well to Germany, the word 'messy' itself does not translate. German has no equivalent word, and the best they came up with in the first project was 'Kaos Kirche', which sounded alarming, entertaining and misleading.

This difficulty illustrates the limitations of our symbols and words, but it also led to an example of the potential within contextualisation that a later German mission initiative has produced. They have built on the commonly known children's chocolate Kinder Surprise and named their new church 'Surprise Kirche', which introduces a subtle but theologically apt meaning in translating Messy Church. It also underlies my contention that, as we unwrap Messy Church, we discover more than we expected.

Underlying outward behaviour and the meanings we put upon it are a culture's values—what is seen as bad, good, better and best. Figure 1 should be used to emphasise that any value system flows in turn from the culture's core world view.

Weak and often misguided mission engagement happens when the missionary focuses on the outer layer, the superficial things that strike us first; missional best practice is to find ways for the gospel to engage and challenge as close to the centre (the world view) as possible. Ideally, good practice connects to the world view, where the gospel can bring transformation. This will then work outwards in a way that is authentic to that culture, to the values, forms and meanings, which in turn affect behaviour.

Traditionally, the assumption might be that such engagement with world view and values would be addressed with argument, story and Christian conceptual truth—an approach to the mind. However, the really interesting thing emerges when we relate the approach of Messy Church to our Western culture, a culture that is perhaps uniquely resistant to arguments of objective truth. Part of the postmodern world view is that all truth is relative and based on individual choice. So Messy Church's short engagement with a Christian message during the celebration element—which has been described by some as 'understated' and 'light'—may be seen as subtle wisdom and rather strategic. Even more notable is the realisation that the way Messy Church most strongly engages with world views and values is precisely through modelling patterns of behaviour and experience which themselves express counter-cultural values. Again, this seems like creative wisdom for our culture, which values experience over ideas.

In a culture that is shaped by a world view of individualisation, Messy Church models community and being together in all its elements, as George Lings has observed.[109] (This model is perhaps weakest in the celebration/service element.) In a culture shaped by a core of consumerism, Messy Church models participation and co-production. In a culture with a world view based on a market economy, whose values primarily work financially and materially, Messy Church invites us into a world where spiritual and social capital rightly return to prime place.

The same approach can be seen in the mission and ministry of Jesus. His is a ministry consistently focused on the kingdom—in other words, a presentation of his alternative world view. In a culture unlike ours, an oral culture that was very open to the truth, he expressed his alternative kingdom through both story and principles. But Jesus also modelled this counter-cultural realm and its associated values in his works of compassion, his community of followers and his embracing of servanthood and worldly powerlessness. The crowds, the Twelve and the 72 were all given a different experience by being around Jesus and observing and living his values.

As well as affirming the culturally sensitive discipleship that is already working out in Messy Church, this framework also provides understanding of and pointers to the ways in which that discipleship may be further enhanced. The analysis provides wider potential to extend the processes of discipleship beyond what may be possible in a once-a-month, event-centred Messy Church.

Within a culture that values experience over objective truth, there are opportunities to add other activities outside the event, such as baby massage and prayer, all-age family prayer workshops, or training and resourcing for family rituals and traditions. Then, in a culture that loves stories almost as much as in Jesus' day, an idea would be to equip families in the art and skills of storytelling with biblical resources such as those found from www.storyrunners.org.

This framework for looking at the nature of culture also helps us to explore how Messy Church may be adapted to different cultures within Western society. It points to the question of how Messy Church might be adapted in working-class contexts. Would the creative element draw more on karaoke than crafts? What should it look like among the marginalised?

Perhaps some pointers here could be found in the 'No Limits' missional community from St George's, Deal, which predominantly engages disabled people. Although it does not use the Messy Church label, it is all-age and expresses all the four elements and all the Messy Church values. It is still about creating together and playing together, but fits with the predominant disabled culture. These elements don't look like the Fresh Expressions DVD clip of Messy Church. The driving aim of the group is for the able and mostly disabled, of all ages, to learn together like Jesus, live and eat together like Jesus, and respond together to God's grace like Jesus. All these aspects work with greatly reduced emphasis on the verbal and conceptual and an increase in participation, facilitation and bodily expression. It is assuredly more 'messy' than most gatherings that bear the name, but also puts the question that some are raising (what is 'pure' Messy Church?) into a whole new perspective.

Three classic processes of learning

The root meaning of the word 'disciple' is 'learner', so, to grasp what is involved in discipleship, we need to understand how learning works. From a 1990 presentation by Ted Ward, Professor of Education at Michigan State University, we came to understand that there are three classic processes of learning: socialisation, formal and non-formal. All three are extremely important for human development, but each works differently and each has different strengths. Jesus made use of all three processes among his learning community of disciples. Professor Ward explained that the three can be related to one another in accordance with the triangle shown in Figure 2. In this triangle, each process can be paired with another that shares a key defining characteristic: socialisation and formal are both traditional, socialisation and non-formal are both practical, and formal and non-formal are both intentional. For each process, then, there is an opposite characteristic, shared by the other two, that it does not display: socialisation's opposite characteristic is 'intentional', non-formal's opposite characteristic is 'traditional' and formal's opposite characteristic is 'practical'.[110]

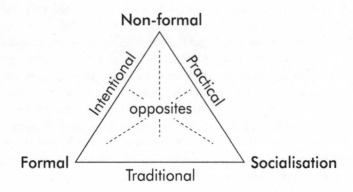

Figure 2. Three processes of learning

Formal learning

This is the learning process that most readily comes to mind for most people. It is typified by the *traditional* learning in schools and colleges, and by a church's sermon series or Christian 'course'. The diagram shows us that one of the two defining characteristics of formal learning is that we *intentionally* engage in it. Typically, we study a subject, and it tends to be 'ladder based'—building from one level to the next level, which depends on the foundational level. It is contrasted with the other two learning processes as being not primarily rooted in practice or practically orientated. There may be practical exercises, but the learning is in a dedicated context. Hence, its character is academic and its main objectives are developing theoretical understanding and enhancing the mind.

Although we do not have records of Jesus employing this learning process in a classic way, his Sermons on the Mount (Matthew 5—7) and the Plain (Luke 6) and his final-week discourses (John 14—17) are, to some extent, in this category. However, it could be argued that their content is mainly moral and about spiritual disciplines, not theoretical theology. In many ways, Jesus built upon the foundations of formal learning in the synagogues.

Socialisation learning

As the name implies, this type of learning happens naturally and spontaneously in the social context of relationships. Hence, by contrast to formal learning, it is *unintentional*. This illustrates that human beings are natural learners. Put us with others and we learn from them and from the interactions between us.

The way we learn languages provides an excellent insight into these first two processes. In growing up, I first learnt English by socialisation. It was entirely *practical*, as each word, phrase and sentence was picked up to help me express myself and make sense of what others were saying. It was also unintentional in that I didn't enrol in a course—there was no systematic plan. Rather, I was immersed in it. By contrast, my formal learning of English at school taught me the structure and science of the language, as I learnt nouns and verbs first, parts of speech and tenses next, and so on. The disciples of Jesus entered a three-year process of socialisation learning as they were invited to 'follow me' (Mark 1:17). They asked, 'Where are you staying?' and received the reply, 'Come and see' (John 1:38–39). Each was chosen 'that they might be with him' (Mark 3:14, NIV). It wasn't a matter of studying forgiveness and conflict resolution this week, prayer and miracles next and servant leadership after that. Theirs was the living laboratory of faith and hope, all expressed through love.

Non-formal learning

The last of the three processes of learning was apparently the last to be identified, described and related to the other two in this framework. Lacking a more descriptive title, the educators called it 'non-formal learning', and the best example is the age-old practice of apprenticeship. It is the way in which master craftspeople passed on their skills, and the way that vocations such as nursing were best learnt.

Using the diagnostic features of Professor Ward's triangle, we see that, like formal learning, it is *intentional*: a carpenter's apprentice enrols with the master and dedicates time to developing the knowledge and skills involved in the trade. It also shares a distinguishing characteristic with socialisation, in that the learning is essentially acquired within a *practical* context: for example, tables, chairs and drawers are made, and measuring, sawing and planing actions are performed.

Once again, we see Jesus involving his followers as apprentices in everyday practical elements of his ministry. We see them instructed ('you give them something to eat', Luke 9:13), directed ('sent... ahead of him to every town', 10:1) and repeatedly given feedback ('you of little faith', Matthew 14:31; 16:8). In turn they repeatedly ask questions, such as 'Why couldn't we heal him?' and 'How should we pray?'

The last defining characteristic in the framework that Professor Ward explained was shared by formal and socialisation learning, and appears along the bottom of the triangle. The word he used was *traditional*, explaining that what is learnt in the social context of the home, village or tribe reinforces traditional patterns and world views. While formal learning processes also tend to reinforce the understandings and values of those institutions, Professor Ward asserted that non-formal processes open up the most potential for change, innovation and new understandings. Even within predominantly formal learning institutions, such as universities, it is in the non-formal relationship of professor to research assistant that innovation usually arises. It may be that someone even has to leave that institution to explore alternative, otherwise rejected, hypotheses.

Here again it is significant that the Gospels show us Jesus working with the disciples in non-formal learning settings as he seeks to bring his radically reinterpreted vision of the meaning of the kingdom of God—nothing less than repentance, *metanoia*, a change of thinking, values and world view.

Characteristic fruits of learning

Before applying this framework to Messy Church, I offer the suggestion that, while each of the three processes delivers complex outcomes with a degree of overlap, it seems to me that the most characteristic fruit of each type of learning is as follows: formal brings understanding, socialisation forms values, and non-formal develops skills. I conclude that socialisation learning requires the longest period of time, because it is unintentional and there is less opportunity to make the learning explicit, as so much is absorbed intuitively. Note that formal learning is facilitated primarily by instruction, whereas socialisation learning occurs mostly through observation with support from execution and instruction. Non-formal learning is enabled primarily by execution with support from observation and instruction.

As I have reflected on the insights of the three processes of learning as they relate to our mission and discipleship and those of Jesus, it seems to me that once a new paradigm has been discovered, the most effective way to propagate such transformation of world view and values is to employ all three processes—as Jesus did. To use only one or two will disproportionately limit the outcome. So the new paradigm needs a community living it, into which others can be invited who will naturally and unintentionally learn through the lived values, practices and lifestyles being modelled in the practical activities together, by socialisation. This process will be powerfully augmented if those who are experienced in areas that exemplify and apply the new paradigm proactively form a team, with one, two or more assistants acting as apprentices, to deliver together their shared practices and aims. Most powerful of all will be if out of these two elements comes the kind of school that develops ways to propagate the understanding of the new paradigm intentionally.[111]

How does this relate to Messy Church?

Firstly, we can use the framework's insights to help us recognise more fully the discipleship elements of church that are already present in Messy Church events. As an overall conclusion, I think that Messy Church is at its strongest in socialisation learning. I have already referred to George Lings' comments that almost all the elements of the events are done together—the coming, being, making, eating and celebrating. I would assess the formal learning as probably the weakest, but note that this may partly reflect a conscious move away from a perceived over-emphasis in traditional church on the long presentational sermon; it may also reflect the philosophy that all-age instruction is best done in such a way that the oldest can learn at the same time as the youngest.

We have to take more than a superficial look to appreciate the extent of non-formal learning in the Messy Church event. First, at a general level, the events are highly intentional as well as practical. Furthermore, there is a measure of apprenticeship that happens with those invited to the events. There is intentional helping of parents to make with and play with their children, as well as passing on the experience and skills of eating together as family. But a really important revelation comes when we recognise that discipleship is not just happening with those who have been invited, but also with the team and the volunteers. Messy Church is strong on non-formal learning as the team and volunteers are apprenticed in planning, preparing and serving, as well as modelling for those invited.

This furthers our thinking about apprenticeship as we continue our quest to expand an understanding of the possibilities of discipleship through these three learning processes. In 2006, when Lucy Moore was sharing with me and my wife, Mary, the challenge of extending discipleship in Messy Church, we added insights that we had gained from a church in Denmark. The Danish church had concluded that the prevailing Western church trend, in which local churches assumed the role and responsibility of discipling the children of church families, was suspect. Rather, they believed that the biblical responsibility for discipling the next generation was primarily that of the family, based on mentoring and apprenticeship by the older for the younger in the home.

As a church, they had therefore shifted the emphasis to providing simple resources to support families doing discipleship in the home. This seems to provide the potential to combine non-formal learning with socialisation learning and does not depend for its delivery on teams and volunteers. There is the matter of providing the resources, but here again the team could look to other local churches or the wider church for support. Using the focus of socialisation can sharpen the issues of discipleship and learning. However, because socialisation learning happens best in spontaneous interaction in family and village, it takes the most time and fits the least well with an occasional event.

Developing socialisation

Thinking through these ideas leads me to believe that there is a progression from an event to a process, to gaining a quality of community, to becoming a place of belonging and a way of life. Jesus' discipleship, which led to his ecclesial community, followed this progression. Part of the journey is a move from attendee to participant to contributor to member. To illustrate this, we could see these progressions as follows:

- At the corporate level: Event — Process — Community — Place of belonging/way of life
- At the individual level: Attendee — Participant — Contributor — Member

Here I raise a loose comparison with, and warning from, Willow Creek Church and the seeker-sensitive approach. This movement came to the UK in the 1990s and gained a significant following, but is now, in most cases, only a memory or an occasional outreach event to enrich inherited church. The similarities to Messy Church are that, as church, Willow Creek was event-centred. It was a resource- and energy-demanding event, although the Messy Church elements are very different, including a meal, craft and play as well as celebration/service. The crucial difference is that Messy Church majors on involvement rather than presentation and spectating, as in Willow Creek. Nonetheless, there must be a warning here that unless the journey from event to community and a way of life can be navigated, sustainability will be a bigger issue than the theoretical question of to what extent an event can be church.

A couple of diagrams may help to develop these principles. First, the matrix in Figure 3 illustrates that increasing the frequency of pre-planned events can develop them into a process with correspondingly increased potential socialisation and other learning. But it is the spontaneous relational elements that create the quality of community. I suggest that Messy Church moves remarkably far in this direction for a monthly gathering, but Messy Church's greatest limitation would seem to be in its difficulties in becoming a place of belonging and a way of life. These understandings also point to how Messy Church could extend itself and overcome the two limitations of frequency and demands noted at the beginning of the chapter.

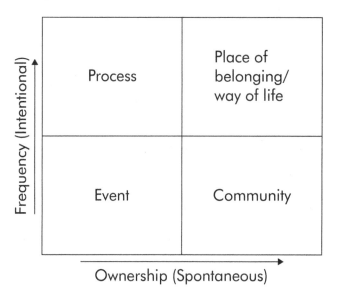

Figure 3. Matrix of developing socialisation

Differentiating attendance and discipleship

The graph in Figure 4 illustrates the fact that Messy Church events, by their nature, are proving highly effective in quickly attracting significant numbers of de-churched and non-churched families. However, they do reach a ceiling in attendance due both to the high level of commitment and resourcing required to deliver these excellent events and to the loss of the essential qualities that occurs above the ceiling. Some key Messy Church qualities that come under threat as numbers exceed this ceiling include the ability to know everyone easily, to fit all together within convenient local premises, and to be less presentational and more participative—not to mention health and safety considerations. By contrast, discipleship learning increases in a slower way and over a longer timescale. Socialisation and non-formal learning take time, and this is limited by monthly gatherings.

Figure 4. Graph of two types of growth

How are these differently paced processes to be worked with?

Lucy Moore commented in 2005 on two constraining factors. Those attending Messy Church are at very different places on their faith journey, and there is a limit to what can be achieved with ten minutes of formal input. On the first count, if all or most of discipleship is to happen within the Messy Church event, then everyone will have to move at the pace of the slowest. If we respond to the few who happen to be ready and hungry for more, we will violate the trust of others who have not signed up for more and have not been led to expect it.

Firstly, if more frequent Messy Church events are to be considered, to move from 'event' towards 'process', inviting the non-churched into the teams would immediately relieve the volunteer constraints. I suggest that they could be given responsibility in all areas of Messy Church. Being part of the planning, and helping to develop the 'spiritual' bits, could be the best apprenticeship learning.

Secondly, even greater strides can be made in moving to 'community', and even a 'place of belonging', if the Messy Church events are complemented by other lighter-weight events and programmes and by more spontaneous engagement of invitees, team and volunteers at other times. If the community of Messy Church is to be further built to be a 'way of life', there should be invitations to one another's homes for meals and social gatherings. Members can take part in so many things outside Messy Church events, with Christians and not-yet-Christians together, family outings and all. Maybe precisely because socialisation learning happens unintentionally, it is implicitly expected to happen most outside the events. If so, it may need to become an explicit expectation of Messy Church that it is more than an event. Is it reasonable to suggest that, if Messy Church is truly to express church, then those involved will do all sorts of everyday things outside of the event together? This could happen in various unplanned combinations and with no separation between leaders and the rest, or between team and attendees.

Moving further, other events and programmes can also be added without needing to be resourced by the Messy Church team or volunteers. They could be run by people from any other church in the area, or by the non-churched where appropriate. Examples could be baby massage and prayer, or an invitation to be part of social ministries in the area such as Besom projects, soup kitchens and support of the marginalised. Such programmes can often be all-age, to remain in harmony with Messy Church values, with children in their schools doing sponsored events to raise money, or collecting clothes and sleeping bags that the family can deliver to those in need. These activities develop the non-formal and socialisation elements and, as Ann Morisy has observed, by taking the non-churched middle classes outside their comfort zone to be alongside those with spiritual resources they may have discounted, this may be one way to open them to the gospel. In her terms, this is the vocational or invitational domain.[112]

Furthermore, emphasising the place of socialisation in learning how to convey conceptual gospel truth gives the relational strength of Messy Church a lot of scope for one-to-one conversations. Rather than relying on presentational mode, there will be plenty of unplanned opportunities to give the reason for our hope in Jesus in spontaneous conversations or informal group discussions.

Focusing back on non-formal learning that is intentional and practically based, Messy Church events provide many opportunities to apprentice the attendees alongside the core team and volunteers. They may be apprenticed to the setting-up and practical team, the cooking team or the craft and games team, as well as the team running the service. They could also be apprenticed outside the Messy Church events in many other family-oriented activities, particularly those outside their experience and comfort zones.

Coming back to the most familiar process of formal learning, based on instruction, I recognise the Messy Church value of 'all-age' and endorse the principle that adults, teens and children can learn together when the teaching is done well. However, as formal learning in Messy Church is accessible to the youngest, there will inevitably be aspects of more complex understanding or mature experience that adults will miss. A partial response can be to have parts of the formal learning in the Messy Church service processed in different age groups, not sending the children out. Some Messy Churches enhance the monthly event by offering a separate 'Messy plus' for those who are older.

In response to today's culture, which is cautious about, if not resistant to, presentation of objective truth, Messy Church's formal learning is strong on story and applied truth. Extending the formal learning outside the Messy Church event can involve courses. Again, obvious examples, such as parenting courses, do not have to depend on overstretched teams and volunteers. But creative imaginations should come up with many ideas of how all-age family life in God's kingdom can be further supported. Examples could include courses in family prayer, family rituals and traditions, conflict resolution and forgiveness in families, and the rhythms of work, rest and recreation in families. Once more, drawing expertise from others, Christian and not-yet-Christian, outside the Messy Church community, prevents problems associated with limited time and resources.

Drawing the threads together

Throughout this chapter I have emphasised that Christian disciple-ship is not a one-way process, which is done by the team and volunteers to the rest. Jesus made this clear in commissioning his disciples to go and make other disciples in the context of genuine relationships of receiving and giving (Matthew 10:7–13; Luke 10:5–9). In fact, the way the gospel is best communicated is reflexively; we are not meant to keep it to ourselves.

This chapter has looked at where discipleship and church are already happening in Messy Church and how they can be enhanced. It has touched on four frameworks to further understanding of human being, learning and doing.

I end with a connection to another familiar fourfold classifica-tion, one that does not always operate in the same order. Firstly, take *belonging* or being part of community. To gain the fullest measure of it, I explored how the Messy Church team and volunteers participate in forming community but also opening up the part that invitees can play. Secondly, there is *believing*, dealing with understanding and conceptual truth. Here again, if we are to see discipleship and church grow most effectively, we should imagine how Christians can all participate in imparting and receiving. Thirdly, in connection with *behaving* there is action and creativity. I have tried to open up how everyone in the Messy Church enterprise and beyond can be involved as doers as well as 'done to'. Fourthly, some speak of *blessing*. Here too I sought to expand the possibilities in Messy Church with additional opportunities for spiritual experience, teasing out how, in this, it is 'more blessed to give than to receive' (Acts 20:35). Messy Church does offer possibilities for both Christians and not-yet-Christians to discover ways of moving deeper into all four aspects. Such are some of the frameworks available to understand its contribution better.

✢

12

Growing, maturing, ripening: what might an older Messy Church look like?

Paul Moore

Paul Moore is Vicar of St Wilfrid's Church, Cowplain, an Anglican church near Portsmouth. He is married to Lucy Moore and is a member of the team that started the first Messy Church in 2004. Paul is also a Vocations Adviser for Portsmouth Diocese with a particular brief for pioneer ministry. He is the author of Making Disciples in Messy Church *(BRF, 2013).*

Many years ago, I was involved in a mission week in Charleston, South Carolina. On our afternoon off, one of our hosts kindly gave our small team a tour of the sights. Having been shown many historic buildings and impressive vistas, we were fast reaching that stage of exhaustion at which Brits abroad crave tea and cake. Our guide gleefully set off down a narrow alleyway, saying, 'Now you *must* see this!' We dutifully followed, and there at the end of the alley was… a red brick wall. We did our best to make politely enthusiastic noises, but we were all thinking the same thing: you see brick walls like this in every town and village in England. 'This is the oldest remaining part of Charleston,' our guide announced proudly. As we respectfully contemplated this 200-year-old section of wall, we suddenly became aware of the vast difference between the US and the UK in the way we perceive time and history.

Nearly 30 years later, I am still involved in mission as the Vicar of St Wilfrid's, Cowplain, a Church of England parish in a suburban area of Hampshire just north of Portsmouth. Here, the first and therefore the oldest Messy Church is approaching its tenth birthday. By any measure, that is not very old, I know; but, in the still relatively new world of fresh expressions of Church, a decade is perhaps long enough for it to be instructive to look back at our history, see how we have changed and developed, note what we have learned, identify some of the questions for which we are still finding answers, and try to have an ear for what the Spirit is saying to the churches, be they of the messy or tidier kind.

So I begin with our experience, describing some of the ways in which our Messy Church has developed and the issues that have come up during this first decade. I then offer some theological reflection on what we mean by growth and maturation in a church context, and what characteristics we might expect to see in an older Messy Church.

Messy Church at ten years old

If you were to visit our Messy Church, which meets on a Thursday afternoon once a month, perhaps, like Charleston's brick wall, it might not seem very different from the many Messy Churches that are springing up in many places around the world. Families are gathering to explore a Bible story or theme through creative activities, then celebrating and eating together.

Essentially we still have the same vision and aim as when we started: to be an all-age expression of Church for those who are not used to going to church (not a bridge into Sunday church), and to be a Christ-centred community where adults and children can encounter Jesus and grow in faith. Our sessions still have the familiar shape of welcome, craft, celebration, then meal. We have the same underlying core values, or DNA, that came into clearer focus during the early years: Christ-centredness, hospitality, creativity, celebration and all-age. With hindsight, perhaps what we really mean by 'all-age' could be better expressed as 'inclusivity'—church for 'all sorts and conditions of men', to echo the vocabulary of the Book of Common Prayer.[113]

So how has our Messy Church developed and changed over these ten years? Firstly, we are more experienced and intentional. We have a better grasp of what we are doing, and we are getting better at it. We still have much the same core leadership team of three or four people who meet each month to plan the craft activities, celebration and meal. They are used to working together quickly and efficiently and have enough experience to know what works well—including things like the need to provide crafts that appeal to dads and boys as well as girls and mums. Roughly half of the helper team of 20 adults and teenagers, who lead the crafts, has changed over ten years, but overall they are more experienced and two-thirds of them have taken part in some training, using *Messy Church: The DVD*. Some of the team have had the exciting experience of running Messy Church sessions with members of other teams from around the country at the Greenbelt festival and elsewhere. Our team are more switched on to what we are trying to do, and more confident in making people feel welcome, chatting with children and adults about the link between the crafts and the Bible theme.

Secondly, we expect God to be working in every part of the session. We want to give people a positive experience of Christian community, and all four parts of the session contribute to this. God is at work through them all, and the celebration is not seen as the only spiritual bit or 'teaching slot'. We have learnt that 'God moments' can happen at any time. For example, in the middle of the noise and chaos of our craft activity, a mother began to open up about the tough time she was having at home, and declared, 'This church is an oasis.' In another craft session on the fruit of the Spirit, people were invited to choose a fruit to have painted on their hand. One boy, who is usually rather quiet and withdrawn, asked for 'the sausage of joy' to be painted on his hand, and went round laughing and showing it to everyone, utterly transformed. We have learnt to look out for these moments when we witness the Holy Spirit at work in people's lives; we try to be ready to make the most of these often brief opportunities to encourage people to respond in faith, perhaps sharing something about our own faith, how prayer helps us in daily life or an aspect of the gospel.

Thirdly, we know being all-age works. Another lesson we have learned is that church with all ages together is not only possible but brings blessing for all, from lonely widows in their 90s to babies in nappies. Of course, it is very different from traditional or inherited church, and we have found that there is much more to being church than just coming together for an hour's corporate worship. George Lings' reflections on what we can learn from the seven sacred spaces of the monastic tradition have helped us to appreciate why the different kinds of spaces we provide at Messy Church for meeting, eating, creativity and worship are vital for developing Christian community.[114]

Fourthly, we have seen more people engage in mission. Potentially one of the most significant byproducts of Messy Church for the wider church in the longer term may be that large numbers of lay people are being released into ministry that is evangelistic in intent, many for the first time, through being asked to help out with a form of church that is mission-focused, outward-looking and not just a haven for the faithful. Team members have grown in their faith and in their confidence to listen and witness to their faith in words and actions; and, most importantly, they have grown in love for those who come along and in the desire for them to know Jesus.

Fifthly, Messy Church has also proved to be a safe place for people to step out in leadership for the first time. Over the last two years, we have deliberately aimed to give more people experience of leading—for example, by bringing a teenager on to the core planning team, using a wider variety of people to lead parts of the celebration and encouraging young instrumentalists to lead the music. It is impossible to run a Messy Church without good teamwork, so we have to learn to work together and how to forgive each other, valuing our unity in diversity as the body of Christ. With all the organising and clearing up to do, there are plenty of small tasks for adults and children to help with and everyone can feel that they are contributing.

Finally, more non-churched families are coming. Although our numbers have remained roughly the same (about 80 children and adults, of whom 24 might be helpers and kitchen team), over the last two years we have seen more families coming along who have no previous church link. Messy Church has been recommended to them by friends. We have no need to advertise, other than to make people aware of the dates. On baptism visits to families in the community, I find that parents have already heard about Messy Church and are keen to come along.

To sum up, Messy Church feels as well established and sustainable as any of our more traditional congregations, and many who come, young and old, have a strong feeling of loyalty, ownership and belonging. Some families have stuck with us from the very beginning, and lasting relationships have been forged. Over ten years we have seen the children grow from tottering toddlers to towering teenagers. What, then, have been some of the main issues for us during this time?

Facing up to issues

Do families grow out of Messy Church?

With any event that focuses specifically on families, there is the likelihood that, as children grow up, they will lose interest in activities that suited them when they were younger, and the family will move on to new things. No doubt, theme parks such as Disneyland spend vast amounts of time and money trying to ensure that they provide rides and facilities that appeal to all the ages and generations. For our Messy Church, this does not seem to have been a major problem, even when children move up to secondary school. As long as the teenagers' friends continue to come, they will too, particularly as Messy Church provides a place for them to meet up regularly with friends who now attend different schools.

I spoke to one of our older teenagers who has been a member of our Messy Church from the beginning. She now sees Messy Church as a place where she serves rather than receives. She is on the helpers' team and usually leads one of the crafts with a friend. She says that she really enjoys seeing the smaller children having a good time just as she did at their age. She agrees that while Messy Church works well for younger teens, it can be harder for those who are 16 plus, especially as some of the younger children often like to latch on to older teenagers and follow them around for the whole session. More positively, she points out that Messy Church provides a place where teenagers can sit and eat with their friends and not have to hang out with their little brother or sister. Teenagers can find space to be themselves within an all-age community.

For many years, the church has attempted to hang on to teenagers by giving them something to do, such as serving at Holy Communion or helping to lead the Sunday school. I remember doing both of these when I was a teenager. Is Messy Church simply using the same rather desperate and unimaginative strategy? Not necessarily, if we give teenagers real responsibility, take their ideas seriously, treat them as full members of the team and encourage, train and support them. At a national level, Messy Church has addressed this issue by hosting 'Young Leaders' days in 2012, with the aim of listening to teenagers' views and encouraging their input.

For us, the point at which families stop coming may be later on, when the teenagers leave home for higher education or a job. For parents to continue coming in such circumstances, they will need to have developed strong friendships with other adults in the church and feel that Messy Church is their spiritual home, where they have a meaningful part to play.

Over ten years, of course, we have seen some families attend for a while and then drift away. Some lose interest; others move out of the area. We have also heard of families who have looked out for a Messy Church near their new home. Often the contact is broken when parents change their working hours or children have sports or other new commitments, making it no longer possible for them to come. Following people up has proved a daunting task when our Messy Church is just one of five congregations requiring pastoral oversight. It really requires a dedicated person or team. Yet all these changes and setbacks happen in parish churches too.

Are we making disciples?

This question is one that people often raise as they consider the pros and cons of starting a Messy Church. The short answer is, yes. Messy Churches in many places have seen new believers baptised and growing as disciples. I have argued elsewhere that Messy Church can be a disciple-making community, but there is a need to remember that many of the unchurched families we are welcoming are starting out from 'a distant country' (Luke 15:13), and their journey to faith may take several years.[115] Discipleship in our Messy Church is very much a work in progress. In Jesus' ministry, people were attracted to him and followed him in the crowd, hearing his puzzling parables about the kingdom of God, observing and experiencing the miraculous signs he did, and, as a result, some from the crowd became disciples. We have observed people gradually becoming more open to faith: a mum taking a moment to pray quietly in the church or children eager to share things for which they want to pray or thank God. As leaders, we need to be prepared for the long haul.

Is once a month enough?

Having many meetings is not necessarily a sign of a mature church. More important in a disciple-making community is the quality of relationships, of love and trust, creating a safe environment where we can learn together how to live out our faith in daily life. It is obviously harder to develop these relationships if we meet only once a month. Doing Messy Church every week would be too demanding for our team, but there are places where it is being done. Some Messy Churches have introduced less elaborate opportunities for families to come together informally during the month, and others have used optional courses such as Journeys, Christianity Explored and Alpha.

In our context, although people are very committed to coming once a month, they are reluctant to come more often—which is, of course, equally true of many who consider themselves to be regular Sunday church attenders. This being the case, we are experimenting with ways of keeping in touch through social networking, developing a Messy Church page on Facebook. More radically, one of our Sunday church families is considering making Messy Church their main commitment and Sunday church an occasional extra, with the intention that they can then focus on befriending and informally mentoring one or two of our unchurched families. From this they might grow a small all-age home group that meets between the monthly sessions to explore aspects of faith and following Jesus. There is a gap in the market for all-age material suitable for enquirers and discipleship courses that might develop alongside a monthly Messy Church.

Over our ten years, it feels as if a lot of seed has been scattered on different types of soil. There have been disappointments, when the seed has not germinated, or has sprouted but failed to take root, or has been choked by the brambles of busy lives. There have also been encouraging signs of green shoots growing, maturing and ripening, although it is still too early to say how big the harvest may be.

Measures of maturity

How should we assess the maturity of a church? What is the measure of maturity? Do we count the numbers of converts, examine the levels of giving, measure the hours of prayer or look for the fruit of the Spirit?

In the New Testament, the obvious place to look for an answer is Ephesians 4, where the process by which Christ intends his church to develop to maturity is described. The ascended Christ gives grace to each believer so that, as his appointed apostles, prophets, evangelists and pastor-teachers equip God's holy people to do their bit of service for building up the body in love, so 'all of us come to the unity of the faith and of the knowledge of the Son of God, to maturity, to the measure of the full stature of Christ' (4:7–13). A mature church is 'rooted and grounded in love', knows the full dimensions of Christ's love and is 'filled with all the fullness of God' (Ephesians 3:17–19). The members are no longer immature, weak or gullible, like children liable to be carried away by the next gust of false teaching or taken in by the latest religious scam; both right belief and right behaviour have become embedded and established.

This picture of the church maturing as the body of Christ reveals that God intends us to grow and mature together in community. Individuals cannot mature apart from the body. How can I grow to be like Christ unless I learn to love, live with and forgive my brothers and sisters as they seek to learn to do the same (see 1 John 4:20)? Believers are urged to grow together as a community in the unity of the Spirit who transforms us into the likeness of Christ's glory (2 Corinthians 3:18). To be able to 'present everyone mature in Christ' (Colossians 1:28) requires every person's engagement with and loving service to the other members of the local church.

The imagery of the body in Ephesians 4 goes deeper, though, than the idea of growing to maturity alongside others. Christian maturity is actually corporate: 'We must grow up in every way into him who is the head, into Christ' (4:15), with every part working properly. To become the living, obedient body of Christ is the goal, the completed state of the church, a sign and precursor of God's eternal plan to 'gather up all things' in Christ (Ephesians 1:10).[116] The church is like a dance group or *corps de ballet* whose goal is to execute the dance perfectly together. This not only requires each dancer to have learnt their own steps, but everyone must rehearse the dance together. Or we might think of an orchestra in which every player needs to develop the musical skill to play their own instrument, but they must all play together, trusting and following the lead of the conductor's baton to perform the maestro's interpretation of the score.

The 'Ephesians 4 test' of church maturity therefore leads us to look for signs of a community that is united in Christ-like actions and words—an inclusive, healing, forgiving, liberating, loving church, where every member is being equipped by the leaders to play their part fully so that the body can build itself up towards the goal of corporate maturity in Christ.

It may be many years before our Messy Church looks remotely like this! Of course, full maturity as described will not be attained until the whole creation is liberated and renewed through Christ. Until then, people will continue to join the church at different times and mature at different rates, and we are unlikely to find a church where everyone is reaching higher levels of maturity together. Indeed, if this happened, it might be indicative that the church has stagnated and become a bonded set with no new believers joining. There will always be a fluctuating pattern of maturity and immaturity in the life of a growing church, because it should be an open set, a welcoming, disciple-making community, incorporating new members who need to be nursed and nurtured by those who are more mature. The 'Matthew 28 test' of church maturity would seek to determine whether a church is making disciples of people from all sorts of backgrounds who then go on to make more disciples. Paradoxically, then, a healthy maturing church should show some signs of immaturity, like the growth of new seedlings alongside saplings and mature trees in a forest. Our Messy Church is still quite a young forest, with a few blasted oaks in it.

At this point I hesitate to introduce yet another analogy for the Church to add to the hundred or so that have been identified in the New Testament,[117] but I wonder if Church can be likened to a range of products within the cheese section of my local supermarket. It offers a bewildering range of cheddar cheese. There is 'mild', 'medium', 'mature', 'extra mature' and 'vintage'. The 'mild' looks like soap and probably tastes bland. The 'vintage' looks cracked and crusty and may prove dangerously pungent, but the point is that it is all sold as cheddar cheese, and it is all maturing. Similarly, in a healthy maturing church we can expect to have a range of Christian commitment and maturity, from new Christians through to vintage disciples, and, even if there are more mild than mature members, it still constitutes real church if the members are working together to build one another up in Christ. Indeed, to have a mixture of levels of maturity is essential. Those less mature in faith need the support, love and mentoring wisdom of more mature Christians, and the old hands need constantly to be refreshed, renewed and sharpened up by the boldness, enthusiasm, struggles and tough questions of the newer believers.

Returning to New Testament images of the Church, this notion of a healthy mixture of immaturity and maturity, of a work in progress, is clearly seen on the building site of 1 Peter 2, where God is constructing a temple of living stones around Christ the cornerstone. The building is visibly going up. Its glorious design and dimensions can already be seen, and it is certainly open for business, but it will remain unfinished until every stone has been put in place. The '1 Peter 2 test' of church maturity looks for a church community knit together strongly by the members' dedication to Christ, celebrating and communicating the transforming power of the gospel and eager to see new believers fully integrated into the life of the church.

Similarly, in 1 Corinthians 3:9, Paul describes the Church as

'God's field, God's building'. Both the growth of the harvest and the construction of the house are ongoing works of God in which Paul and others play their parts—planting and watering, then leaving the growth to God, or laying foundations, then handing over to other builders. Fields of crops and building sites are usually muddy and messy places where there is always more work to be done. If a degree of mess is a sign of a growing church, we can expect that an older Messy Church will still look messy.

Four marks of the Church

In *Mission-Shaped Church*, four words from the Nicene Creed, 'one', 'holy', 'catholic' and 'apostolic', were put forward as a model or test for the health and authenticity of different expressions of Church. They were described in terms of four dimensions of a journey: 'up' towards God (holy), 'in' towards unity in diversity (one), 'out' in mission (apostolic) and 'of' the wider church (catholic).[118] The problem with this test, as George Lings has more recently pointed out, is that, historically, the Church has interpreted these terms in many different ways, which reduces their usefulness. Nevertheless, Lings has suggested a further adaptation of the four marks to encapsulate the essence of Church. In my view, given the huge importance of the quality of relationships and the experience of community in Messy Church, a real strength of this new formulation is that it is couched in relational terms:

A group may be called Church when a diverse community is formed by transformative encounter with Jesus Christ. Called to follow him, this community lovingly responds through the prompting of the Holy Spirit, seeking to live and act as signs of God's Kingdom. Their call to be the people of God for a place or culture, will be shown by the following:

> 1. *By their presence, acts and words they communicate the reality of Jesus Christ, to continue his **mission**.*

2. *Living out faithful commitment to one another, they reflect the loving and diverse **oneness** in the Trinity.*
3. *Knowing they are an integral part of Christ's **universal** people, they love, learn from, and support Christians beyond their own group.*
4. *By their worship of God the Trinity, they encourage transformation into his **holiness**, including the practice of Baptism and Communion.*[119]

All four of these marks of the Church are evident in our Messy Church to different degrees. Firstly, as a fresh expression of Church, we have a strong mission focus and motivation, and an older Messy Church would, we hope, continue to have this sense of being on the edge, being welcoming and inclusive.

Secondly, we are seeking to give people an experience of Christian community, of the love that unites us in the Lord. Christ-like love is perhaps the clearest sign of a maturing church: Jesus says that when we love one another as he has loved us, all people will recognise us as his followers (John 13:35).

Thirdly, fresh expressions of Church are often criticised for having little sense of being part of the wider Church. However, we, as the first Messy Church, are very aware of the privilege of being part of something much bigger, and we rejoice to see how God is blessing people through Messy Churches in many places throughout the UK and abroad. We regularly welcome visitors from different counties, countries and denominations, and we have worked in partnership with other Messy Church teams to put on special events.

Fourthly, we see ourselves as a disciple-making community where baptism marks a new beginning and Holy Communion nourishes us with grace for spiritual growth and progress on the journey of faith. We have baptised two young adults, one with learning difficulties, at Messy Church. Other families are considering baptism, having spent some time with me during Messy

Church exploring what baptism is all about. If they do decide to go ahead, it is likely that they will prefer to have the service on a Sunday so that the wider family can attend. This may be no bad thing, as it will highlight catholicity—that baptism brings us into the extended family of faith, not just a local Messy Church.

Holy Communion happens at Messy Church once a year, often in the run-up to Easter, sometimes as part of a Passover-style meal that recalls the story of the exodus and Jesus' death and resurrection. Personally I feel that we should be including Holy Communion more often, but we continue to struggle with the wordiness of the liturgy we are required to use, and wish that we could be allowed to develop a simpler, indigenous form. We adhere to Anglican practice in offering a blessing to those who are not communicant members, and have been pleasantly surprised that this does not create a feeling of 'us' and 'them'. This is probably because many of the adults and children have rarely, if ever, experienced someone praying for them specifically, and so for everyone it feels like a special time of drawing near to Jesus with faith and receiving blessing.

The Messy Church of the future

If this is our Messy Church at ten years old, very much a work in progress, what might an older maturing Messy Church look like?

Community

I said earlier that our aim in Messy Church has been to welcome people into an experience of a Christ-centred community. If Messy Church is to be a taste of God's kingdom, then clearly a maturing Messy Church must develop a depth of belonging and a quality of relationships that model Christ's welcome and love.

My hope would be that, like the early church in Acts 2:42–47 and 4:32–37, Messy Church would gain a reputation in the wider community as a group of people who are learning to live out an alternative set of kingdom values, such as love, acceptance, forgiveness, justice, generous giving and sharing of possessions—values that are radically different from those of our individualistic, consumerist culture.[120]

The creativity encouraged by Messy Church might lead to creative solutions to contemporary problems. For example, a Messy Church might run a food bank, set up a debt advice service or rent an allotment and grow vegetables to give away. I can also see potentially fruitful links with ideas from new monasticism, where we find a similar aim to rediscover the essence of church and shape a counter-cultural, inclusive disciple-making community, 'an environment where it is easier to be good', modelling interdependence as an alternative to individualism.[121] Perhaps, in the future, maturing Messy Churches will be encouraging people to adopt a Messy Rule of Life.

Discipleship

A maturing Messy Church will be geared up for welcoming all and growing disciples, with a team that has grasped the vision and values and is well trained and confident in its various roles, making the most of every opportunity to live out and chat about the gospel. Team members will be committed to Messy Church as their own church, rather than seeing it as one of many meetings where they help out, and they will therefore have time to build relationships with people. Christian families will befriend and mentor unchurched families and share in leading all-age courses for seekers and new believers. Baptisms of adults and children will be taking place regularly, and new Christians will be brought into leadership. Teenagers will be given opportunities to develop their own creativity in worship. Local liturgies and home-grown songs of praise will be composed. Parents will be well supported and resourced to help their families to practise their faith at home and in daily life.

Structures

Most Messy Churches are started by a team from a parent church that provides leaders, buildings, finance, insurance, oversight and prayer support. A significant number are ecumenical projects, which brings particular blessings and challenges.[122]

I suspect that we should expect a maturing Messy Church to be moving towards financial independence, paying its own way, perhaps having its own buildings and contributing to mission elsewhere. Most Messy Churches would find financial independence a struggle, even those that are led entirely by volunteers. Our Messy Church currently receives sufficient income from donations to cover the food each month, but for everything else we are dependent on St Wilfrid's, and there are many hidden costs, especially for the premises and all the facilities we use. Nevertheless, a maturing Messy Church should be teaching about and demonstrating Christian giving and generosity, perhaps supporting a Messy Church in a more deprived area with finance, prayer, advice and willing helpers.

Personally, I think it is important that Messy Churches continue to be part of larger church organisations in order to remain firmly rooted in our Christian tradition, but we also need to develop a more interdependent relationship with parent churches over time. Our Messy Church is led by a small core team of lay people, but we provide an update on our activities for each meeting of the Church Council, so there is accountability and opportunity for wider ownership and prayer support. We try to keep all our different congregations informed about what is happening in Messy Church, and it is encouraging that several members of our Sunday congregation who do not come to Messy Church have become keen ambassadors for us when talking to people from other churches.

If Messy Church continues to be a major growth point for churches, it seems likely that, in the future, churches will increasingly be asked to target their budgeting in order to encourage this growth by improving church facilities and increasing support for Messy Church activities. But Messy Church needs to continue to be part of the mixed economy. Together we are rediscovering important aspects of Christian mission through hospitality and growing disciples in community, with Christ at the centre, that will be important both for fresh expressions and for the ongoing tradition.

Conclusion

Over the ten years since we started Messy Church, we have kept the vision to build a welcoming Christian community where adults and children can experience and explore the Christian faith through creativity, celebration and eating together. We now have a much better understanding of the task before us and the long spiritual journey that we are encouraging people to join. We are continually conscious of the importance of the quality of our community life and the depth of relationships needed to be a disciple-making community. We have begun to explore ways of developing mentoring relationships and bridging the gap between meetings. We have seen people opening up to the gospel and becoming disciples.

Just as a mature forest must contain immature trees if it is to continue to grow, so a mature church must continually be incorporating new members. Messy Church may grow up, but it must not lose its messiness as a work in progress or its vision to be on the edge of the church, welcoming all sorts of people in to enjoy being creative while finding out about our great Creator God and his love for a glorious but messed-up world.

Celebrating our Messy Church's tenth birthday seems a historic landmark to us, but, of course, against the backdrop of 2000 years of church history it is as unremarkable as a few bricks in a wall in Charleston. But what a vast number of bricks of so many different shapes and sizes are being built into a spiritual house on this messy building site! We celebrate the work of the Master Builder, who still has many more living stones to add to his grand design before it is complete.

Case study: St Andrew's Church, Bebington: the journey of an older Messy Church

Marie Beale

Marie Beale leads a Messy Church in the north-west of England.

Let me take you back to 2008. We had been blessed for some years with a thriving, over-subscribed toddler group called Little Fishes. Many of the Little Fishes families went on to the church primary school, and we had some key church members with good links and relationships at the school gate. We were running a half-termly dads-and-kids group and inviting the families to our monthly family service. We were also providing a support group mainly for mums finding family life stressful, a women's Bible study and a monthly mums' coffee and craft group.

For many, the jump to a Sunday morning service felt too great, and we were relating mainly to mothers, not the whole family unit. Also, while we were building excellent relationships with families with preschoolers, we found it hard to sustain our links once the children were at school.

At this time I had left work to have my own family and essentially served as a voluntary families' worker for a ten-year period, seeking to develop our relationships and ministry in this area. I had been particularly struck by a statistic that if the father in a family becomes a Christian, in 90 per cent of cases the rest of the family will come to faith; when it is the mother, the figure is more like 17 per cent.

One evening, I had been praying and exploring different possibilities for reaching families, googling different churches and family ministry ideas, when up popped the Messy Church website and the original Fresh Expressions DVD featuring Messy Church. I felt that it was a gift from God tailored for our situation. A week later, three of us were booked on a Messy Fiesta, full of questions about when, who and how. Two months later, in October 2008, we started our own Messy Church on a Saturday afternoon, from 4.00pm to 6.00pm, with an enthused group of church families.

As well as seeking to follow the Messy Church values of 'create, chill, chomp and celebrate', our aim was to provide an accessible, high-quality place for families to come together to meet with others, and to introduce Jesus through hospitality, friendship, stories and worship. We sent flyers out to Little Fishes and other contacts and waited to see what would happen.

106 people attended the first session, of whom 28 people were serving, including eight teenagers and eight adults without children. There were twelve church families, ten fringe/non-church families, and three families from other churches. This resulted in 21 male adults, 31 female adults and 54 children/teens.

Our Messy Church has now been running for almost four years: that's 43 sessions, about 450 crafts and 4500 meals. We have yet to advertise beyond the group. Around 100–140 adults and children come regularly, and their feedback tells us that they really appreciate the family time together and with God. We regularly have visits from interested local churches, and this year our daughter church, Townfield Church, has started its own Messy Church based in the church school.

What is distinctive?

We are constrained by our premises to doing craft, celebration and eating all in the same room. This leads to a degree of chaos at transition times. However, visiting churches have commented that it also gives a very natural feel to the move to celebration, and everyone remains involved. We don't always find it easy to bring out the spiritual aspects of the activity during our busy craft time (and some are better at leading that than others), but we try to reinforce them in a plenary group at celebration time.

We are an evangelical church and have had a gospel focus in our teaching themes, but four years on we have started to bring in more discipleship teaching and content, particularly when we manage (inconsistently) to send material or tasks home to do.

The last four years: observations and learning

Reaching dads

We still get more mums and their children attending, but we do also see many dads. Football is important here, and during the season we have found that dads go to the match and then arrive at Messy Church to be with their family towards the end of the session. That gives us valuable time to catch up, and they are often very grateful that the rest of the family is busy and happy as part of the church community.

We had a very successful Messy meal for just the grown-ups, again following the 'chill, chomp and celebrate' principles. This gave us a great chance to get to know our couples without children. We must do another one! I also wonder about the potential of a Messy house group—several families on a Sunday afternoon, say, going for a walk and sharing a meal and some teaching together.

Growing kids

When we started, most of the children of our core church families were between six and nine years old. We talked to this core group of children about modelling Messy Church routines and behaviour, and this really helped us to establish the pattern of Messy Church. Those children are now 10–13. They have grown up in Messy Church and many of them are now naturally acting as helpers and leaders.

Engaging boys and youth

There is no doubt that all-age/craft-based activities often appeal more to girls. We have worked hard at developing a more science-based approach to activities, and offering challenges and games that appeal to and engage the boys. This has worked for some but not all. We've also tried to give some technical jobs to some of our older boys.

Our youth work is currently in transition, and I would like to involve our youth team more as we develop. As some of our older children are not from churched backgrounds, I wonder if there is scope to have a youth discipleship session running in parallel with the main worship time, or perhaps to involve the young people more in leading the younger children in the celebration. This takes time, and needs to be a priority for us.

Too separate?

Should the Messy congregation and wider church come together, and, if so, how? We have run a few whole-church events with the Messy Church values as their basis. All have enjoyed the mixing, although we have found that it is the established church members who struggle to know how to be in the wider group.

A place to serve

Our church has been experiencing some challenges over recent times, and for some it has been a difficult place to be. Messy Church is not just an accessible, non-threatening place for unchurched people to come to, but has also proven to be a safe place where people have felt free to serve and support each other, and it provides a vision that all can buy into.

Sustainability

One measure of the success of a fresh expression of Church is that it is no longer dependent on one or two key individuals. The effort to deliver a high-quality Messy Church to 100–150 people within the constraints of our building is huge, and I do worry about the long-term sustainability if a few key folk were to move on. We need to involve and develop others and, in particular, make the most of the creativity and ability of our young people. Also, as our Messy congregation now mucks in much more in serving and tidying, I would like to develop their service.

Has it been worth it? Will we continue?

Yes! At the start, we prayed that our Messy Church would not be just another activity group or club. We are thankful that it has developed into a Christian community that shows evidence of God's love and grace. Our prayer is that we will all become increasingly rooted and grounded in that love. There is plenty to do, and at times we are stretched, but we are also encouraged to see God at work.

✥

13

Why we might expect mess, not merely tolerate it

George Lings

Mess in creation and fall

From these twin foundational features in Christian thought, we derive an expectation that many things are both good and spoilt. Nothing and no one is perfect. The sun shines; we smile, and then get sunburnt. It rains; crops grow, and we hope not to be flooded. People are beautiful and then some have untimely deaths. Everything is partial, and perhaps some elements are intentionally incomplete. Each of us is made in the image of God and yet each person is of but one gender within a wider humanity that includes the other. So, much is provisional and time-tainted. Nothing lasts for ever, including forms of Church—hence the need for reimagination, emergence and fresh expressions of Church, each of which, in time, can go stale. Messiness is one word for this complex reality.

Perfect order is rare, and perfected thought even scarcer. Historically, much of church doctrine has been formulated in reaction to events. Even within the New Testament this occurs: for example, the evolution of understandings of the Trinity, the identity of Christ or atonement. Theology is intended to make sense of new experiences of, and revelation by, God. We begin in not knowing and not understanding, and edge forward from there.

This process has continued through engagement with further cultures. Here, the elusive but essential task is seeking both to keep faithful to the enduring past and to connect with the emerging present. Ecclesiology has thus been said to have a nose of wax. A classic example is the Catholic writer Avery Dulles, charting the changes in essential images of the Church and the rise of five models since 1940. As if to underline the pace of change, in the second edition of his book, he pens a sixth model, and so the creativity continues.[123] If 'messy' is taken to mean chaos and disorder, then rightly it will be repudiated. But if it is taken to mean a healthy untidiness, rooted in humility about our fallen state and our intended incomplete understanding as noted in 1 Corinthians 13, the word 'messy' may be a good reminder.

Paul Bayes' chapter in this book looks at this messy incompleteness from the other end of the telescope, recognising that the inherent problem in theology is that it is forced to deal with the sort of God who is greater than our capacity to comprehend him, and yet has too often resorted to intellectual rigour to respond. He points up by contrast how children can delightfully reframe our approaches, remind us of the value of curiosity and offer surprising shafts of truthfulness in the face of the undiluted incomprehensibility of God. All this, Messy Church aids and abets.

Mess in the 'now' and 'not yet' kingdom

The kingdom of God offers an enabling framework in which to think about why life is messy. Its dynamic interweaves with an untidy eschatology, summarised in the tension inherent in the well-worn phrase 'already—not yet'. The tension between these two, neither end of which must ever be relinquished, is expressed on the one hand by Jesus' comment in Mark 1:15, 'the kingdom of God is at hand', and on the other by his insistence in the Lord's prayer that we are to pray, 'Your kingdom come' (Matthew 6:10).

Such a tension offers an explanation for why the good things we know of, which come to us as signs of God's breaking into the world and his activity, are also partial. They, too, are part of the already and the not yet. That is why they are best seen as signs.

Their nature is to point to something beyond and greater than themselves. Thus they are indicative but never exhaustive.

Pointers can also fail to fulfil their purpose. The signs can go sour. In the ecclesial realm, splendid young churches are planted, all seems well—then a leader goes off the rails, or a scandal fatally damages their reputation, or a person involved in the structures throttles the life out of them. Or it may be that the partial nature of the promise is patent. Some weeks, in the life of the young church, it seems that the door to heaven is open, the presence of God is obvious, the love in the community is palpable, the serving is sacrificial, and its witness is compelling. Then at other times bitter conflict breaks out, vision is disputed, or the members erect a glass ceiling on what can happen by undue introspection. Perhaps a local good example continues, but, compared to the whole, it seems insignificant; there are still so many other poor signs that seem to deny the very spiritual reality of the transforming Christ that they allegedly point to. Some of the young churches may lack the maturity, stability, sustainability, gravitas or full range of practices that older churches seem to ask for. Their messiness and partial development is taken against them.

How do these dynamics contribute to an acceptable kind of messiness? The nature of the kingdom has this mixed 'now and not yet' quality. But equally, because I think that the kingdom points to what the face of the Church should look like, the nature of the kingdom should affect our understanding of the Church. The kingdom, if it is to be visible, must be embodied by the lives of those who live for the King. So, in this way, at least in theory (though sadly rarely luminous in practice), the Church is intended to be both a sign of the kingdom and a foretaste of eternal life in Christ. I have no expectation that the church will be either equal to or ever more than the kingdom, but the aim should be that the gap between the two narrows. The values of the kingdom are to be translated into the practice of the Church. Even if it is done well, though, there will still be a 'now and not yet' feel to this, that is not far from messiness. Some churches may think they have arrived and are 'already/now' churches, whereas some young ventures may be castigated as 'not yet' churches. Yet is it not more true that all churches will have the 'already/not yet' tension within them? Does not messiness stalk us all? Those in glass churches should not throw stony ecclesiology.

Mess in an aspect of Christology

Orthodox historical Christology came to accept that the incarnation is marked by the birth of God the Son, and rejected the heresy of adoptionism—the view that Jesus only became the Son of God at the time of his consciousness of it, usually located to the event of his baptism. Yet it was also the case, in the historical period leading to the resurrection and ascension, that his identity and divinity were only gradually disclosed to others. This process is an intriguing example showing that inner identity and others' outward recognition of it do not have to be contemporaneous from the outset.

Christians have always accepted the body of Christ as one foundational model of the church. If Church is being formed in new ways for new cultures and groupings, should not a similar discontinuity between identity and recognition be allowed? The vocabulary of 'emerging church' explicitly adopts this view. If the Church, the body of Christ, is being formed for a fresh group of people, and Jesus was content for gradual disclosure to take place for himself, why should a similar discontinuity not be permitted? Present incomplete recognition should not become a bar to future gradual disclosure. Perhaps we should pray and expect that more of today's church leaders follow the steps of Peter at Caesarea Philippi, suddenly having it revealed to them that it is Christ and his Church being formed among such communities. The connection to this chapter is not that the Christological identity was messy, but that recognition of it took time. Messy Church as a phenomenon is not yet ten years old. It is quite possible that its full gifts and its identity still await further disclosure.

The eschatological framework can embrace, and live with, untidiness in the dynamics of being church. We must hold together the promise of creation and the tragedy of the fall. We live with the 'already/not yet' tension inherent in the kingdom: we believe that Christ has come, Christ comes among us now and Christ will come again. We know that even the disclosure of Christ himself took time and was only partially perceived, as the chapter in this book by John Drane teases out.

Mess in salvation and sanctification

We also teach such a process of untidy and messy stages in relation to salvation. Years ago, evangelical preachers such as John Stott would teach that in Christ we have been saved from the penalty of sin, yet still we are still being saved from the power of sin, and we are yet to be saved from the very presence of sin. We know similar painful tensions in connection with the process of sanctification; we are grateful for changes made by grace, but are more than conscious of how much further there is to go. Indeed, one characteristic of the great saints was their awareness of their frailty and the incompleteness of their journey in Christ. It is normal to be glad of our acceptance and that we have been made new in Christ, but it is healthy to acknowledge that spiritual life and death continue to work within us, and to long for the final day when the process is completed. It seems consistent to hold a similar long-term view of Church, with its inherent incompleteness and messiness. Ecclesiological fundamentalism has never been attractive, and there are increasingly good reasons to think it is not compelling.

If, within the doctrines of creation and fall, the kingdom of God, Christology, and salvation and sanctification, there is room for messiness over what emerges, is it not likely that it is institutional resistance, rather than good theology, that has put up barriers to forms of emerging church through history and denied them legitimisation until they conform to all past external marks? Where is the intentional room for proper messiness, for partial disclosure and the patience encapsulated in the 'wait and see' humility of Gamaliel (Acts 5:38–39)?

Wider issues

It is almost certainly true that Messy Church is the single most common form of fresh expression of Church that we have observed in the last ten years.[124] Along with other kinds, it is sharply raising important questions in relation to the boundaries of what used to be thought as safe and incontestable to say about Church. In particular, there are changes related to whether churches must be clergy-led, how people become disciples and more than attendees, and what needs to be present if a fresh expression is to count as an example of Church.

Leadership

The Western church is facing an enormous change over what leadership looks like. A harbinger has been the fate of the Roman Catholic Church in countries like France, where clergy are very thinly spread indeed. We, too, have seen epoch-making changes in numbers and deployment. In the Anglican Church in the UK, for years the default response to decline in the number of full-time serving clergy has been reliance on the euphemistically named 'pastoral reorganisation' tactic. Most recently, a mixture of shortage of vocations compared to retirements, leading to a prospective 30 per cent reduction by 2020 in some places, and the prospect of declining revenues in the face of ageing congregations, stretches this response to the point of incredulity. We have slowly shifted from the inherited pattern, last fully operative in the early 1970s, of a stipendiary clergy person serving each parish to the emergence of a localised episcope in which a stipendiary is, in practice, a mini-bishop to anything from a handful to well over a dozen local churches. We are approaching the point where the Christendom model of ministry is crushing those called to keep it going. In one Welsh diocese, they are looking at a scenario of over 300 churches served by 60 clergy. This is ridiculous and unsustainable. Moreover, in some of those churches, the impression given is that they would rather slowly die as they are than embrace significant change.

Mission and ministry in, and to, many of these churches is not adequately addressed by the desperate search for those who can provide an adequate level of eucharistic provision and keep the occasional offices going. Until now, to do this we have multiplied ordained designations, although we have never agreed between dioceses which ones universally count (such as Ordained Local Ministers); we have turned to the generation of early retirers to bail us out by finding their vocations late in life, and we have relied heavily on the already retired clergy to keep the system going.

For 20 or more years I have observed processes for finding and freeing local people to become self-supporting clergy. Too often, both local church people and wider selectors look for those who could become liturgically competent and pastorally adept. What is omitted is a search for strong leaders and those capable of turning churches inside out to face outwards in mission. Thus these schemes are but provision of palliative care to elderly and declining churches, based on seeing sacramental ministry as the heart of ordination. The latter is not wrong, but it is not enough and may not even be central. There are significant wider issues to face, about what ordination is for and how it connects to effective leadership for a missionary church in a post-Christendom society. The recently trumpeted census that disclosed a 59 per cent nominal Christian figure, which came in lower than most mission pundits expected, and a 'No religion' figure of 25 per cent, would be an indicator of this.

In stark contrast is recent research data from the world of fresh expressions of Church, in which the single most reported kind of leader is spare or part-time, a lay person of either gender, without any formal training but with a small team, meeting monthly with a significantly higher proportion of de-churched and unchurched people than is usually seen anywhere else.[125] The most common examples are Messy Churches. Stories about some of those are told in the case studies in this book. The missional potential is enormous and the leadership is fragile and often not well supported. Yet such a scenario in the earliest church, in the mind of Roland Allen (the early 20th-century missionary and thinker), and in much of the two-thirds world today, might be thought entirely normal. It sounds like an echo of the upstart leaders who were effective in the westward spread of the gospel and church in 19th-century America[126] and are now common in China.[127] This is an unlooked-for and welcome challenge.

The area of leadership is untidily changing, historically driven more by context than conviction, and likely to change even more. The phenomena of the leaders of Messy Churches and the deeper questions of what kind of leaders we need in local churches are contributors to a future discernment. We will need to have the courage to put down unsustainable patterns from the past, freedom to question whether they may be seen only as embodiments of a Christendom context, and vision to look for whatever deserves to be affirmed among emerging situations. What we must not do is to look back to the highly trained clergy who have failed to solve our missional problems in the past. The presently defended borders, over who is ordained and what the non-ordained are allowed to do, are bound to be more severely tested than ever before. Messy Church practice is an unintentional contributor to this ferment.

Discipleship

I have been glad to hear every insistence that people being in Christ is about much more than church attendance. I have been unconvinced for a long time that the virtues promulgated by some devotees of Anglican ecclesiology actually deliver in practice. Being parochially based and so serving the wider community; engaging with place; gathering publicly, weekly and mainly eucharistically; using centrally authorised liturgies and lectionary-driven homilies;

and engaging with synodical structures and a diocesan framework are all very well in themselves. However, they do not seem to me, in themselves, to deliver the goods in terms of discipleship.

In over 60 years of parish life, with 22 of them as a leader, and living with all those virtues as part of the furniture, I am sad to say that I have met too many regular church people who are without a living faith, lacking any sense of eternal assurance, with no working knowledge of the atonement, vastly ignorant of the themes of the Old Testament, sadly living lives without a working discipline of private prayer, operating at the level of tipping God for goods and services, never sharing any faith they do have, entertaining un-checked prejudices against others, harbouring bitterness towards fellow Christians, dominated by a mean and critical spirit and caught up in ecclesial trivia including time-consuming committees. The list is long and rather worrying. In fairness, I know that I am not very quick at being changed; I know also that there is far I still have to travel; but something is wrong. No wonder, as the wag said: 'Most people outside the church are there because of those of us who are inside.' This kind of church life is frankly the sort of mess we are in and can do without.

So I welcome the rising call for discipleship to be seen as core to the church—but what does this freshly emphasised word mean? I want to go further than some and link it to *theosis*, a strand of New Testament texts and patristic thought that is very serious about our becoming more like Christ in calling, character and even nature than we usually think possible. Thus, both bar and hope are raised.

A significant number of the chapters in this book engage with this area. Judy Paulsen showed how the experience of Messy Church led to changes in behaviour, belonging and believing for those who attended, each made practical and measurable by a clutch of parameters. The changes were most notable and widespread in behaviour, only to some extent in belonging and least widespread in relation to belief. But I think Judy is right to look across all three, as well as to be realistic that we have to start somewhere.

I also wondered what changes, or lack of them, across the three dimensions might be reported by whatever is the standard parish. John Drane examined the messiness of discipleship among the Twelve and the spectacular highs and lows of Peter's rollercoaster ride to a more settled faith. I myself recall Bishop Michael Marshall commenting that Peter might have been more aptly named Sandy! Drane also unpacked the way in which Messy Church fits well in life that is inherently messy, and in a changing culture that has gone well beyond love of Enlightenment values. Discipleship no longer usually proceeds from a background in believing, drawn from a working Christendom, that is followed by a Damascus road experience. Rather, many people's journeys are untidy, non-linear, experiential and experimental. Messy Church is at home with all this, aided by its giving full place to children within families, where spontaneity, curiosity and fun all have their messy place.

Beth Barnett questioned our uncritical adoption of Western, so-called adult views of maturity, contrasting them with the images Christ chose to use. For her, the words 'messy' and 'mature' are not just a paradox to hold together but a combination that is both biblical and essential. Both Tim Waghorn and Bob Jackson celebrated the beginnings that Messy Church has made down the path of discipleship and urged for ways be found to develop this area, or to grow out beyond just the Sunday monthly gathering. Bob Hopkins drew out how Messy Church engages with different levels of culture and how it fares compared with very different sorts of learning, in which formal learning is but one of three essential ways in which we all learn. He noted how well Messy Church operates at the level of socialisation, and how that contributes to building values as well as offering non-formal learning that fosters skills. This is an important contrast with approaches to discipleship that are reduced to courses favouring formal learning and the acquisition of knowledge, but which all too often fail to see changes in behaviour.

All of these authors have contributed to a re-evaluation of what is meant by discipleship, and most have pushed the Church way beyond a dry acquisition of theological information and towards lasting Christ-centred transformation of life and lifestyle. Paul Moore reflected on the longest local Messy Church story, back in Portsmouth, and what is slowly maturing there. He sees a more fully orbed community growing because of a wider way to be church than one that focuses on public worship. Its width and informality foster a safe place for gifts and ministries to be tried, as well as drawing more unchurched people than do other ways of being church. He admits that discipleship with them is a long haul, made more difficult by the monthly pattern, but continues to look for something that would be appropriate and sustainable between those times. Messy Church, by its values—belief in interaction, participation, creativity and hospitality—is helping to redraw our assumptions of what Christian discipleship is about, how it happens and what the endgame is. These authors have added to that conversation.

Is Messy Church really church?

The shortest answer is, 'It all depends.' It depends partly on who is asking the question. Is it an unchurched newcomer, is it the local leader or team member, or is it the bishop or a theological college staff member? Across this variety, the criteria required will vary, and so will the answers.

It depends, too, on which example is under the microscope. I might be regarded as so Messy Church-friendly as to admit all examples, but precisely because I take the two words in its name seriously, that is exactly what I will not do. The Church Army Research Unit's sponsored continuing survey of fresh expressions of Church in selected dioceses has had to meet this question head on. Across the five dioceses examined so far, my team and I have had to exclude 53 per cent of the Messy Church cases offered to us. We have used the same generic criteria for genuine fresh expressions of Church that we drew up before the process started.

Some are about sheer practicality. If cases we examine do not even meet monthly, there is no realistic prospect of building community, growing corporate identity or producing disciples; thus they are excluded. If they have not yet started, they cannot be considered. Some criteria are about intention. Something that is begun for existing Christians falls outside the missional aspect of the definition of a fresh expression of Church. Something to bring people back to the existing church is not aiming to become church with its own identity. It falls outside the ecclesial aspect of the definition of a fresh expression of Church.[128] So here, the fact that we are handling things called 'Messy' is not used as an excuse for being sloppy.

Similarly, some of the authors in this book want to offer meaningful criteria to take forward this serious question. They do not assume that all things named Messy Church are true to the values of Messy Church. My own chapter presents why it matters to work with those values—which I liken to DNA—rather than merely copying the shapes, and I outline what is lost if that counsel is ignored. Indeed, the chapter argues that part of the inherent untidiness involved happens because the reproduction of churches is rightly non-identical. Therefore, what a church will look like if it emerges for a fresh culture or context will be a matter of bold discernment, not bald definition.

Claire Dalpra has also been involved in Church Army's research of fresh expressions of Church across a diocese, the application of our criteria, and the assessment of which cases really are church. She knows at first hand that examining aspiration, rather than just achievement, matters, and that this is more subtle, although more penetrating and useful. So, to assess the intention to be Church, she offers further questions by which to arrive at clarity. Is the new venture intended to be a bridge back into existing church or to become church in its own right? Do those who attend see it as their primary place of church, and are issues of discipleship handled there?

Claire also draws on the way *Mission-Shaped Church* explored the creedal marks of Church, seen as four interconnected relationships, not just dimensions (the vocabulary used back in 2004). Because such values need to become visible, she looks for evident growth of community, advance in Christlikeness, growth through serving, a journey towards including the sacraments, representation in the decision-making councils of the wider church and outreach beyond itself.

Paul Moore's chapter does some similar work as he reflects on the team's own ten-year story of running Messy Church in Portsmouth. A basis for discerning whether particular cases are church, using a Christ-centred view of the four creedal marks, has certain virtues. It obviously shows the desire to relate to the living tradition and its enduring values; it deals in a common currency; and it contributes to re-engagement with how these seminal words are understood today. That is theology being practised. This approach gives room for intentions; it offers space for generosity of interpretation but without the lack of boundaries that would allow the baptism of anything that moves.

Steve Hollinghurst adds some further rigour to this question by examining the attitudes and views of some adults presently attending Messy Church events, and the limits to their involvement. Where the practice of the shape and visible opting out by parents from the most obviously 'spiritual' bits of the session are dominant, he argues that it is more plausible to see such examples as mission projects, not fresh expressions of Church. They participate in Messy craft, meal and outreach, but dip out of Messy worship. However, this view could be akin to saying that where any Christian community has a problem with nominalism, then it is not Church. That would exclude many parish and free churches across the land. It is so easy to tip over from proper questions of health and maturity into judgmental attitudes over identity. Paul's strongly worded letters to the Corinthian church, which was plagued with many deep and disturbing problems, never make this error.

Hollinghurst also explores whether the combination of elements in Messy Church is an unhelpful departure from standard fresh expressions of Church theory. This theory holds that it works best to keep separate the stages of building community, exploring evangelism and evolving worship, for then no one is conned or coerced into the later stages before they are ready. The alternative view is that the intentional combination of these stages in Messy Church is genius in the face of postmodernity, drawing on the evangelistic significance of experience, which shortens the journey to faith. Thus some criteria are offered to decide when and whether particular cases do count. Yes, 'it all depends', but we may now know enough about what it depends upon.

Where have we come to?

My hope is that this book takes further the conversation on these three interconnected topics: Church, discipleship and leadership. The theory and practice of Messy Church are prompting deeper re-examination of our understanding, and offer ways to overcome past distortions led by Enlightenment assumptions.

We are clear that by no means all practice of so-called Messy Churches is healthy, adequate or (in some cases) even authentic. However, a Reformation tag, 'The abuse does not take away the use', reminds us that a movement and its founding concept deserve consideration when seen in a good light. The chapters offer several facets on why we should be more tolerant of mess, untidiness and incompleteness without abandoning a search for coherence, consistency and Christlikeness. This mixture has not been easily adopted by systematic theology or much ecclesiology. Messy Church, by its name, makes such a consideration more pressing, but the rise, over the last 30 years, of differing ways to be Church and a greater emphasis on living with diversity while seeking unity are similar trajectories.

The three words 'messy', 'church' and 'theology' can be combined differently. It is proper to ask, what is the theology of Messy Church, and does that lead us to conclude that it (when following its DNA) is truly an expression of being Church? It is equally legitimate to explore why theology itself, and therefore the theology of the church, is messy. The different chapters have offered contributions to both those clusters of questions. Perhaps the final point is to note that one gift of Messy Church has been to connect the two sets. For this, I, at least, am grateful.

Afterword

Lucy Moore

I am deeply pleased with this book. I'm grateful that such thoughtful, insightful and experienced practitioners in different fields have been generous enough to lend their considerable powers of intellect to those of us who are also conjuring up meals for 90 and working out how to convey the meaning of perichoresis using three kitchen roll innards and a small chemical reaction.

The authors of the different chapters have written in a clear, powerful, often passionate and sometimes playful way on their areas of expertise, making it an enjoyable book to read as well as one packed with thought-provoking material and challenges for how we can make our Messy Churches even more effective. I find it reassuring that contributors like Bishop Paul Bayes have taken the trouble to visit their local Messy Churches and write from a grounded knowledge of vegetable modelling. With the case studies from Messy Churches themselves, I think the book captures a sense of the varied and rich state of play across the Messy world at this stage of its development. A TV documentary about the rock band Queen featured a group of literature professors sitting in a university college library debating the lyrics of 'Bohemian Rhapsody' and deciding that whatever the lyrics meant, Freddie Mercury would have been deeply tickled to know they were taking him that seriously. And I suppose the part of me that still sees Messy Church simply as enormous fun finds it humbling but also amusing that our own high-powered expert chapter writers are taking such an anarchic idea so seriously.

We deliberately chose to invite a messy selection of writers, people with whom we didn't necessarily see eye to eye, in order to keep the book from becoming sycophantic. We wanted to try to tease out the truth of the various arguments presented, not produce a 'look how wonderful Messy Church is' tome. For example, should Messy Church happen weekly rather than monthly, as Tim Waghorn suggests? I feel that this would be an impossible commitment to sustain—if done properly—for the majority of us. It is also hard to see how there would be space for reflection and development of ideas between sessions. Equally, the frequency changes the dynamic: a monthly session is a special event, albeit a regular one, something to mark in red pen on the calendar; and for people at the start of their faith journey, once a month is a good enough toe in the water of something as unfamiliar as church. More importantly, the once-monthly nature of Messy Church gives space for a church community to be decentralised, truly to become a priesthood of all believers, involving all members rather than simply the 'experts'. In the spaces between celebrations we need to take responsibility for our own prayer life, our own Bible study, our own family disciplines.

But while I personally feel that Messy Church becomes a different animal when it is held once a week instead of once a month, Tim's chapter reflecting on his own experiences with a weekly Messy Church community has many valuable points. It is important that we air different perceptions of what God is doing so that readers can draw their own conclusions and fight their own way to the best route forward for their own church, Messy or otherwise. Similarly, Bob Jackson and I have a long-running (and I hope amicable) debate about whether God is interested in numbers or not and whether now is the right time for published resources on discipleship, but his chapter is nonetheless a treasure chest of empirical data, uncomfortable challenges and profound affirmation. I need more time to digest the truths, rebukes, warnings and exhortations in each chapter, to take on board the research of Claire Dalpra, Bob Jackson and Steve Hollinghurst about the bigger question of church in its historical context; to ponder Beth Barnett's cheerful applecart-upsetting of 'givens'; to muse with George Lings upon the implications of Messy Church having a DNA rather than an unalterable shape; and to wonder with Judy Paulsen, Tim Waghorn, John Drane, Bob Hopkins and Paul Moore what the implications of messy discipleship might be in and beyond Messy Church.

Overall, this book feels to me like lights being shone on to the Messy Church 'body' by benevolent companions: we might wince and blink a little under their glare, but we are delighted they have taken the trouble to shine for us. Some of the lights are like a doctor's anglepoise lamp, showing up disease or decay in that body, or perhaps even a surgeon's laser beams painfully cutting away at the rot for the health of the patient. Other lights shine backwards and help us to notice and celebrate what God has done so far; others shine ahead and point out the choice of paths we could take in the future. Still others cheer us, warm us and give us the 'Ahhhh!' moment of awe and wonder, like children marvelling at Christmas lights, as the writers articulate for us what God has done, is doing now and wants to do with his messy world.

✛

Notes

1   www.freshexpressions.org.uk/sites/default/files/what-would-success-look-like-for-fresh-expressions.pdf

2   S. Croft, C. Dalpra and G. Lings, *Starting a Fresh Expression of Church* (CHP, 2006).

3   We would also include any examples of evangelistic ministry that began without intending to plant a fresh expression of Church but recognised the need to create one because the cultural divide between new converts and existing church meant that discipleship after conversion was not taking place. Sometimes, only as missiological engagement is effective is it discovered that fresh expressions of Church are needed.

4   G. Cray (ed.), *Mission-Shaped Church* (CHP, 2004), p. 32.

5   As well as the birthing of new churches, the term generously included existing churches that were renewing and redirecting their current life—for example, developing a cell or cluster model. By encompassing this 'renewal of existing' in their definition, the fresh expressions of Church language in *Mission-Shaped Church* left room for subsequent confusion, as the phrase had been interpreted in different ways.

6   Cray (ed.), *Mission-Shaped Church*, pp. 127–129.

7   The growth and significance of midweek church is also discussed in M. Moynagh, *Changing World, Changing Church* (Monarch, 2001), p. 128.

8   B. Carter and M. McGoldrick, *The Expanded Family Life Cycle, Individual Family and Social Perspectives* (Allyn and Bacon, 1998), ch. 2.

9   L. Singlehurst, *Sowing, Reaping, Keeping* (Crossway, 1995).

10 C. Dalpra, 'Small beginnings', *Encounters on the Edge* No. 31 (Church Army, 2007), p. 14.

11 A. Dulles, *Models of the Church* (Image, 1978), pp. 129–144.

12 G. Lings, 'Unravelling the DNA of Church: how can we know that what is emerging is "Church"?', *International Journal for the Study of the Christian Church*, Vol. 6, No. 1 (2006), p. 109.

13 Cray (ed.), *Mission-Shaped Church*, pp. 98–99.

14 G. Lings, *International Journal for the Study of the Christian Church*, Vol. 6, No. 1, p. 112. Differing views are taken, for example, by M. Moynagh in *Church for Every Context* (SCM, 2012), pp. 106–114, and A. Smith & C. Walton, *Fresh Expressions in the Mission of the Church* (CHP, 2012), p. 114.

15   Cray (ed.), *Mission-Shaped Church*, p. 99.

16   G. Lings, 'Discernment for mission', *Encounters on the Edge* No. 30 (Church Army, 2006), p. 14.

17   www.acpi.org.uk/Joomla/index.php?option=com_content&task= view&id=37&Itemid=65 (accessed 30 March 2012) is a helpful short summary of Venn's three-self principle and its implications for church planting and fresh expressions of Church.

18   The 37 included many in the early stages of thinking about starting a Messy Church.

19   *Forgotten Families* (Contact a Family, 2011): www.cafamily.org.uk/ media/381636/forgotten_isolation_report.pdf.

20   N.T. Wright, *The New Testament and the People of God* (SPCK, 1992), p. 360.

21   Revd Joan Foster in an email, June 2012.

22   Featured in G. Lings, 'Sweaty Church', *Encounters on the Edge* No. 56 (Church Army, 2013).

23   J.W. Drane, *The McDonaldisation of the Church* (DLT, 2000).

24   J. Paulsen, *Messy Church: Growing missional connections through multi-generational worship and learning* (Fuller Theological Seminary, D. Min. Final Project, 2012).

25   A. Kreider, *The Change of Conversion and the Origin of Christendom* (Trinity Press International, 1999), pp. xv, 22.

26   R. Williams, *The Wound of Knowledge* (DLT, 1979), p. 1.

27   G.W. Lathrop, *Holy Ground: A liturgical cosmology* (Fortress Press, 2003), pp. 64–65, original emphasis.

28   Quoted by John Pritchard in A. Richards & P. Privett (eds), *Through the Eyes of a Child* (CHP, 2009), p. vii.

29   C. Handy, *The Age of Unreason* (Arrow Press, 2002), p. 53.

30   Letter to God, by Lulu, aged six (March 2011).

31   Hollenweger discusses this in his *Conflict in Corinth: Memoirs of an old man* (Paulist Press, 1982).

32   Many times in training seminars and in conversation, but also in his *Come, Holy Spirit* (Hodder & Stoughton, 1985), ch. 33.

33   John Keats, in his letter to George and Thomas Keats, 21 December 1817.

34   www.archbishopofcanterbury.org/articles.php/2389/the-archbishop-replies-to-lulu-aged-6.

35   L. Moore & J. Leadbetter, *Starting Your Messy Church* (BRF, 2012), p. 13.

36   For details of what we did, see G. Lings, 'Soft cell', *Encounters on the Edge* No. 20 (Church Army, 2003).

37   R. Fabian, 'The scandalous table' in S. Burns (ed.), *The Art of Tentmaking* (Canterbury Press, 2012), pp. 150–151.
38   www.messychurch.org.uk/messy-blog/spirituality-parents.
39   A.M. Ramsey, *The Gospel and the Catholic Church* (Longmans, Green & Co., 1936), p. 122 (emphasis added).
40   R. Williams, 'Catholic and Reformed', paper presented 1993, quoted in T. Hobson, *Anarchy, Church and Utopia* (DLT, 2005), p. 63.
41   Athanasian Creed, vv. 9, 12 (extracts).
42   J. Shore, *Penguins, Pain and the Whole Shebang* (Seabury, 2005), p. 69.
43   See R. Bauckham, *Gospel Women: Studies of the named women in the Gospels* (Eerdmans, 2002).
44   R.V. Peace, *Conversion in the New Testament: Paul and the Twelve* (Eerdmans, 1999), p. 5.
45   One of the more comprehensive studies of this is still J. Finney, *Finding Faith Today* (Bible Society, 1992).
46   For more on this, see J. Drane, *After McDonaldization: Mission, ministry, and Christian discipleship in an age of uncertainty* (DLT, 2008), pp. 82–86.
47   Taken from P. Torday, *Salmon Fishing in the Yemen* (Phoenix, 2007), pp. 205–206.
48   J. Drane, *Faith in a Changing Culture: Creating churches for the next century* (Marshall Pickering, 1997), ch. 4.
49   For the classic and original works, see J.W. Fowler, *Stages of Faith: The psychology of human development and the quest for meaning* (Harper & Row, 1981); J.W. Fowler, *Becoming Adult, Being Christian* (Harper & Row, 1984); J.W. Fowler, K.E. Nipkow & F. Schweitzer (eds), *Stages of Faith and Religious Development* (SCM Press, 1992).
50   Stage 1 ('intuitive/protective'), correlating with Peter's upbringing within Judaism; stage 2 ('mythical/literal'), the point at which he met Jesus and decided to explore him further; stage 3 ('synthetic/conventional'), Peter's confession at Caesarea Philippi, aligning himself with what others believed; stage 4 ('individuative/reflective'), the episode in the high priest's garden, working out the nature of commitment at a deeper level; stage 5 ('conjunctive'), as Peter wrestled with the issues over Cornelius and, more broadly, Gentiles/Jews, and therefore personal identity; stage 6 ('universalising'), as Peter went on to become a global missionary in his own right, ultimately prepared to give his life for the cause.
51   J.O. Hagberg & R.A. Guelich, *The Critical Journey: Stages in the life of faith* (Sheffield Publishing, 2005), pp. 6–7. More controversially for some, at least one author has utilised this approach as a way of

understanding Jesus' own self-consciousness: see R.W. Kropf, *The Faith of Jesus: The Jesus of history and the stages of faith* (Wipf & Stock, 2005).

52   Hagberg & Guelich, in *The Critical Journey*, offer a more biblically nuanced understanding of faith as a staged journey and one which takes more seriously the retrograde steps as well as the progress.

53   See N. Slee, *Women's Faith Development: Patterns and processes* (Ashgate, 2004); A.Phillips, *The Faith of Girls* (Ashgate, 2011)

54   D. Bosch, *Transforming Mission* (Orbis, 1991), pp. 190–191.

55   I use the term 'pristine' here to describe what I understand to have been the original vision. Many examples of Messy Church that I have experienced appear to adopt the terminology as a more trendy way of describing what they have always done in outreach to children—a form of rebranding rather than a radical reimagining of what holistic mission might look like in an intergenerational context.

56   On church and personality types, see J. Astley & L. Francis (eds), *Christian Perspectives on Faith Development* (Gracewing/Eerdmans, 1992); L.J. Francis, *Faith and Psychology: Personality, religion, and the individual* (DLT, 2005).

57   For the ways in which Enlightenment culture skewed the understanding of discipleship, see C. Armstrong, 'The rise, frustration, and revival of evangelical spiritual resourcement', in *Journal of Spiritual Formation and Soul Care* 2/1, 2009, pp. 113–121, where he argues that, in their zeal to defend faith against a rationalistic critique, apologists of the early 20th century focused on defending important doctrines and, in doing so, 'had come to identify the Christian life with cognitive beliefs' (p. 114). Discipleship was then equated with doctrinal orthodoxy, which in turn demanded a style of church life based on a patriarchal educational paradigm to sustain it.

58   See O.M. Fleming Drane, 'The Holy Fool: clowning in Christian ministry' in *The Bible in Transmission* (Spring 2011), pp. 17–19.

59   Mark's Gospel in particular was almost certainly intended to be performed interactively in the early church rather than being merely read. See W. Shiner, *Proclaiming the Gospel: First-century performance of Mark* (TPI, 2003); A. Clark Wire, *The Case for Mark Composed in Performance* (Cascade, 2011); D. Rhoads, J. Dewey & D. Michie, *Mark as Story* (3rd edn, Fortress Press, 2012).

60   G. Land & B. Jarman, *Breakpoint and Beyond: Mastering the future today* (HarperCollins, 1992).

61   These examples are quoted in S. Orchard and J.H.Y. Briggs (eds), *The Sunday School Movement* (Paternoster, 2007), pp. 10–12.

62 The estimates can all be found in M. Griffiths, *One Generation from Extinction* (Monarch, 2009), pp. 45–47.

63 R. Gill, *Churchgoing and Christian Ethics* (CUP, 1999).

64 Source data in Brierley (ed.), *Religious Trends* 2000/2001 No. 2, Table 2.15.

65 I have met the analogy in many conversations with other theorists in the fresh expressions of Church/emerging church field. It was used as a search for a transferrable ecclesial essence by several authors within S. Croft (ed.), *Mission-Shaped Questions* (CHP, 2008) (see Angela Tilby, p. 79; Loveday Alexander, p. 141; Alison Morgan, p. 154; Steven Croft, p. 189). I drew upon it myself and began to explore the different uses to which it is put: see G. Lings, 'Unravelling the DNA of Church' in *International Journal for the Study of the Christian Church*, Vol. 6 No. 1.

66 L. Moore, *Messy Church* (BRF, 2006), p. 21.

67 Moore, *Messy Church*, pp. 35–39.

68 Moore, *Messy Church*, pp. 21, 37–38.

69 Moore, *Messy Church* (pp. 49–53) explores possibilities for many kinds of creative church: Green, Sports, Performing Arts, Music, Photography, Cookery, Mechanical, Community Action. In *Messy Church 2* (BRF, 2008), p. 12, she expresses disappointment that some of these have not yet appeared.

70 Moore, *Messy Church*, p. 21 (emphasis added).

71 Moore, *Messy Church 2*, pp. 50–62.

72 Moore, *Messy Church 2*, p. 57.

73 Lucy Moore, *All-Age Worship* (BRF, 2010), p. 39.

74 I recall Bishop Colin Buchanan drawing this comparison in lectures in the 1970s.

75 G. Lings, 'Seven sacred spaces', *Encounters on the Edge* No. 43 (Church Army, 2009).

76 Moore, *Messy Church 2*, pp. 17, 20–34.

77 For example, Philip Mounstephen and Kelly Martin were the CPAS advocates; Daphne Kirk applied it to Cell thinking; Margaret Withers wrote *Mission-Shaped Children* (CHP, 2006).

78 Moore, *All-Age Worship*, ch. 1, pp. 13–36, especially pp. 25–34.

79 Lucy Moore agrees that there are legitimate times and needs for doing things separately. Moreover, the choice of any time or day for Messy Church will exclude some: *All-Age Worship*, pp. 49–50.

80 The analogy of DNA, seen firstly as essence of church and secondly as its method of reproduction, I developed in two lectures in Toronto, in 2008. They can be found at http://institute.wycliffecollege.ca/author/george-lings/feed/

81   One such would be: S. Murray, *Church after Christendom* (Paternoster, 2004).
82   They include Cray (ed.), *Mission-Shaped Church*; Drane, *Mcdonaldisation of the Church*; M. Riddell, *Threshold of the Future* (SPCK, 1998); Moynagh, *Changing World, Changing Church*; A. Frost & M. Hirsch, *The Shaping of Things to Come* (Hendrickson, 2003); M. Nazir-Ali, *Shapes of the Church to Come* (Kingsway, 2001); Moynagh, *Church for Every Context*.
83   M. Percy, 'Losing our space, finding our place?' in S. Coleman & P. Collins (eds), *Religion, Identity and Change* (Ashgate, 2004); or, in more depth, in his *Salt of the Earth: Religious resilience in a secular age* (Sheffield Academic Press, 2001).
84   A. Smith & D. Walton, *Fresh Expressions in the Mission of the Church* (CHP, 2012), p. 114.
85   This is written up in G. Lings, *Sweaty Church: Church for kinaesthetic learners* (Church Army, 2012).
86   Dulles, *Models of the Church*, pp. 16–17.
87   Dulles, *Models of the Church*, p. 17.
88   I argued in a 2009 PhD thesis that the Church universal has within it a calling and capacity to reproduce. Available within SCOLER—an online resource from Church Army's Research Unit: www.churcharmy.org.uk/ms/sc/SCOLER/sfc_27197.aspx.
89   Moore, *Messy Church*, p. 22, and *Messy Church 2*, p. 8. Perhaps, in retrospect, it was not helpful that the shape was given such a prominent feature in the early section of the second book.
90   Lucy Moore is rightly proud to be the founder of something that has worked well for so many and concurrently dislikes the danger of celebrity culture and becoming seen as 'Mrs Messy'.
91   Moore, *Messy Church*, p. 10.
92   In 2006, Graham Tomlin wrote a lecture for Holy Trinity, Brompton, on the 'Implicit Theology of Alpha'. It argued that the process and values are the deepest feature and make up the implicit content.
93   A. Walls, *The Missionary Movement in Christian History* (T&T Clark, 1996), p. xvi.
94   Cray (ed.), *Mission-Shaped Church*, p. 104.
95   The monograph by J. Fowler, *Stages of Faith*, has been broadly influential in religious education. In the absence of other models, it remained mostly unchallenged for the remainder of the 20th century. In postmodern critiques of developmentalism generally and with the resurrection of Vygotsky's thinking in educational philosophy, the work of the stage theorists generally has undergone much revision. Meanwhile, Fowler's

stages have passed into the popular imagination, due to their congruence with the assumed norms of the Enlightenment zeitgeist.

96   For a more extensive exploration of the range of biblical images of the child, see Marcia Bunge, 'The child, religion, and the academy: developing robust theological and religious understandings of children and childhood', *Journal of Religion* 86, no. 4 (October 2006), pp. 549–579.

97   www.mainlymusic.org.au. Mainly Music is a Christian-based children's music programme for preschoolers. Please visit the website for more information.

98   Leviticus 19:18 declares, 'Do not seek revenge or bear a grudge against anyone among your people, but love your neighbour as yourself. I am the Lord' (NIV).

99   www.anglican.org.au/content/home/about/students_page/What_are_ordained_Ministers.aspx

100   www.melbourne.anglican.com.au/mission/theologicaleducation/network128/Pages/Year-of-Discernment.aspx. This section of the Anglican Diocese of Melbourne's website is for pathway planning for people seeking ordination.

101   www.whychurch.org.uk/trends.php, sited 06/06/2012.

102   T.S. Reigner, *Surprising Insights from the Unchurched and Proven Ways to Reach Them* (Zondervan, 2008).

103   www.anglican.org.au/docs/commissions/liturgy/The%20Prague%20Report.pdf

104   J. Hebenton, 'Youth and Liturgy: an Oxymoron? A summary of a study into how and why Anglican liturgy and the Anglican liturgical tradition are being used in worship targeting young people within the Anglican Church (Tikanga Pakeha) in New Zealand', Department of Theology and Religious Studies, Otago University, Dunedin, New Zealand (November 2009), p. 7.

105   Hebenton, 'Youth and Liturgy', p. 9.

106   www.messychurch.org.uk/messy-church-directory.

107   www.acpi.org.uk: click 'Articles', then 'MessyChurch – Nurture and Discipleship'.

108   L. Kwast, 'Understanding Culture: Perspectives on the world Christian movement' (Institute of International Studies, 1981).

109   G. Lings, *Encounters on the Edge* No. 46 (Church Army, 2010).

110   T.W. Ward, L. McKinney & J. Dettoni, *Effective Learning in Non-Formal Modes* (Institute for International Studies in Education, Michigan State University, 1971).

111 For an example, see G. Lings, *Encounters on the Edge* No. 53 (Church Army, 2012), pp. 19ff.

112 S. Croft (ed.), *The Future of the Parish System* (CHP, 2006), pp. 131–132.

113 Moore, *Messy Church*, pp. 27–38; G. Lings, 'Messy Church: Ideal for all ages?' in *Encounters on the Edge* No. 46, pp. 6–7.

114 G. Lings, 'Seven sacred spaces', *Encounters on the Edge* No. 43.

115 Paul Moore, *Making Disciples in Messy Church: Growing faith in an all-age community* (BRF, 2013).

116 A.T. Lincoln, *Ephesians* (Word Biblical Commentary) (Thomas Nelson, 2010), p. 256.

117 P.S. Minear, *Images of the Church in the New Testament* (Westminster Press, 2004).

118 Cray (ed.), *Mission-Shaped Church*, pp. 96–99.

119 Lings, 'Unravelling the DNA of Church', *International Journal for the Study of the Christian Church* Vol. 6, No. 1, pp. 104–114.

120 G. Cray, *Disciples and Citizens: A vision for distinctive living* (IVP, 2007).

121 G. Cray, I. Mobsby & A. Kennedy (eds), *New Monasticism as Fresh Expression of Church* (Canterbury Press, 2010), pp. 6–28.

122 See the report 'Ecumenical Messy Church' (2011), www.ctbi.org.uk/pdf_view.php?id=732.

123 A. Dulles, *Models of the Church* (2nd edn, Gill & McMillan, 1988).

124 We know of nearly 20 kinds of fresh expression of Church, some of which overlap with others, so no one type will be a majority. However, across five dioceses that the Church Army's Research Unit have surveyed in the last two years, Messy Church is commonly one in five of all cases recorded. It is easily the largest single group.

125 In Liverpool these lay leaders make up 36 per cent, in Canterbury 37 per cent, in Leicester 53 per cent, in Derby 39 per cent, and in Chelmsford 36 per cent.

126 See R. Clapp and R. Finke, 'How the Upstart Sects Won America 1776–1850' (*Journal for the Scientific Study of Religion*, March 1989, 28:1), pp. 27–44.

127 Articles about the contemporary Chinese church have recently appeared in *The Bible in Translation* (Bible Society, 2012).

128 The shortest generic list of criteria for fresh expressions of church is 'missional, contextual, ecclesial, formational'. The last is shorthand for 'making disciples'. Our ten criteria develop this list: one form of it is found in G. Lings, 'A Golden Opportunity', *Encounters on the Edge* No. 50 (Church Army, 2011), pp. 19–21.